Американской Администрации Помощи
в Крыму

Мы женщины-матери Южного района гор. Севастополя преисполненные горячей благодарностью, шлем свое сердечное спасибо за помощь и заботу оказанную в такое тяжелое время нашим детям. Слезы умиления выступают на глазах при виде того как бледные, измученные личики детей, благодаря заботам братской Американской помощи делаются свежими и здоровыми. Дети счастье и радость матери в настоящем и опора и надежда в будущем. Да, благословенны будут сердца идущих навстречу этому и да же оскудеет рука дающего.

Гор. Севастополь
Марта 14го дня 1923г.

THE RUSSIAN JOB

THE RUSSIAN JOB

THE FORGOTTEN STORY OF
HOW AMERICA SAVED THE
SOVIET UNION FROM RUIN

Douglas Smith

FARRAR, STRAUS AND GIROUX | NEW YORK

Farrar, Straus and Giroux
120 Broadway, New York 10271

Grateful acknowledgment is made for permission to reprint the following material:
Excerpts from *The Big Show in Bololand: The American Relief Expedition to
Soviet Russia in the Famine of 1921*, by Bertrand Patenaude; copyright © 2002
by the Board of Trustees of the Leland Stanford Jr. University. All rights reserved.
Used by permission of the publisher, Stanford University Press, sup.org.

Illustration credits can be found on pages 301–303.

Library of Congress Control Number: 2019017677
ISBN: 978-0-374-25296-0

Designed by Richard Oriolo

Our books may be purchased in bulk for promotional, educational,
or business use. Please contact your local bookseller or the Macmillan Corporate
and Premium Sales Department at 1-800-221-7945, extension 5442,
or by e-mail at MacmillanSpecialMarkets@macmillan.com.

www.fsgbooks.com
www.twitter.com/fsgbooks • www.facebook.com/fsgbooks

1 3 5 7 9 10 8 6 4 2

To Stephanie

It burns and scorches, the midday heat,
All life here has died. In slumbering peace
The earth lies mute, guarding its secret.
Not a sound, save the occasional whirlwind.
A column of fire, rushing over the field,
Rises heavenward and vanishes like smoke.
Severe and stern the infinite sky:
It's empty, the gods have all died
And are now deaf to the suffering of men.
The earth's parched: no dew, no rain.
Our fertile fields, vast like the sea,
Whose bounty once brought comfort,
Fill our hearts with joy no more.
Death stalks the land, bringing with it endless sorrow.

—A. GELEZHE, BUGURUSLAN, RUSSIA, 1922

Trying to kill people may sound more exciting than trying to keep them alive, but don't you ever believe it's so.

—GEORGE McCLINTOCK, AMERICAN RELIEF ADMINISTRATION, SAMARA, RUSSIA, 1922

CONTENTS

THE RUSSIAN JOB

PROLOGUE:

MR. WOLFE'S HORRIFYING

DISCOVERY

T HE STORIES BEGAN TO APPEAR in the Soviet press in the autumn of 1921, each one more gruesome than the last. There was the woman who refused to let go of her dead husband's body. "We won't give him up," she screamed when the authorities came to take it away. "We'll eat him ourselves, he's ours!" There was the cemetery where a gang of twelve ravenous men and women dug up a fresh corpse and devoured the cold flesh on the spot. There was the man captured by the police after murdering his friend, chopping off his head, and selling the body at a street market to a local restaurant owner to be made into meatballs, cutlets, and hash. And then there was the desperate mother of four starving children, saved only by the death of their sister, aged thirteen, whom the woman cut up and fed to the family.

The stories seemed too horrific to believe. Few could imagine a hunger capable of driving people to such acts. One man went in search of the truth. Henry Wolfe, a high-school history teacher from Ohio, spent several weeks in the spring of 1922 traveling throughout Samara Province, several hundred miles southeast of Moscow on the Volga River, intent on finding physical evidence of cannibalism. In the district of Melekess, officials told him about a father who had killed and eaten his two little children. He confessed that their flesh had "tasted sweeter than pork." Wolfe kept on searching, and eventually found the proof he had been looking for.

At first glance, it appears to be an unremarkable photograph of six individuals in winter dress: two women and four men, their expressions blank, betraying no particular emotion. But then our eyes catch sight of the grisly objects laid out across a wooden plank resting unevenly atop a pair of crates. There are two female heads, part of a rib cage, a hand, and what appears to be the skull of a small child. The adult heads have been

cracked open and the tops of the skulls pulled off. Along with the human flesh, cannibals had feasted upon the brains of their victims.

Wolfe stands second from the right, surrounded by Russian interpreters and Soviet officials. There's a faint look of satisfaction on his face at having accomplished his goal. Here, at last, was the incontrovertible proof he had set out to find.

Wolfe may have found the answer he had been seeking, but to us, a century later, the photograph raises a number of questions. What was Wolfe doing in Russia in the first place? What had led this young American to a remote corner of the globe, half a world away, in search of such horrors? And why would the Soviet government, the newly formed socialist state of Vladimir Lenin and his Bolshevik Party dedicated to world revolution and the overthrow of the capitalist order, have helped Wolfe to uncover, much less document and publicize, its miserable failure at feeding its own people?

If we look closely, a clue to answering these questions is to be found in the three letters stamped on the box in the center of the frame: "ARA."

Facing one of the worst famines in history, the Soviet government invited the American Relief Administration, the brainchild of Herbert Hoover, future president of the United States, to save Russia from ruin. For two years, the ARA fed over ten million men, women, and children across a million square miles of territory in what was the largest humanitarian operation in history. Its efforts prevented a catastrophe of incalculable proportions—the loss of millions of lives, social unrest on a massive scale, and, quite possibly, the collapse of the Soviet state. Having completed their mission by the summer of 1923, the Americans packed up and went home. Before the ARA left, the leaders of the Soviet government showered the organization with expressions of undying gratitude and promises never to forget America's help.

"An act of humanity and benevolence," Machiavelli wrote in his *Discourses on Livy*, "will at all times have more influence over the minds of men than violence and ferocity." Machiavelli was wrong. The Soviet government quickly began to erase the memory of American charity, and what it could not erase, it sought to distort into something ugly. But it wasn't just the Russians. Back in the United States, where Americans had followed the work of the ARA with great interest, knowledge of Hoover's achievement faded. By the time Hoover was voted out of office a decade later, during the Great Depression, the story of this extraordinary humanitarian mission had been forgotten. Now, almost a hundred years later, few people in America or Russia have ever heard of the ARA. *The Russian Job* seeks to right this wrong.

1921

RUSSIAN
APOCALYPSE

T HE RAINS DIDN'T COME IN THE SPRING OF 1920. It was unusually hot, and by planting season the ground had been baked hard. The dry weather carried on throughout the summer and into the autumn. The harvests proved small. That winter saw scant snow covering the land, followed by a second parched spring. The worst drought in thirty years gripped much of Soviet Russia in its deadly grasp: nearly the entire length of the Volga River Basin, from Nizhny-Novgorod in the north all the way to the Caspian Sea in the south, and from Ukraine in the west to the edge of the Ural Mountains in Asia. Villages were starving. Over a hundred thousand peasants left their homes in search of food. Russia was facing a catastrophe.

Life for the Russian peasant had never been easy, even after the end of serfdom in 1861. The peasants eked out a meager existence not much beyond subsistence levels. Farming methods were primitive, the land was overcrowded, taxes were heavy. In the late 1880s, the Russian state began a massive program of industrialization, to be financed by the sale of grain abroad. *Ne doedim, no vyvezem*—we may not eat enough, but we'll export—became the motto of the effort to bring tsarist Russia up to the modern lifestyle of the West. Tax collectors were sent out into the countryside to redouble their efforts; peasant farmers were forced to hand over an ever larger share of their rye, wheat, and barley. Between 1881 and 1890, the average yearly export of major grains almost doubled.

And then, in the late summer of 1891, the crops failed following a horrendous drought. Peasants ran out of food and survived on what they called *goly khleb*, hunger bread: an odious loaf made from a small dose of flour mixed with some sort of food substitute, usually *lebeda*—saltbush or orache—that when consumed for any length of time causes serious illness. By December, the Ministry of the Interior estimated more than ten million people would need government relief. Leo Tolstoy, the conscience of the nation, publicized the extent of the famine and organized relief, thus helping to let the world know of the full scale of the disaster. America was among the countries to come to Russia's aid. A group of Minnesotans sent a ship full of Midwestern grain that was greeted by fireworks and a jubilant crowd when it arrived at the Baltic port of Libau* in March 1892. In the end, the people of Minnesota donated over 5.4 million pounds of flour and $26,000 worth of supplies to combat the famine on the other side of the globe. The generosity of the Americans was commemorated by the artist Ivan Aivazovsky, the great master of Romantic seascapes, in two paintings that he himself delivered to America in 1893 along with other gifts of thanks from Tsar Alexander III. The paintings hung for decades in the Corcoran Gallery until First Lady Jacqueline Kennedy saw them and had them moved to the White House.

The Russian government mounted its own relief effort, which, though

---

* Now Liepāja, Latvia.

bedeviled by setbacks and inefficiencies, at its peak provided more than eleven million people with supplemental food. The state was joined in its efforts by a great many in educated society. Moved by the plight of the hungry masses, Anna Ulyanova, a twenty-seven-year-old noble-man's daughter from the town of Sim-birsk on the Volga River, distributed food and medicine to the needy, like so many others of her background. Her brother Vladimir, however, was an exception. Not only did he refuse to aid the suffering, he welcomed the famine, since he believed it would help destroy the people's faith in

Vladimir Lenin

God and the tsar. Revolution, not charity, would save the peasants, he said. "The overthrow of the tsarist monarchy, this bulwark of the land-owners, is their only hope for some sort of decent life, for an escape from hunger, from unending poverty." Vladimir, better known as Lenin, his revolutionary nom de guerre, understood even as a young man the con-nection between food and power.

Russia in 1921 was confronting more than a drought. Indeed, the lack of rain played only a secondary role in the famine. Much more important had been seven years of war and revolution. By the end of 1916, after two years of brutal fighting in the First World War, Russia was experiencing grain shortages and bread riots in major cities. In February 1917, factory women protesting the high cost and lack of bread in the capital of Petro-grad sparked the revolution that led to the fall of the tsarist regime the next month. The food crisis and the state's inability to address it had been directly responsible for the death of the three-hundred-year-old Romanov dynasty.

After overthrowing the interim Provisional Government in October, the Bolsheviks set about establishing a monopoly of power, arresting and killing their political opponents. Their actions plunged Russia into a civil war of unspeakable barbarism that would last several years. Foreign forces—including the British, French, Americans, and Japanese—landed on Russian territory, first in the hope of keeping Russia in the war against Germany, and then offering nominal support to the White armies fighting against the Bolshevik Red Army. Complicating matters still further, Great Britain's Royal Navy established a blockade in the Baltic Sea that isolated the new Soviet government from the West for many months.

The Bolsheviks knew from the start that bread was crucial to their survival. If they didn't solve the food problem, the revolution would fail. Leon Trotsky, the great revolutionary and prominent Soviet official who, among other things, was then head of the Extraordinary Commission for Food and Transport, told the Central Executive Committee of the Soviets in April 1918: "I say it quite openly; we are now at war, and it is only with guns that we will get the grain we need. Our only choice now is civil war. Civil war is the struggle for bread [. . .] Long live the civil war!" A key tactic in the effort to seize the grain was to stoke class warfare in the villages. The Bolsheviks created Committees of Poor Peasants (*Kombedy*) to confiscate the grain of the wealthier peasants, the so-called kulaks, and hand it over to the state. Often composed of outsiders, the *Kombedy* terrorized the local population, stealing their personal property, making summary arrests, and further destabilizing rural life, an effort Lenin endorsed as part of a larger goal of destroying age-old and, in his eyes, backward peasant culture. A Provisioning Army (*Prodovol'stvennaya armiya* or *Prodarmiya*), consisting largely of unemployed Petrograd workers, was also created and sent out into the countryside, both to spread Bolshevik propaganda and to help in the requisitioning of grain. Fyodor Dan, a leader of the Menshevik Party,* called it "a crusade against the peasantry."

Lenin, however, was only getting started. In August 1918, he ordered that wealthy peasants be taken hostage and executed should the requisition targets not be met. He sent this directive to the Penza Soviet:

---

* A wing of the Russian socialist movement that advocated a more moderate program than Lenin's Bolsheviks.

The kulak uprising in your five districts must be crushed without pity [. . .] You must make an example of these people. (1) Hang (I mean hang publicly, so that people see it) at least 100 kulaks, rich bastards, and known bloodsuckers. (2) Publish their names. (3) Seize all their grain. (4) Single out the hostages per my instructions [. . .] Do all this so that for miles around people see it all, understand it, tremble.

Even fellow Bolsheviks were aghast at what was being done to the peasants. "The measures of extraction are reminiscent of a medieval inquisition," commented one official after witnessing a requisition brigade at work in southern Russia. "They make the peasants strip and kneel on the ground, whip or beat them, sometimes kill them." In June 1918, Joseph Stalin traveled to Tsaritsyn* with two armored trains carrying 450 Red Army soldiers to secure food for the capital. His initial success was not enough for Lenin, who felt Stalin had been soft and ordered him to "be merciless" toward their enemies in the hunt for food. "Be assured our hand will not tremble," Stalin replied. "We won't show mercy to anyone [. . .] We will bring you bread."

The grain quota established by the central government grew ever higher. By 1920, it had risen from eighteen to twenty-seven million poods.[†] The peasants called that year's requisition campaign "The Iron Broom," for it swept the villages clean of practically every last kernel of grain, leaving the peasants with almost nothing. Local authorities could not believe what they were seeing and sent back reports to their bosses in Moscow that such actions were "senseless and futile." Even though the war against the White armies had largely ended with the defeat of General Pyotr Wrangel's forces in late 1920, still the campaigns against the peasants raged on.

Peasants responded to the brutal policies of the Bolsheviks in a number of ways. One was to hide their grain, be it under the floor, down the

---

* Now Volgograd.
[†] A Russian pood equals approximately 16.4 kilograms or 36 pounds.

well, stuffed in thatched roofs, or behind fake walls and secret compart-
ments in their huts. The men of the *Prodarmiya* soon caught on to the
peasants' tricks and became relentless in ferreting out their hidden stores,
regardless of the damage they caused. A second response was to reduce
the land under cultivation and grow only the bare minimum necessary
for their own survival, thus denying any surplus for the state. Between 1917
and 1921, as much as a third of the arable land in the main agricultural
regions of Russia was removed from production. The harvest of 1920 was
just barely over half that of 1913.

And some peasants decided to fight back. Revolts against grain requisitioning first erupted in the summer of 1918 and grew as time went on.
The uprisings turned into an actual war in the summer of 1920, when
a former factory worker and schoolteacher by the name of Alexander
Antonov organized the Partisan Army of the Tambov region. Eventually
growing to some fifty thousand men, many of them Red Army deserters,
Antonov's peasant army swept out of Tambov and soon spread into the
lower Volga region—Samara, Saratov, Tsaritsyn, and Astrakhan—and
even into western Siberia. "Banditry has overwhelmed the whole province,"
wrote terrified Bolshevik leaders in Saratov in a telegram to Moscow. "The
peasants have seized all the stocks—3 million poods—from the grain
stores. They are heavily armed, thanks to all the rifles from the deserters.
Whole units of the Red Army have simply vanished." The fire of revolt
seemed unstoppable, and the Soviet government was losing control over
ever more territory.

Toward the end of 1920, the Cheka—the Soviet political police, pre-
cursor to the KGB—admitted that, except for areas around Moscow,
Petrograd, and the Russian north, the entire country was convulsed with
unrest. The situation grew worse in early 1921. The chairman of the
Samara Province Cheka wrote to his superiors in Moscow in a top-secret
memorandum: "The masses now have a hostile attitude to the communists [. . .] Cholera and scurvy are raging [. . .] Desertions from the gar-
rison are growing." Lenin was beside himself. The peasant war, he warned
his colleagues, was "far more dangerous to us than all the Denikins,

Kolchaks, and Yudeniches put together."* The key to the fate of the Soviet government, in other words, lay with the country's rebellious peasants.

And it wasn't just the peasants. The Bolsheviks began to lose support in the cities, too, among workers and soldiers, once their most devoted followers. In January 1921, bread rations were cut by as much as 30 percent in a number of cities. Angry and hungry, the workers of Petrograd went on strike. Demonstrations quickly devolved into riots. Cheka detachments had to be dispatched to restore order; martial law was declared in late February 1921. The following month, the sailors at the Kronstadt naval base rebelled against what they called the "Communist autocracy," characterizing the country's rulers as "worse than [Tsar] Nicholas" and issuing a call for their own "third revolution." Lenin saw to it that the mutiny was crushed. Over two thousand men were sentenced to death, more than six thousand sent off to prison.

To save the regime, Lenin announced at the Tenth Party Congress in March a strategic retreat from the extremist policies of the past. "War Communism," as the initial phase of the revolution came to be known, was to be replaced by the New Economic Policy (NEP), a concession to capitalism and market forces that allowed for private property and ownership of retail trade and small industry. Most important, NEP ended the forced grain requisitions in favor of a tax in kind (i.e., grain or other agricultural products). Henceforth, peasants would know exactly what their obligation to the state was, thus giving them the incentive to grow as much as possible, keeping any surplus for themselves.

Meanwhile, the war against Antonov's peasant army raged on into the summer of 1921. An army of one hundred thousand led by General Mikhail Tukhachevsky mounted a campaign of ruthless terror that included the use of heavy artillery and airplanes against what the state called "bandits." Soldiers were given orders to shoot on sight any person who refused to give his name. Families guilty of harboring bandits were to be arrested and deported from the province. Their property was to

---

* Commanders of the White forces: Anton Denikin, Alexander Kolchak, and Nikolai Yudenich.

be seized, and their eldest son executed forthwith. Tukhachevsky's army took thousands of hostages and interned them in *kontsentratsionnye lageria*—concentration camps. By August, ten camps in Tambov Province alone held over thirteen thousand prisoners. Lenin ordered his general to suffocate the enemy: "The forests where the bandits are hiding must be cleared with poison gas. Careful calculations must be made to ensure that the cloud of asphyxiating gas spreads throughout the forest and exterminates everything hidden there."

Eventually, the Red Army gained the upper hand. Although Antonov would not be caught—and killed—until June 1922, the last of the rebels were being mopped up by the autumn of 1921.

The Bolsheviks, however, had vanquished one foe only to face another, much more dangerous one. In terms of sheer numbers, the famine of 1921 was the worst Europe had ever known. The Soviet government estimated that some thirty million people were facing death. The concessions to the peasants made in March at the party congress had come too late to alter the situation. Lenin had said then: "If there is a harvest, then everybody will hunger a little, and the government will be saved. Otherwise, since we cannot take anything from people who do not have the means of satisfying their own hunger, the government will perish." Two years of drought, and several more of war and senseless cruelty, meant whatever harvest there might be would never come close to feeding a hungry Russia.

THE GOVERNMENT HAD been receiving reports of the growing crisis since the beginning of 1921. One Cheka report from January described the famine sweeping over Tambov Province, which it attributed to the "orgy" of requisitioning in 1920. The waves of refugees fleeing hunger throughout the Volga Basin became too large to ignore.

Yet that is just what the government did. Any official mention of the famine was forbidden until July 2, 1921, when the newspaper *Pravda* published the following notice on the back page: "This year the grain harvest will be lower than the average for the last decade." It went on to add that there had been "a feeding problem on the agricultural front."

A family of refugees
in search of food

Orwellian language if ever there was. Ten days later, *Pravda* printed a
fuller and more honest story that characterized the famine as "a catastrophe for all of Russia that is having an influence on every aspect of the
country's economic and political life." It instructed readers in the famine
zone to stay where they were and not to add to the "wave of refugees" or
give in to the panic and rumors that represented such a "very large danger" to the country at present. The bourgeois West had been informed of
the famine, *Pravda* went on, but it cautioned readers against placing any
hope in the "capitalist predators," who would not only be overjoyed to see
the working people of Russia starve, but would use their suffering as a opportunity to organize a counterrevolution against the Soviet government.

The West had indeed been made aware of the catastrophe early that
month, in two separate appeals for help. One had been issued by Tikhon,
patriarch of the Russian Orthodox Church, addressed to the pope, the
archbishop of Canterbury, and other world religious leaders. The other had

been made by the writer Maxim Gorky. Apparently, the idea had not belonged to Gorky, who was no great champion of the peasantry. (He even published a book the following year called *The Russian Peasant* in which he wrote of "the half-savage, stupid, and heavy people of the Russian villages" and expressed the hope that they would die out and be replaced by "a new tribe" of "literate, sensible, hearty people.") Friends of the writer convinced him to use his considerable moral authority to speak with the Kremlin about issuing an open appeal to the world. Lenin, it seems, did not take much convincing.

In "To All Honest People," dated July 13, Gorky wrote: "Gloomy days have come for the land of Tolstoy, Dostoevsky, Mendeleev, Pavlov, Mussorgsky, Glinka and other world-prized men [. . .] Russia's misfortunes offer humanitarians a splendid opportunity to demonstrate the vitality of humanitarianism [. . .] I ask all honest European and American people for prompt aid to the Russian people. Give bread and medicine." He included mention of the unprecedented drought afflicting his country, but said nothing about capitalist predators or counterrevolutionaries. Gorky sent the appeal initially to Fridtjof Nansen, the famous Norwegian explorer, scientist, and humanitarian, but Nansen replied that the Russians would be better advised to concentrate their efforts on the Americans, for they alone had the resources to help.

On July 22, 1921, a copy of Gorky's appeal published in the American press landed on the desk of Herbert Hoover, the U.S. secretary of commerce. As soon as he had read it, Hoover knew what had to be done.

2

THE CHIEF

THE HUBERS LEFT THEIR NATIVE SWITZERLAND for the American colonies in the first half of the eighteenth century. At some point they anglicized their name to "Hoover" and abandoned the Lutheran Church for the Religious Society of Friends, the Quakers, drawn to the Friends' revulsion to slavery. The family moved west with the young nation, eventually settling in a small cottage by Wapsinonoc Creek, in the rolling farm country of eastern Iowa. It was here, in August 1874, that Herbert Hoover was born.

Jesse Hoover was the blacksmith in the village of West Branch; Hulda, his wife, taught Sunday school and served as secretary in the Women's Christian Temperance Union. They were simple, industrious folk. The family motto was "What matter if we descended from the highest unless we are something ourselves. Get busy." Little Bertie, as he was called, was a sickly boy, often afflicted with the croup. Once, they thought he had died and laid him out on the table, a dime over each eye. Suddenly, Bertie stirred. "God has a great work for that boy to do," said his amazed grandmother; "that is why he was brought back to life." In 1880, Jesse died, followed by Hulda four years later. At the age of nine, Bertie became an orphan.

He was sent off to live with his uncle in Oregon. Life there was as serious as in his parents' home. A fellow Quaker, Bertie's uncle impressed upon the boy the importance of individual responsibility, hard work, and self-improvement. At school, Bertie was asked by his teacher to consider questions such as whether more men's lives had been destroyed by liquor or by war. In 1888, Bertie, now just fourteen years old, was sent to Salem to be an office boy for the Oregon Land Company, where he acquired the fundamentals of business and proved an excellent worker. In 1891, he joined the inaugural incoming class at the new Leland Stanford Junior University, dedicated, in the words of its founder, "to promote the public welfare by exercising an influence in behalf of humanity and civilization." When Hoover graduated four years later, with average grades and a B.A. in geology, none of his classmates held out any great hopes for his future. Yet the fundamental elements of his character that would make him a successful businessman and then a great humanitarian—a keen mind, boundless energy, a nascent sense of his uncommon talents, undeniable ambition, and a commitment to duty and service—were already in place.

Hoover set off to work as a mining engineer in the gold fields of the Australian outback (what he called "hell") and then moved on to China, where he managed to put together what was perhaps the largest mining transaction in the country's history, all before the age of thirty. He was in Tianjin in 1900, during the Boxer Rebellion. Refusing to be evacuated to safety, he delivered food and supplies on his bicycle to other members of the foreign settlement, with bullets whizzing past his ears. This marked young Hoover's first relief mission, which, though modest, was not free of personal danger.

He was made a partner in the British engineering firm Bewick, Moreing and Company two years later and traveled about the world setting up and reorganizing mining operations in sixteen countries. He had a knack for making lackluster operations profitable and discovering new opportunities. In 1905, Hoover invested his own money into an abandoned mine in Burma, and under his management it quickly became one of the world's richest sources of silver, zinc, and lead. He gained an international reputation for his administrative talent, technological understanding, and way with finances. After a few years, he parted company with the firm and went off on his own, operating simply as "Herbert C. Hoover," with offices in New York, San Francisco, London, Paris, and St. Petersburg.

Hoover first visited Russia in 1909, and over the next several years he invested considerable time and money in the country. He was involved in oil fields around the Black Sea, copper mines in the Kazakh Steppes, gold and iron mines in the Ural Mountains. At one point, he was even asked to manage the Romanov Imperial Cabinet's mines. He returned to Russia two years later to check on his investments. Although pleased with the state of his various operations, Hoover was disturbed by what he saw of Tsar Nicholas II's Russia. He described as "hideous" the social tensions rumbling just beneath the surface. The sight of a chain gang being marched off into Siberian exile made him shudder. The brutality of the tsarist system haunted Hoover: he couldn't shake the feeling that, in his words, "some day the country would blow up." Hoover sold off his investments before the country exploded under the joint pressures of war and revolution. Russia, for Hoover, was a land filled with "annoyance and worry."

The outbreak of World War I in 1914 found Hoover and his wife and children living in luxury in London. Forty years old, Hoover had amassed a fortune and now commanded the highest engineering fees in the world, but the fun had gone out of it. He retired from business. It appears that Hoover had undergone some sort of crisis. Money and worldly success were no longer enough for him; he wanted something different, something more. The old family values of doing good, being of service, aiding one's fellow man pricked his conscience.

That year, Hoover was approached by the U.S. consul in Britain and asked to help Americans trapped in Europe by the war. Hoover set to work immediately and managed to arrange safe passage home for 120,000 people. Hoover's career in public life had begun.

He next turned his attention to the crisis in Belgium. Ignoring its neighbor's neutrality, Germany had invaded Belgium early in the war. In what became known as the Rape of Belgium, the German Army massacred thousands of civilians and burned their homes. The international outcry was enormous. With the country occupied by the Germans and cut off from supplies by a British naval blockade, the people of Belgium were soon running low on food. Mass starvation looked like a horrifying possibility.

Hoover set up the Commission for Relief in Belgium to bring food and supplies to the approximately nine million people living under German occupation in Belgium and northern France. But first he had to convince the warring nations to agree to his plan. The British, led by Minister of War Lord Kitchener, First Lord of the Admiralty Winston Churchill, and Prime Minister David Lloyd George, objected to the idea, fearful the Germans would take the food for themselves and thus prolong the war. Hoover, however, managed to convince them that the CRB's agents would control the transport, storage, and distribution of all supplies, thus minimizing the possibility that the food would end up in German hands. At the same time, he also convinced both Britain and Germany that it was in their own best interest to allow the aid to go through, since this would go a long way to improving public opinion in America—still a neutral party—and so, perhaps, help to win the United States to their side in the conflict. Although no one in London or Berlin cared to listen to the arguments of some American businessman, in the end they all agreed.

For the next two and a half years, the CRB distributed over 2.5 million tons of food to the people of Belgium and northern France. There had never been an organization like it before. The CRB was the biggest, most ambitious relief effort in history, run by an outfit that was neither wholly private nor wholly public. One British Foreign Office official called it "a piratical state organized for benevolence." It had its own fleet of ships, and even its own flag. The men of the CRB had been gathered from among Hoover's business associates, Rhodes scholars, and U.S. Army officers, all of

whom served with unquestioned devotion the man they called "The Chief."
His agents had complete freedom from
the various European governments to
operate as they saw fit, and their boss entrusted them with enormous leeway in
their day-to-day operations.

Herbert Hoover

At the same time, Hoover insisted
on complete control over the entire
operation. An undertaking of this size
and complexity demanded the organizational skills of an exceptional businessman and the absolute power of a
dictator. "Famine fighting is a gigantic
economic and governmental operation
handled by experts," he insisted, "and not 'welfare' work of benevolently
handing out food hit or miss to bread lines [. . .] Some individual with
great powers must direct and coordinate all this." "Some individual"
meant, naturally, Hoover himself. With every minute of the day devoted
to famine relief, Hoover had no time left to manage his personal financial affairs, but he didn't worry. "Let the fortune go to hell," he said. He
wrung money out of everyone he could to support the CRB. He even
managed to talk Britain and France into subsidizing his effort, to the
tune of over $300 million. Not everyone was impressed by Hoover's ef-
forts. Senator Henry Cabot Lodge of Massachusetts deemed the CRB a
criminal act by an individual citizen who was usurping the authority of
official United States diplomacy. He threatened an investigation.

In the end, the CRB proved an enormous success. It disbursed over
$880 million in aid, more than the typical annual budget of the United
States government before the war, and saved millions of lives. "The Savior
of Belgium," as Hoover became known on both sides of the Atlantic, had
won the admiration of people across Europe and America.

After the United States entered the war in April 1917, Hoover gave up
his position at the CRB and returned home, where President Woodrow

Wilson made him the head of the United States Food Administration established that summer. Dubbed "the food dictator" by the press, he was now in charge of the food chain for the entire nation. With singular focus, he pushed efficiency, standardization, and measurement to minimize waste. Every American learned to "Hooverize" for the sake of the war effort. At war's end, Wilson invited Hoover to join him at the Paris Peace Conference as an unofficial adviser. To help sustain the hungry, war-torn continent and begin the process of economic reconstruction, Hoover urged the president to create the American Relief Administration, funded by a $100 million appropriation from Congress early in 1919. As its general director, Hoover undertook relief operations in thirty-two countries, not only offering food and clothing but rebuilding devastated infrastructure and acting as a quasi-intelligence and diplomatic organization for the Allied powers. Upon learning that Europe's telephone and telegraph systems had been largely destroyed, Hoover created an effective wireless network using U.S. Navy vessels and experts from the Army Signal Corps. Nothing would stand in the way of accomplishing the mission. Over the course of nine months, the ARA distributed over $1 billion in aid.

The establishment of the ARA symbolized the arrival of the United States on the international stage. Its creation was an expression of Americans' growing confidence in their ability to project American power and values around the globe. Hoover shared Wilson's belief in America's mission to improve the world. Yet, unlike the president, whose practical knowledge of life abroad was quite limited, Hoover had lived outside the United States for many years and so had a much better understanding of the world and how difficult improving it was going to be.

Wilson, like many presidents after him, mistakenly believed America could redeem humanity; a wiser, more knowledgeable Hoover was content to ease its suffering. "The sole object of relief," Hoover remarked in December 1918, "should be humanity. It should have no other political objective or aim other than the maintenance of life and order."

That said, he was convinced that neither life nor order could be secured in nations that fell to the new threat: Bolshevism. He made it clear in a memorandum in November 1918 that the first order of business in the reconstruction of Europe was the need "to stem the tide of Bolshevism," which could only be achieved through the peace and stability that adequate food made possible. Wilson agreed, writing to the chairman of the House Appropriations Committee in early 1919: "Bolshevism is steadily advancing westward, is poisoning Germany. It cannot be stopped by force, but it can be stopped by food." Food, the two men correctly understood, was a weapon.

Many in the United States, intent on "making the Hun pay" for the war, were not so clear-sighted. The U.S. Senate went out of its way to forbid the use of any of the appropriation for the ARA in the defeated enemy states. Hoover had fought against the restriction, and had also spoken out against the Versailles Treaty's harsh treatment of Germany. Forcing the Germans to accept the blame for the war and to pay punitive reparations, the treaty, in his opinion, reeked of "hate and revenge" and was bound to lead to resentment and political instability. Not to be stymied by the small minds of the Senate, Hoover outwitted his own government by moving aid through a byzantine network of organizations, thus making it impossible to follow exactly what the ARA was up to. In the end, Hoover managed to direct over 40 percent of the ARA's relief supplies to Germany and the former Austro-Hungarian Empire.

The economist John Maynard Keynes, representative of the British Treasury to the peace talks, stood in awe of Hoover and the ARA:

> Never was a nobler work of disinterested goodwill carried
> through with more tenacity and sincerity and skill, and with
> less thanks either asked or given. The ungrateful Governments
> of Europe owe much more to the statesmanship and insight of
> Mr. Hoover and his band of American workers than they
> have yet appreciated or will ever acknowledge [. . .] It was their
> efforts, their energy, and the American resources placed by the
> President at their disposal, often acting in the teeth of European
> obstruction, which not only saved an immense amount of human
> suffering, but averted a widespread breakdown of the European
> system.

Keynes and Hoover, who met at the conference, were of the same mind about the treaty. Keynes was convinced that had there been more diplomats in possession of Hoover's "knowledge, magnanimity, and disinterestedness," they would have been able to secure "the Good Peace."

ALTHOUGH HOOVER UNDERSTOOD how Bolshevism spoke to the Russian people after centuries of oppression, he was an unbending foe of communism, and would remain so for his entire life. He was against official recognition of Lenin's Soviet state, what he called "this murderous tyranny," not only since he believed this would encourage radicalism in the West, but also given the Soviets' refusal to assume tsarist debts* and his conviction that the Bolsheviks would never protect American lives or property—views shared by Wilson.

Nevertheless, Hoover did not support military action by the United States. He wrote in a memorandum to Wilson on March 28, 1919: "No greater fortune can come to this world than that these foolish ideas should have an opportunity somewhere of bankrupting themselves." In the meantime, however, he was not against offering aid to those then waging war against Lenin and the new Soviet Russia. He wrote Secretary of State Robert Lansing from Paris in August 1919 that the ARA should support the White Army forces of General Nikolai Yudenich, convinced that the Whites represented Russia's best hope for a constitutional government and the defense of personal liberty. When Yudenich marched on Petrograd in the autumn, Hoover supplied him with food, clothing, and gasoline. The grateful general wrote to thank "Mr. Hoover, Food-Dictator of Europe," and informed him that his army was "now existing practically upon American flour and bacon," which was no less important for their success than "rifles and ammunition."

Hoover later tried to cover up his support of the Whites, but Lenin and the rest of the Soviet leadership knew about it. Understandably, the

---

* Soon after seizing power, the Bolsheviks renounced the $187 million the U.S. government had extended to the Provisional Government and the $86 million loaned to the tsarist regime by American banks.

true motives of America's great humanitarian remained under a cloud of suspicion.

AFTER READING GORKY'S appeal on July 22, 1921, Hoover, now secretary of commerce under the new president, Warren G. Harding, wrote to Secretary of State Charles Evans Hughes: "I feel very deeply that we should go to the assistance of the children and also provide some medical relief generally." He stated that he wished to reply to Gorky's appeal. "I believe it is a humane obligation upon us to go in if they comply with the requirements set out; if they do not accede we are released from all responsibility."

Hoover could not have been surprised by Gorky's appeal. In the first week of June, the ARA received reports on the severity of the Russian crisis. Hoover communicated to his top subordinates in the ARA that operations in other countries were to be halted so that they could begin building up supplies for a possible mission to Russia. He wanted to be ready, should the Soviet government collapse or be overthrown, to show Russia the goodwill of the American people. His motives were twofold: the desire to fight both hunger and Bolshevism.

On July 23, Hoover wired a lengthy telegram to Gorky, explaining that he had been moved by the suffering of the Russian people and laying out what had to happen before any aid might be considered, as well as a necessary general understanding of principles. First, he noted, all American prisoners in Russia had to be released immediately. Next, the following items had to be agreed to: (1) that the Soviet government must officially state that it was requesting the assistance of the American Relief Administration; (2) that Mr. Hoover was acting not as secretary of commerce but in an unofficial capacity, as the head of a relief agency, so that help from the ARA in no way signaled official U.S. government recognition of the Soviet state; (3) that the ARA would operate in Russia as it did in all other countries: namely, its workers would have complete liberty to come and go and travel about, free of interference; that they would have permission to set up local aid committees as they best saw fit; and that the

Soviet government would cover all costs associated with the transportation, storage, and handling of ARA supplies. In return, the ARA promised to give food, medical supplies, and clothing to one million children "without regard to race, creed, or social status." Finally, Hoover affirmed that the representatives of the ARA would refrain from any political activity.

If the Soviet leadership had any doubts, reports from the provinces that month may well have convinced them to put them aside. In the middle of July, the vice-chairman of the Samara Province Executive Committee sent a secret telegram to Lenin, outlining in clear terms just how dire the situation had become: "There are no more grain reserves in the district capitals. State dining halls are all closing. Children are starving in the orphanages [. . .] The cholera epidemic has taken on terrifying proportions [. . .] Samara is now the breeding ground of a contagion, the consequences of which threaten the entire republic [. . .] The population is fleeing from Samara Province, the train stations and wharfs are overflowing with refugees. Famine, epidemic."

From the start, the ARA mission to Russia was subject to political pressure back at home. When word of Hoover's reply to Gorky became public, the ACLU objected in the pages of *The New York Times* to linking the offer of aid to any political conditions. *The Nation* criticized Hoover along similar lines, noting that surely there were Soviet citizens in U.S. jails, and so who were we to expect the Soviets to release Americans if we did not do the same to Russians. Some on the right saw in the famine the opportunity to strike a blow against Bolshevism. John Spargo, an erstwhile socialist turned rabid Republican anti-Red crusader, wrote Secretary of State Hughes, "The present crisis presents an opportunity which, if rightly used, may lead to the liquidation of the Bolshevist regime and the beginning of a restoration." He recommended they work together with the newly created All-Russian Committee for Aid to the Starving, an organization that included many anti-Bolshevik intellectuals and prerevolutionary political and cultural leaders, which Lenin had reluctantly agreed to sanction, although chiefly for cynical public-relations efforts in the West. Lenin let the other Soviet leaders know that a close watch would be kept on the committee, and that as soon as it had served its function, it would be closed and its members dealt with. As for Spargo, he, like some other opponents of the Soviet regime, thought the committee could become the basis of a representative government in Russia once the Bolsheviks had fallen.

Paul Ryabushinsky, an adviser to the embassy of the Russian Provisional Government in Washington, D.C., met with Hoover's assistant Christian Herter to tell him in secret that Russian émigrés were prepared to provide money and supplies to the ARA that it could funnel to the All-Russian Committee for Aid to the Starving. Their goal was to use the ARA to help undermine the Soviet government and replace it with the committee once the Soviets had been overthrown. Herter declined to endorse Ryabushinsky's plan.

All of this was taking place in the shadow of the Red Scare that had gripped the United States in 1919–20. After the war, the country had experienced a wave of strikes and worker agitation, and there was the fear that Bolshevik influence might spread outward from Russia to destabilize the West. The U.S. Senate organized a subcommittee to investigate the threat of the "Red Menace" to civilization. In the spring of 1919, anarchists began a bombing campaign against key politicians, state officials, and businessmen, including John D. Rockefeller. One bomb was mailed to the home of U.S. Attorney General A. Mitchell Palmer. An enraged Palmer responded with the so-called Palmer Raids. By December, 249 radicals had been caught and placed on a ship leaving for Finland, whence they would be free to make their way to Bolshevik Russia. Among them was the "Red Queen," Emma Goldman. One of the young agents hired by Palmer to hunt down the radicals was a nineteen-year-old civil servant by the name of J. Edgar Hoover. In the end, thousands of suspected radical subversives were deported. Palmer announced that the Reds planned to overthrow the U.S. government on May 1, 1920. When the day came and went with no revolution, Palmer's credibility took a hit. Still, the violence, and the hysteria, continued. On September 16, a bomb exploded on Wall Street, killing thirty-eight people.

Staunch anti-Bolshevik though he was, Hoover appears to have looked upon the hysteria of the Red Scare as misguided and overblown. Even though the Red Scare had calmed down by the summer of 1921, many Americans still saw no difference between the Bolsheviks and the Russians, so that helping one was helping the other. But Hoover always insisted on keeping the two separate: "We must make some distinction between the Russian people and the group who have seized the Government." Moreover, Hoover's reputation as an enemy of Bolshevism was just the thing for an American trying to win support for a relief operation to Russia: it immunized him against the charge that his ultimate goal was to help save the young Soviet regime.

On July 26, a mere three days after sending his list of conditions, Hoover received a reply from Gorky stating that the Soviet government looked favorably on his offer. Two days later, Lev Kamenev, an old Bolshevik, a longtime comrade of Lenin, chairman of the Moscow Soviet, and head of the Committee for Aid to the Starving, sent Hoover an official letter of acceptance of relief on behalf of the government. He promised that the American prisoners would be freed and proposed that the two sides immediately sit down to agree on the conditions necessary to begin the enormous task of feeding the hungry.

3

THE RIGA
AGREEMENT

NEGOTIATIONS BEGAN IN THE BALTIC CITY of Riga, capital of the newly independent state of Latvia, on August 7. Walter Lyman Brown, the London-based director of the ARA for Europe, represented the American delegation, together with his assistants Cyril J. Quinn, head of the ARA in Poland, and Philip Carroll, ARA chief in Germany. The Soviet team was led by Maxim Litvinov, deputy chairman of the People's Commissariat for Foreign Affairs. The chain-smoking Litvinov spoke fluent English and was an intelligent and highly skilled negotiator—persuasive, wily, and tough. Once, Litvinov's revolver fell from his coat pocket and crashed onto the negotiating table. Quinn worried that if all Bolsheviks were like Litvinov, they were in big trouble.

Two days before the negotiators met, Lenin instructed Kamenev to hurry up with the release of the American prisoners, and the Soviet government did manage to accomplish this in time. But no sooner had the two sides sat down than Litvinov pushed back on two of the ARA's key demands: a voice in determining which regions to serve, and the right to set up local relief committees without Soviet interference. Disagreements also arose over questions concerning the ARA's freedom of movement about the country and who would have ultimate control over the distribution of food and other relief: the ARA or the Soviet authorities. As for the Americans, Brown wanted to backtrack on Hoover's reference, in his telegram to Gorky, to helping one million children, proposing instead that they drop any mention of a specific number and promise only to feed as many as possible. He also added the stipulation that, as in other countries served by the ARA, all warehouses, offices, vehicles, trains, and kitchens be prominently marked as belonging to the "American Relief Administration" and that, wherever possible, these identifications include the image of their boss, Herbert Hoover. If the ARA was going to go to the considerable trouble of aiding the people of Russia, it was going to make certain everyone there knew just who it was who was helping them.

A wall of mistrust divided the two sides. The Americans worried about compromising the independence of the operation and simply handing over relief supplies to the Soviets to disperse as they saw fit, without American control. They would offer aid on their own terms, feeding as best they could everyone in need, not just loyal supporters of the regime, and were careful not to let themselves be used by the Soviet government for their own designs. The Soviets worried about a good many things, chiefly that the true goal of the operation was the overthrow of their government.

Lenin, in declining health and suffering from insomnia and horrible headaches, nervously followed the talks from Moscow. He sent Litvinov a radiogram on August 11: "Be careful. Try to gauge their intentions. Do not let them get insolent with you." He insisted on being kept informed of every detail during the talks. Lenin seethed with anger when he heard the Americans' demands, especially about noninterference with the ARA men once they were inside Russia. Hoover and Brown were "impudent liars," he wrote the same day to Vyacheslav Molotov, secretary of the Communist Party throughout the 1920s and then foreign minister under Stalin. Lenin insisted, "Hoover must be punished, he must be *publicly* slapped in the face so *the whole* world can see." He demanded Litvinov set "very strict conditions: for the slightest interference in internal matters—expulsion and arrest." The *Red Newspaper* captured the mood with an article titled "The Greek Hoover and His Gifts": the ARA was a modern-day Trojan horse presented to foment counterrevolution; if the ARA was permitted into Soviet Russia, the newspaper demanded, it would have to be not only watched but placed under tight government control.

The most fanciful comment on the ARA came from Leon Trotsky, the brilliant Marxist theorist and ultimate master of spin, in a speech before the Moscow Soviet. While acknowledging that Russia was facing a serious famine, Trotsky assured his audience that the government could handle it without outside help. No, he proclaimed, it wasn't Soviet Russia that needed the West, but the other way around: the capitalist world was facing a commercial and industrial crisis of unprecedented scale (the depression of 1920–21 had indeed been bad, but the worst was over by then), and its only chance at survival was in finding a way to draw Russia back into the world economy. "What is at stake is the very basis of bourgeois rule," Trotsky told his audience. In other words, America would not save Russia, but Russia might well save America. The offer of relief by the ARA had nothing to do with a real concern for human welfare; rather, it amounted to nothing more than an aggressive move by the missionaries of American capital, who were certain to be followed by businessmen, traders, and bankers.

There was one gaping hole, however, in Trotsky's depiction of the current situation: if the government truly could handle the famine without Western help, why, then, was it willing to make "big concessions," as he characterized them, to the ARA, especially if the Americans posed such a serious counterrevolutionary threat? To this, the great Marxist dialectician had no answer. In fact, Russia could not get by without outside help, as Kamenev had made quite plain in a speech the month before, admitting, with all seriousness: "We know that our resources aren't enough to

even begin to halt this disaster. We must have help from abroad, especially
help from foreign workers and also all kinds of public organizations in Europe and America that are able to recognize the necessity of help regardless of our political differences."

An article titled "Stemming the Red Tide" that had appeared that
spring in the journal *The World's Work* seemed to validate Soviet suspicions of the ARA. The author, T.T.C. Gregory, a brash lawyer from San
Francisco with an inflated sense of his role in world events, had served in
the ARA in Central Europe after the war. Gregory described how he and
Hoover had hatched a plan to overthrow the communist government of
Béla Kun in Hungary by withholding food relief to Budapest in the summer of 1919. "Way down in my heart," Gregory wrote, "I knew that we
were not only feeding people but also were fighting Bolshevism." His actions had shown the incredible power of food "as modern weapons." After
his cunning maneuver to stop the spread of the "Red Menace," as Gregory saw it, no one could deny that "Bread is mightier than the sword!"

Though it's true that Hoover could not stomach the Kun regime,
Gregory's boast was pure fancy. (The imaginative Gregory also claimed
he prevented the Habsburg restoration after the fall of Kun: "My blood
was up . . . A member of the Habsburg family? Not while I could have a
word to say, at any rate!") The Hungarian Soviet Republic, which lasted
a mere 133 days, collapsed of its own making, largely because of the regime's military aggression toward its neighbors, and not the derring-do of
T.T.C. Gregory, attorney-at-law. Nevertheless, the article, soon reprinted
in *Soviet Russia*, confirmed the Russians' darkest fears about Hoover and
the ARA.

Gregory's piece gave ammunition to the American left as well. *The
Nation* took up the story and accused Hoover of putting politics ahead
of people. Another left-wing magazine commented, "Everything that is
known about Mr. Hoover [. . .] conveys ample assurance that he would
use his position in Russia for political purposes." While negotiations were
under way in Riga, the American Labor Alliance held a rally in New
York City at which the main speaker openly accused Hoover of planning

to overthrow the Soviet government by taking control of the country's food supply.

Attacks also came from the right. Henry Ford's *Dearborn Independent* maligned the mission and attacked the ARA as poorly administered and venal. There were nasty suggestions that the ARA was controlled by Jews and Bolsheviks. Another Midwestern newspaper asked why America should "interest itself in perpetuating a dynasty of darkness that is dying because of its incompetence." Criticized by both left and right, Hoover let his men know that the ARA would avoid politics at all costs. He sent a cable to Brown in Riga on August 6, a day after Herter's meeting with Ryabushinsky:

> I wish to impress on each one of them [employees of the ARA] the supreme importance of their keeping entirely aloof not only from action but even from discussion of political and social questions. Our people are not Bolsheviks but our mission is solely to save lives and any participation even in discussions will only lead to suspicion of our objects. In selection of local committees and Russian staff we wish to be absolutely neutral and neutrality implies appointment from every group in Russia and a complete insistence that children of all parentage have equal treatment.

Along with instructions to his agents, Hoover also maintained an ARA public-relations department, led by George Barr Baker in New York, that put out a steady stream of uplifting press releases, maintained good relations with the Western press, and sought to counter any negative publicity. Hoover was not about to let anyone tarnish his reputation or that of the American Relief Administration if he could help it.

IN RIGA, TALKS had reached an impasse. On August 12, the local newspaper published an interview with Litvinov in which he affirmed that the Soviets would "never agree to any conditions that may have the slightest effect of discrediting our government. We will never let any foreign administration use the terrible conditions in the Volga District to force the Workers' and Peasants' Government to accept conditions that are against our honor." The following day, he sent a cable to his boss, Georgy Chicherin, people's commissar for foreign affairs: "I have the impression that the ARA has come to us without any ulterior motives, but still we're going to have plenty of trouble with them." The two sides had had no success in coming to any sort of agreement over the ARA's autonomy and who would be in charge of handing out the food. Litvinov kept reminding Brown and the other Americans, in his heavily accented English, "Gentlemen, food iz a veppon." Of course, Litvinov knew this well from recent history. The Soviet government had given extra rations to social groups that supported the regime and denied food to its enemies, both real and imagined. They had used food as a weapon in the struggle to win the revolution and create the first communist state. And they needed food now to prevent the state from collapsing, but the question was: if food was a weapon, whose finger was going to be on the trigger?

Brown wired Hoover on August 15 that the talks were deadlocked and they would have to make some concessions. At first Hoover refused, but he soon realized it would be best to do whatever he could to make a deal. He agreed that the ARA would not hire any non-Americans without the approval of the Soviet authorities, and that the ARA would fire from its staff anyone the Soviet government complained about, if there was the least bit of evidence of any political or counterrevolutionary activity on that person's part. The Americans also agreed to permit the Soviets to expel any person caught engaging in political or commercial activity and granted them the right to search premises in which they believed a crime had taken place, and reinstated the reference to feeding one million children first made in Hoover's telegram to Gorky. Nonetheless, the Americans refused to concede the point about the Soviets' obligation to cover all the costs of transporting, storing, and administering the aid, as well as the ARA's right to work in those terrorities it deemed needing assistance. Litvinov, after hearing of Hoover's concessions, had no trouble agreeing to this: "Money, gentlemen, ve vill give you a carload; if necessary, ve can put the printing presses on an extra shift."

After almost two weeks of negotiations, the two sides agreed to terms on August 20. The following day, at a ceremony presided over by the president of Latvia and attended by various officials and members of the world press, the Riga Agreement was signed. Litvinov told the gathering that this was an occasion of great political significance, expressing the hope that it signaled the rapprochement between the United States and Soviet Russia. Brown chose to ignore Litvinov's comments in his own remarks. As Hoover had insisted, the ARA mission to Russia was to be above all politics.

LENIN HAD FOLLOWED the talks closely. Having to accept help from capitalist America was a bitter pill. On August 23, he sent a secret letter to Molotov: "In light of the agreement with the American Hoover we are facing the arrival of Americans. We must take care of surveillance and intelligence." He instructed the Politburo to set up a special commission that could come up with a plan. "The main thing is to identify and mobilize the maximum number of communists who speak English so that they can be inserted into the Hoover commission, as well as coming up with other forms of surveillance and intelligence." Two weeks later, Lenin, now even more alarmed at the thought of so many Americans entering the country, wrote Chicherin: "As for the 'Hooverites,' we must shadow them with all our might [. . .] and we ought to 'catch' and entrap the worst of them (a certain Lowrie?*) in such a way as to produce a scandal around them. This calls for war, a brutal, *unrelenting* war."

As a way of deflecting attention away from the ARA, Lenin created the International Workers' Committee for Aid to the Starving in Russia (*Mezhrabpom*, in Russian) that same month. The appeal to the world proletariat to come to the aid of the first communist state did little to help

---

* A reference to Donald Lowrie of the ARA, who'd caused a minor scandal in Petrograd when he tried to stop stevedores from pilfering small amounts of grain.

the starving—its total relief effort amounting to a mere 1 percent of that marshaled by the ARA—but *Mezhrabpom* did function as a useful propaganda tool, especially in the United States, where it operated as the Friends of Soviet Russia. In the middle of August, a meeting was convened in Geneva by a number of Red Cross societies to discuss the possibility of organizing aid to Russia. They established the International Committee for Russian Relief and elected Fridtjof Nansen, to whom Gorky had first sent his appeal for help, as its high commissioner. The Nansen mission, as it was known, brought together relief organizations from over twenty countries. Among the groups that came to Russia's aid were the British Society of Friends, the Save the Children Fund, the Red Cross of Sweden, Norway, the Netherlands, Czechoslovakia, and Belgium, and His Holiness the Pope.

Nansen left Geneva for Moscow, where he was warmly embraced by top Soviet officials, in large part because he was much more cooperative than Hoover and the ARA. Nansen had no serious experience in relief operations, nor did he have a large organization at his disposal, and so he offered to turn over to the Soviet government whatever supplies he managed to gather. The Soviets could not have been happier. The relief provided by the Nansen mission was significant, although modest when compared with what the ARA provided: approximately 90 percent of all aid delivered to Russia came from the Americans. Nevertheless, Nansen was fêted by the Kremlin as a true friend of the Soviet state on both of his two brief visits to Russia. Some in the West viewed the Norwegian as a naïve tool of the Soviet regime, and the exaggerated praise showered on Nansen—and his associate Vidkun Quisling, the notorious president of Norway during the years of Nazi occupation—drove the ARA men mad. Nansen's being awarded the Noble Peace Prize was but more salt in the wounds.

After the troubles dealing with the Americans in Riga, Lenin was in no mood to bargain with Nansen. He wrote to Stalin, then both commissar for nationalities and commissar for the workers' and peasants' inspectorate (*Rabkrin*), on August 26: "Nansen will be given a clear 'ultimatum.' We'll put an end to this game (*with fire*)." To show Nansen in no uncertain terms that he was not playing around and that the Soviet leadership was in complete command of the situation, Lenin also instructed Stalin to shut down the All-Russian Committee for Aid to the Starving before the Norwegian left Russia. On August 27, Cheka agents moved on the committee, arresting its non-Bolshevik members and charging the group with secretly negotiating with "foreign powers" behind the government's back and even trying to establish contacts with the remnants of Antonov's peasant army. Two of the committee's leaders were sentenced to death (later commuted), and the rest were exiled from Moscow—to towns without any rail connections—and placed under surveillance. Lenin ordered that the committee be denounced in the harshest terms in the press no less than once a week for the next two months. Foreigners were arriving in Moscow, and Lenin was going to make certain no critics of the government would be there to meet them.

Indeed, around 6:00 p.m. that same evening of the 27th, the first group of ARA men arrived by train in the Soviet capital. The mission had begun. As the Americans were approaching Moscow, Walter Lyman Brown wrote to Hoover: "It is going to be by far the biggest and most difficult job we have yet tackled and the potentialities of it are enormous, but I think we can pull it through." Neither Brown nor anyone else in the ARA had any idea just how big or difficult the Russian job was going to be.

4

GOING IN

L ATE ONE AFTERNOON IN JULY during the sweltering summer
of 1921, two young American men sat whiling away the day at the
Café du Commerce in the small French town of Château-Thierry.
Charles Veil—fighter pilot for the Lafayette Flying Corps in the war,
turned playboy-adventurer in peacetime—was reading the Paris edition
of the *Chicago Tribune* when he looked up at his friend and casually
remarked: "There's a famine in Russia and an appeal has been made to
America for aid. It seems the American Relief Administration may go in."
J. Rives Childs took the paper and read Gorky's appeal. In an instant,
Childs was seized with the idea of signing up and heading off to Russia.

"If the deal goes through, there will be big news," a grinning Childs told Veil. "Right now Russia is a closed book."

Childs was a son of the South, born in Lynchburg in 1893 to an old Virginia family. His father had served as a messenger for General Lee in the Civil War and then went on to a career in business that ended badly, in a bank failure. His mother was the stronger, more influential of his parents. A college graduate, she was the first white woman in Lynchburg to teach in a school for black children, much to the displeasure of the local white superintendent. She made sure her son got an education, sending him to the Virginia Military Institute, then Randolph-Macon College, and finally on to Harvard College for a master's degree in English. Young Childs had dreams of becoming a writer. One day, the radical journalist John Reed came and spoke to the class about his dangerous experiences on the Eastern Front. Childs's head was filled with the allure of foreign adventures.

Soon after, in the summer of 1915, he and a friend volunteered for the American Ambulance Corps and sailed for Europe. For several months, he ferried wounded French soldiers under the distant rumble of heavy guns from Compiègne to the College of Juilly, not far outside Paris. After the United States joined the war, Childs was commissioned as a second lieutenant and sent to intelligence school, then served with the American Expeditionary Force in the Bureau of Enemy Ciphers in Chaumont, France. In December 1918, he was assigned to the American delegation to the Paris Peace Conference as a radio intelligence officer. There he watched his hero, President Wilson, parade down the Champs-Élysées amid wildly cheering crowds. Wilson's idealism, his progressive political agenda, and his vision of a new world order based on democracy and national self-determination inspired Childs and would become signposts in his life. As Wilson rode past, Childs was so overcome with emotion he had to walk away from the crowd and try to collect himself in private.

Childs fell in love with Europe, and when his job in Paris ended, he began looking about for anything that would keep him from having to return to the States. He heard about the newly established American

Relief Administration and was hired on to help feed hungry children in Yugoslavia. It was just the posting he had been looking for. "The Balkans were remote and romantic," he later recalled. The job ran until the autumn of 1919, when he reluctantly returned home. His disappointment was somewhat lessened after he won a job as the White House correspondent for the Associated Press. He met his idol on a few occasions, but then was nearly crushed with despair at the 1920 election of the Republican Warren G. Harding, whom he characterized as "a ponderous piece of flesh" and "a great tragedy for the American people." Childs's choice for president had been Eugene V. Debs of the Socialist Party of America. He was now more eager than ever to get back to Europe. In the spring of 1921, Childs managed to land a writing assignment that would take him to France for several months. He jumped at the opportunity.

ON AUGUST 1, Childs made his way to the American Express Office at 11 rue Scribe in Paris. In the Visitors' Writing Room, he wrote a letter to Walter Lyman Brown in London, reminding Brown how the two had met back in 1919, before Childs shipped off for Yugoslavia, and offering his services for the job the ARA was preparing to undertake in Russia. He told Brown that serving with the ARA had been a great honor and no other work in his life had given him such satisfaction. He was prepared to come to London at a moment's notice to discuss with him in person the chance of going to Russia. He closed his letter by remarking that he already possessed a fair conversational knowledge of the Russian language. This was a lie, but, then, Childs was willing to do just about anything to return to the ARA.

Two days later, Brown cabled Childs, inviting him to come to London. Childs was overjoyed. He immediately wrote his mother: "There seems to be the prospect of a spirited adventure in Russia and you may be sure that if it is possible I shall be heading that way before returning home." He made no mention of the famine, or of communism, or of potential business opportunities, only that a job with the ARA would provide him with "some interesting material for stories." Childs's motivation for heading off

to Russia—the prospect of adventure, the
lure of the exotic and the unknown, a motivation shared by many, if not most, of the
young Americans who signed up for the ARA
mission—never once crossed the minds of
Soviet officials. After three revolutions and
three wars in two decades, the Russians
had had plenty of "adventures," more than
most nations experience in the course of a
century or two. They could not even con-
ceive of a country where life was so steady
that its young men sought out the world's
troubled spots merely in the hopes of quick-
ening their pulse. A cloud of misunderstanding obscured the Americans from the

J. Rives Childs

Russians, and it never lifted, not even after years of close work together
in the fight against the famine. Childs was in Vienna on the 20th when
he received a wire informing him an agreement had been made with the
Soviet government and instructing him to head to Riga by the shortest
possible route. He nearly burst with excitement. "It will be a tremen-
dously big job and one which any man should be proud to have a hand
in. To be among the first expedition I consider a boon sent directly from
Heaven," he wrote his mother. He had a sense based on his previous work
for Hoover that they'd be engaged in more than just famine relief. Hoover's
true aim, he seemed certain, was "the ultimate economic reconstruction of
the country." Childs hadn't felt so alive since his days in Yugoslavia. "The
old fever to be among stirring scenes and a part of great events is once
more about to be satisfied."

Armed with a Russian dictionary, Childs set off for Riga by way of
Berlin. He asked his mother to send him his wool socks, three suits of heavy
underwear, and a carton of Camel cigarettes. On the 27th, he reached
Riga. There he met Emmett Kilpatrick, a friend from his Paris days.
Kilpatrick had been taken prisoner by the Red Army while serving with
the Red Cross in southern Russia and spent nearly a year in Moscow's

Lubyanka Prison, much of it in solitary confinement. Childs seemed shocked that his old pal was no longer the fun-loving prankster of former days. Over lunch, Kilpatrick told him of the horrors he had gone through in prison—the filth, the lice, the cold, hunger, and brutality. He had stayed sane by repeating the famous lines of Richard Lovelace's "To Althea, from Prison"—"Stone walls do not a prison make, nor iron bars a cage." Childs noticed how his "eyes roved restlessly about him like those of a hunted animal." Late on the night of the 29th, Childs left for the station and boarded his train for Moscow. At last, he was on his way into what he called "that strange, mysterious world" of Soviet Russia.

Among the small party of Americans with Childs was a middle-aged professor of Russian history from Stanford. Frank Golder had been born in Odessa and immigrated to America as a boy with his family, most likely soon after the bloody pogroms of the early 1880s. As Jews, the Golders hoped for a better life across the ocean, but getting by in New Jersey proved a struggle. Frank's father, a Talmudic scholar, made little money, and Frank was forced to sell household wares on the street to support the family. One day, he met a Baptist minister who was so impressed by the boy's work ethic that he persuaded the Golder family to let him give them money to allow Frank to go to school.

As a teenager, Golder studied philosophy at Bucknell University and then went on to Harvard, from which he graduated in 1903, before enrolling in graduate studies in Russian history. After earning his doctorate in history in 1909, he took a position at Washington State College, in the town of Pullman, amid the rolling hills of the Palouse. Golder dreamed of working in Russia's archives, and he managed to travel to St. Petersburg in the summer of 1914, just as war was breaking out across Europe. He was back again in March 1917, and witnessed the collapse of the Romanov dynasty with his own eyes. Like many, he greeted the February Revolution as a necessary step toward a freer, more just Russia, only to be disillusioned at the chaos and violence that soon followed. He could not believe how quickly a country could go to pieces.

In 1920, Golder was hired by the new Hoover War Collection (later the Hoover War Library and now the Hoover Institution Library and

Archives) at Leland Stanford Junior University to help build a collection of documents on the history of the Great War. Stanford would become his home for the rest of Golder's life, both as a professor and as director of the Hoover Library. Golder traveled all over Europe, buying up manuscripts, libraries, and ephemera for Hoover. Everywhere he went, he was met with open arms. Modest, soft-spoken, a good listener who never tried to impose his views on others, Golder developed an enormous network of contacts among the continent's intellectual elite, including in Russia. Few if any Americans in 1921 could boast of a

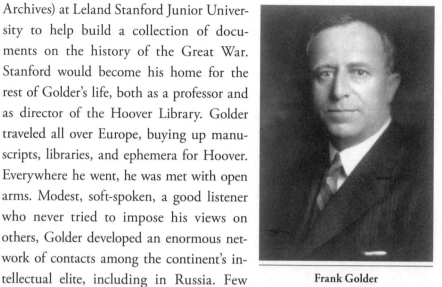

Frank Golder

more thorough knowledge of Russia—its history, culture, and politics—than Frank Golder, and it was for this reason that his employer, Herbert Hoover, sent him back to Russia that summer, to continue his collecting and to assess the famine as a special investigator for the ARA. "Doc" Golder, as he was affectionately called by the ARA men—all a good deal younger, and almost all a good deal less educated than he—would cover more ground over the next two years than any other American in his search to discover the full extent of the famine.

The electricity on the train had gone out, so the men rode through the night by candlelight. When they crossed the frontier, Childs was shocked to see that everyone was dressed in rags. The faces of the Russians seemed to betray a dull-wittedness the likes of which he had never seen before in Europe. Trains loaded with refugees from Moscow passed them along the way. Their locomotive was so underpowered that it failed to summit a few small hills along the route. Twice the engineer had to back up the train a good ways and give it all she had to get over the gentle inclines. After a forty-hour trip, the train finally pulled into Moscow on the afternoon of August 31; here they were met by Philip Carroll.

The first group of ARA men had "gone in," as one called it then, several days earlier. Russia had been almost completely cut off from the rest of the world for over three years. A palpable sense of excitement, mixed with foreboding, had filled their car as they crossed the border. They were entering a strange new land and had little idea what lay ahead. A man from Universal News came along to film their progress behind the Red Curtain. There were seven of them, led by Carroll, acting chief of the Russian mission, a longtime ARA man from Hood River, Oregon. He'd been sent in with no specific instructions from either the New York office or Hoover. As would be the case in much of the mission to come, the men on the ground had to make it up as they went along. The Soviet officials meeting them at the station were shocked: they'd been told to expect only three men and had no idea where they were going to put up an extra four. It seemed a bad omen. With a bit of work, Carroll managed to secure a large gray stone mansion at 30 Spiridonovka, just blocks from Patriarch's Ponds, later made famous by Mikhail Bulgakov's *The Master and Margarita*. Once the luxurious, state-of-the-art residence of a wealthy Armenian sugar baron, its thirty rooms had been reduced, in Carroll's words, to "an absolute state of filthiness." The central heating was kaput, the electricity dead, and the plumbing, one ARA man put it, "only a memory." No one bothered to remove their heavy coats or gloves after moving in. Fifty portable oil-burner heaters were immediately ordered from London.

At the station, Carroll picked up Childs, Golder, and four others on the team in one of the ARA's freshly painted Cadillacs. Childs noticed how the Muscovites stared as they drove through the city. When they pulled up at their new home, Childs thought Spiridonovka had the look of a dark and massive prison. Carroll seems to have read Childs's mind, commenting as they went in, "It should be able to withstand a long siege."

The next day, Childs went out to explore. "I wish that I might give a faithful picture of my impressions of this strange unreal city of Moscow," he wrote his mother, "but for the difficult portrayal the extraordinary emotions which it awakens there is demanded the morbidly-minded genius of a Poe or E. T. Hoffmann. It is like some great city upon which a pestilence has settled and in which the population moves in hourly ex-

ARA headquarters in Moscow, on Spiridonovka Street, with its fleet of Cadillacs and their drivers. The automobile assigned to Colonel William Haskell, who arrived in Moscow in late September to replace Philip Carroll as head of the Russian operation, distinguished by the license plate "A.R.A. 1," is on the far right.

pectation of death." Everywhere were signs of artillery and machine-gun fire, craters where once had been buildings, formerly exquisite shops all now boarded up and cobwebbed. Several years' worth of trash lay in the streets, and the ground floors of the abandoned structures served as public toilets. Yet more striking than the physical image of the city was the sight of its inhabitants. Childs could not get over "the apparent absence of a heart and soul with which one is struck so forcibly and pathetically. I think that perhaps the briefest and most just characterization of Moscow would be to say that it is a city without love." Nowhere did he encounter a laugh, or even a smile, as he walked along. There was "rust and corrosion upon the heart and a pall of fear upon the soul."

The Americans got to work straightaway. On September 1, the SS *Phoenix* arrived in Petrograd from Hamburg, bearing seven hundred tons of ARA rations. Five days later, the first ARA food kitchen opened, in School No. 27, on Moika Street. The first kitchen in Moscow opened on the 10th, in the former Hermitage Restaurant, a beloved establishment for the city's wealthy in the days before the revolution. Given the great distance food had to be shipped, the meals consisted of products that could be easily packaged and stored and offered lots of calories, usually corn grits, rice, white bread, lard, sugar, condensed milk, and cocoa.

Golder had spent the first two days running around to meetings with Soviet officials in order to make arrangements for a trip to the heart of the famine on the Volga River. No one on the Soviet side seemed to be in charge, and he was having a devil of a time getting any concrete answers about exactly when preparations would be ready for him to depart. Finally, late on September 1, he was told to go to the station for a train leaving at midnight. With Golder were his fellow ARA men John Gregg and William Shafroth, as well as a Soviet liaison officer, two Russian porters, and a driver for the Ford camionette they'd be taking along with them on the train.

They awoke to heavy rain the next morning. Golder noted that the landscape reminded him of northern Idaho, although the desperate, hungry faces at the stations they passed through left him no doubt he was in Russia. Late on the morning of the 3rd, they pulled into the city of Kazan, the old Tatar capital on the Volga, some 450 hundred miles east of Moscow. The men were now inside the famine zone. Hungry refugees from the outlying villages thronged the station, all "huddled together in compact masses like a seal colony, mothers and young close together," in Golder's words. The children were surviving on a bit of soup and one small piece of bread from the public kitchens. The city itself was a ruin. In the streets they encountered "pitiful-looking figures dressed in rags and begging for a piece of bread in the name of Christ."

The Alexander Palace at Tsarskoe Selo
near Petrograd. Part of this famous
building were used to feed the local
Children.

A wing of the Alexander Palace at Tsarskoe Selo, home of Tsar Nicholas II
and his family, was converted into an ARA kitchen that fed more than two
thousand children a day. The kitchen was run by one of the tsar's
former cooks and several servants of the last Romanovs.

They went to the offices of the Tatar Autonomous Soviet Socialist
Republic to introduce themselves to the local authorities. The Tatars
received them with an air of suspicion, as if they'd been warned to be on
guard. When they learned, however, that Golder was a teacher, as the Tatar officials themselves had been before the revolution, and spoke perfect
Russian, their caution melted away. Together the men went off to tour
the local hospital. The conditions were abysmal: filthy and lacking the
most basic of medicines, the rooms overcrowded with persons afflicted
with tuberculosis, scurvy, typhus, and dysentery. Upon returning to their

railcar, they found it was besieged by begging children and their wailing parents—a pitiful sight that made it impossible for the men to eat or rest. On the 5th, Gregg sent a wire to headquarters in Moscow: "The need for relief in this country is beyond anything I have ever seen. Speed is of utmost repeat utmost importance as without exaggeration children dying [of] actual starvation every day." The situation was much worse than anyone had imagined.

That month, Golder traveled throughout the famine region. Everywhere he went, he encountered the same scenes of hunger and despair. At one small station on the way to Simbirsk, two militiamen told him they had not been paid in months and received nothing from the government but one bowl of watery soup a day. They had taken to making a bread substitute out of grass and acorns, which Golder mistook for horse manure.

When they were a few days out of Kazan, their train stopped because of a wreck up the line. Golder went out to have a look and found the flatbed conveying the ARA Ford crowded with peasant women who had climbed on. They told him they had left home in search of potatoes, and shared their stories. Desperate mothers had abandoned children they could no longer feed in the Simbirsk marketplace, in the hope that the state would take the children in. Others had even killed their offspring and then taken their own lives. Everyone they met seemed resigned to their fate. Only the subject of the Soviet government agitated the women: they blamed it for their misfortunes. Golder noted that life had been hard under the tsars as well, but they rejected the comparison. Yes, the tsar's officials had stolen and robbed, they admitted, but back then they all had so much they didn't really notice. Now it was different. All the Soviets knew how to do was take—an attitude Golder encountered often during his trip. He gave them each a bit of chocolate cake, which they carefully wrapped up and put in their pockets, saving it for their children back home. Finally, the line was cleared, and the train started up again. As they rode along, Golder looked out and saw sparks pouring out of the stack; they landed on the peasants and set their raggedy clothes ablaze.

Golder and his party stopped at the wharf near the village of Khra-

Refugees crowd the top of a train, fleeing the famine.

shchevka. The villagers, who had come down to the river to beg for food from passing boats, told them how the Communist Party had sent workers from the cities to crush a peasant revolt there in 1918. Golder had heard similar tales as they passed through villages along the way. All about them were pitiful scenes. Golder was especially moved by the sight of an old woman crawling in the mud on all fours, fighting with several pigs over bits of pumpkin rind. They happened upon a local dentist, and she told them there was not a single toothbrush in the entire village. The peasants, having eaten up all the remaining dandelions, wild mustard, and onions, had come down with scurvy, and she could do nothing but watch their teeth fall out.

On the 14th, they reached the city of Samara. "Dirt and ruins are everywhere," Golder wrote in his diary. "Windows are smashed; streets torn up and littered with rubbish and dead animals. Hotels, which at one time compared well with the best of Europe, are today empty shells; church steeples are turned into wireless stations and palatial homes into barracks. In brief, the city is a wreck, a shadow of its former self." The people were surviving on rinds, potato peelings, and bones. The rail station was

A common scene from a children's home inside the famine zone

crowded with people trying to flee to Siberia, where they'd heard there
was plenty of food. Others crowded the beach, hoping to escape by boat to
Ukraine. The authorities, however, were doing everything in their power
to keep people from leaving and spreading panic and disease as they went.
Weakened by hunger, the people lay about and slept and waited; their little
remaining strength they devoted to searching the bodies of their loved
ones for lice. "I shall never forget the sights I saw in September, in Samara,"
Shafroth later wrote.

The scenes in the hospitals and orphanages were particularly disturbing. Typical was one children's home built for 30 that now held 450. The
men mistook the stinking rags on the floor for discarded clothing, only
to realize that they concealed, in Golder's words, the "cadaverous bodies of young children with such old, shriveled faces that they look like
mummies."

It was by now obvious that although the ARA had not provided medical relief in its other operations, it would need to do so in Russia. The
most basic supplies were lacking: aspirin, chloroform, ether. Old news-

paper had replaced bandages for wrapping wounds and surgical incisions. Before the month was out, the ARA made an agreement with the American Red Cross for $3.6 million worth of medicines and supplies. The scope of the medical relief would grow during the mission and become a large part of the ARA's work in Russia.

On the last day of the month, Golder headed back to Moscow. The train was covered with refugees who were trying to flee the area. They rode on the roofs of the cars, on the steps, the bumpers; many even clung to the undercarriages, their bodies just inches above the rails. Golder remarked that it looked as if the train were covered with insects. When one sickly-looking man got too close to their compartment, the Soviet liaison officer pulled his gun and threatened to shoot. "Shoot!" the poor man screamed. "Do you think it makes any difference to me whether I am shot or die of hunger?" The train stopped at the bridge over the Volga, and the militia pulled all the refugees off. But no sooner had the train crossed to the other side when another mass of refugees, "waiting, shouting, swearing, and pushing," lunged at the train and climbed on before it could get back up to speed.

From Moscow, Golder wrote to a colleague back in the history department at Stanford:

> The famine is bad beyond all imagination, it is the most heart breaking situation that I have ever seen. Millions of people are doomed to die and they are looking it calmly in the face. Next year millions more will die [. . .] To see Russia makes one wish that he were dead. One asks in vain where are the healthy men, the beautiful women, the cultural life. It is all gone and in place of it we have starving, ragged, undersized men and women who are thinking of only one thing, where the next piece of bread is coming from [. . .] In all these wanderings and through all the discomforts there is one blessed thought: that I have another land to go to.

When news of the horrors on the Volga reached Moscow, Carroll decided to send a team to begin operations in Kazan as soon as possible. The plan was to prepare a train with fourteen cars loaded with enough food to feed thirty thousand children for a month. In addition, there would be a large flatcar to carry two ARA trucks and a Cadillac touring car, a railcar with kitchen, and two saloon cars for the ARA men, their interpreters, chauffeurs, and cook, and a group of American newspaper reporters. The train was scheduled to leave Moscow on Wednesday, September 14.

As would soon become clear to the Americans, setting a schedule and sticking to it were two very different things in Soviet Russia. First, there was a series of unexplained delays in finding the required railroad cars. Finally, when several did appear at the station, they were too filthy and broken-down to be of any use. It was at this point that the Americans learned a crucial lesson about working in Russia: the Cheka could be a friend as well as an enemy. The Cheka agent Bublikov, according to Childs a sinewy figure with "superabundant nervous energy" and "the cold penetrating eye of one devoid of the instinct of mercy," picked up the phone and demanded that the necessary cars be delivered to the station within two hours or those responsible for the delay would be arrested. Sure enough, the cars arrived on time; late on the afternoon of the 15th, the train set out for Kazan.

Besides Childs, the ARA men included Vernon Kellogg, Ivar Wahren, and Elmer Burland. The press was represented by Walter Duranty of *The New York Times*, Ralph Pulitzer of New York's *The World*, Floyd Gibbons of the *Chicago Tribune*, and Bessie Beatty, the noted journalist who had witnessed and reported on the Russian Revolution firsthand. Also on the train was the Australian-born adventurer and onetime British member of Parliament Arthur Alfred Lynch. By the next day, their train was already passing through small railroad stations crowded with refugees. Childs noticed how the people outside his window, so weakened and hopeless-looking, showed "scarcely any vestige of human expression." The little boys and girls with grotesquely bloated stomachs made him think of hideous freaks of the kind one might see displayed in a museum.

Once, without thinking, Childs carelessly tossed some apple peelings out his window; a pack of children set upon them as if they represented a great treasure. Lynch, however, seemed strangely untouched by the misery.

Young famine
victims photographed
in a refugee camp in
Samara Province

Childs noticed how he would leap from the train at each stop and shout, "Long live the Soviets!" One wonders what the poor, starved Russians made of this spectacle.

They arrived in Kazan in a cold drizzle the night of the 17th. Looking about, Childs could see nothing but mud and misery. He was reminded of a line from Thomas Moore's "Oft, in the Stilly Night"—"I feel like one / Who treads alone / Some banquet-hall deserted." In the gloom of the station, he caught sight of a young boy struggling to pull a cart bearing a coffin. The next day, Childs and Wahren went to meet Rauf Sabirov, chairman of the Tatar Central Executive Committee, and Kashaf Mukhtarov, chairman of the Council of People's Commissars of the Tatar Republic.

The meetings went well, and the men immediately established an easy rapport. That very day, less than twenty-four hours after arriving in Kazan, the ARA began feeding children in a makeshift location. A few

One of Kazan's muddy main streets on a day in early May

days later, they set up a full feeding operation capable of handling a thousand young people.

On the 20th, Wahren left Kazan with a boatload of relief supplies for villages out in the countryside, followed by Burland and Kellogg the next day. Childs stayed behind to set up their offices and housing. The days were long, but Childs was excited to finally be at it. He wrote his mother that it filled him with pride to be involved in a large effort aimed at saving lives—not taking them, as had been his mission during the war. One of his first days at his desk, with paperhangers scurrying about and office furniture and supplies being delivered, the Cheka showed up and arrested Childs's interpreter. No explanation was given, and he never saw the man again. That afternoon, a smart-looking young man in a Red Army uniform marched into the office, saluted, clicked his heals, and introduced himself as William Simson, Childs's new interpreter. Born in Estonia, Simson had been educated in England and worked as a valet in London's Savoy Hotel, where he perhaps anglicized his name, before returning to Russia to join the Red Army. He had been arrested and sentenced to death as a counter-revolutionary spy more than once before being exiled to Kazan. His English was flawless. Childs naturally, and certainly correctly, assumed that the Cheka had sent Simson both to interpret for and to spy on Childs, but this didn't bother him in the least: in his estimation, he and the ARA had nothing to hide. What's more, with the others gone, Childs was terribly lonely. He hugged Simson and begged him to join him for dinner. The two men soon formed a close bond and were rarely apart. Later, Childs would even save Simson's life.

Most of Childs's time in the first days was spent trying to put together the personnel vital to the ARA mission. The total number of Americans in Russia never surpassed more than two hundred at a time, and so the great bulk of the work had to be done by the local population. The ARA office in Kazan was inundated with applications, but only a few of the applicants possessed the requisite skills. Among those to beat a path to their door was the granddaughter of Generalissimo Alexander Suvorov, famed field marshal under Catherine the Great and one of Russia's greatest military commanders, along with her son and daughter. They were dressed in rags, and their gaunt faces bore all the signs of prolonged hunger. He hired the daughter, since she spoke English and French and could type, but had no use for the other two. The poor mother, who at one time had been received at the tsarist court, pleaded through her tears with Childs to hire her. She refused to leave, and for the rest of the day haunted the office with her presence. Childs didn't know what to do, never having encountered before persons whose nerves were so "hopelessly disordered."

Accompanying the Russians' desperate wish to be hired by the ARA was an almost equally strong fear that working for the Americans would lead to future trouble with the Cheka. There was talk in the city that the ARA would be around for only a few months, and that once it pulled out the secret police would arrest individuals who had had anything to do with the Americans. Everyone was convinced the Cheka had planted agents throughout the organization and was keeping close tabs on its operations and personnel. Childs, dangerously naïve in such matters, called these fears unfounded. When he brought the matter up with local officials, they assured him that such concerns about retribution were baseless. (Some of these same officials would themselves later be arrested and shot as counterrevolutionaries under Stalin.) The Latvia-born John de Jacobs, hired on in Kazan as another interpreter, later commented that the Russian staff was riddled with Cheka informers. They even proposed to Childs the idea of putting some of their desks in his private office, which the unwitting Childs happily accepted.

Working eighteen-hour days, Childs had built up a staff of fifty by the end of September. Even though he was solely responsible for their training, he still managed to find time to expand the feeding operation to fifteen thousand children. The strain was enormous, and at times he thought he was about to break under the pressure. He felt horrible having to turn away so many seeking jobs, for he knew that, without the money and rations provided to ARA workers, many would perish in the coming winter. Moreover, reports from the provinces made it clear that the operation would have to expand to include the feeding of adults. The famine was much worse than they had ever imagined, a fact that he feared the ARA bosses back in London and New York did not understand. Childs did his best to raise the alarm. "I cannot permit part of the responsibility for the death of thousands to rest on my head," he recorded in his diary. A bit of relief came with the arrival of two Americans: John H. Boyd, a tall and lanky Southerner with considerable experience in aid relief in the Near East, and, a bit older and more sedate than Boyd, Van Arsdale Turner, a preacher's son who had come to Russia in search of adventure. Childs noted that Turner "had the language of romance on his tongue," and was an "impractical, idealistic type for whom America has no corner to which to turn." Boyd took charge of transport and supply for the Kazan district; Turner and Childs divided the children's feeding operations between them.

5

FAMINE SHOCK

I T WASN'T LONG BEFORE LENIN began to see the good the Americans were doing. He wrote to People's Commissar for Foreign Affairs Georgy Chicherin in mid-October: "*Hoover* is a real asset [. . .] Agreements and concessions with the Americans are extremely important to us: with Hoover we have *something* (and it's not a little)." When Lenin learned that Cheka agents from Novorossiisk had boarded and then searched an American destroyer with "Hooverites" aboard and treated the Americans "most rudely," he was outraged. He sent an angry letter to Chicherin, reminding him that they were anticipating necessary American food and supplies via the Black Sea, and that measures had to be taken to rein in the Cheka, or else there would be "the most serious trouble"

Alexander Eiduk

with the Americans. Chicherin, Lenin let him know, had been too soft and slow in addressing the matter. It was imperative that they "arrest these rotten Chekists, bring the guilty ones to Moscow, and shoot them."

On September 2, *Izvestiia* had published an order from Mikhail Kalinin, the titular head of the Soviet government, addressed to all people's commissars and directors of the provincial executive committees, instructing them to carry out every request of the ARA within forty-eight hours, since the work of the Americans was "extraordinarily urgent and demanded the commitment of a military operation." Any attempts to slow up, much less block, the ARA's work would be punished "according to all the severity of revolutionary justice." Later that month, the Central Executive Committee set up a liaison organization to assist the ARA in its operations. When the original representative plenipotentiary proved ineffective, he was replaced by Alexander Eiduk.

A fearsome Latvian, Eiduk had been a revolutionary practically his entire life. Exiled from tsarist Russia after the Revolution of 1905, he apparently returned after the Bolsheviks seized power and joined the Cheka, quickly rising in the ranks to become one of its leaders, a figure notorious for his cruelty and bloodthirstiness. A killer with an artistic side, he supposedly penned the following verse for a collection titled "The Smile of the Cheka"—"There's no greater joy, no better music, / Than the crush of broken lives and bones." All manner of gruesome stories were told about Eiduk. He was dubbed "the executioner" for the many White officers he was reported to have executed with his own gun. A member of the ARA claimed he had "one of the cruelest faces I have ever seen."

Eiduk was immediately impressed with the ARA's efficiency, administrative talent, and organizational know-how, all of which only highlighted the shortcomings of the Soviet government, especially at the local level. In the early months of his work with the ARA, Eiduk tried to tackle the bureaucracy, inefficiencies, and fears lurking inside most Russians (of taking initiative, of acting without written orders from above, of foreigners, of unfamiliar ideas and new ways of doing things) that hindered the ARA's efforts. He saw to it that Russian ARA personnel were given government food rations, and permitted Americans to keep guns for their personal safety. Yet at the same time, he ordered strict surveillance over the ARA men and their Russian staff. Eiduk was going to help the ARA get its work done, but he was going to make certain it didn't get up to anything beyond its stated mission.

Meanwhile, Carroll, the temporary acting head of the ARA mission in Russia, had been replaced by Colonel William Haskell, the new permanent director. The stiff and taciturn Haskell was a military man through and through. A West Point graduate, he had served in the Philippines and then with the Second Army Corps in France in the First World War. Given the forty-three-year-old Haskell's proven leadership experience and his lack of any involvement in politics, yet his unequivocal anti-Soviet

Colonel William Haskell and Cyril J. Quinn

attitude, Hoover deemed him "the ideal man" for the job, although many longtime ARA men thought he was too quick to impose military order and hierarchy on the loose, informal, and historically flat structure of the organization. Haskell arrived with a staff of seventeen. Captain Thomas C. Lonergan was appointed executive officer, and he was soon joined by Cyril J. Quinn as the second executive officer.

Among Haskell's first tasks was finding more space for the expanding operation. Spiridonovka was fine for the ARA's offices, but it wasn't going to be big enough to house all the men, whose numbers were growing rapidly. The ARA offices in London and New York were inundated with applications, and Quinn was busy scouring for worthy hires among the U.S. Army forces stationed at Koblenz and the Rhodes scholars at Oxford. Over the two-year mission, some 380 American men would eventually work in Russia. And men they were: American women were not even considered, on the assumption that the work

Emma. Following the racial prejudice of the day, the ARA photographer did not bother to record her surname.

was too dangerous for them. Nor were Jews, again supposedly for their own good, the argument being that, should disorder break out, they would likely become targets of anti-Semitic pogroms. Given America's stringently enforced system of white privilege, it is not surprising that no other racial and ethnic minorities were welcome among the ranks of the ARA, either. But the mission was not an entirely all-white, all-male affair: among the ARA's archives are two photographs of an African American woman identified simply as "Emma."

She was from Washington, D.C., and had somehow ended up in Moscow, where she was hired on as the ARA's laundress. According to the caption on one of the photographs, Emma was "excellent" at her work, and she had "a white husband"—which must have seemed an objectionable arrangement to most of her American compatriots in Russia.

Haskell located two large mansions that he wished to use for housing the ARA men. Once homes of Russia's wealthy elite, they had been nationalized and turned into state museums under the control of Natalya Sedova, Trotsky's wife, as head of the so-called Museum Division of the People's Commissariat for Enlightenment. Madame Trotsky wouldn't hear of renting the museums to the Americans, given their valuable art and furnishings. One of these, at 8 Bolshoi Znamensky Lane, had been the home of the famous collector Sergei Shchukin, and fabulous works by Monet, Picasso, and Matisse still covered the walls. Haskell refused to back down, and promised in writing that no damage would be done to any of the properties; in the end, Madame Trotsky acquiesced. Eventually, the ARA occupied five buildings along with their headquarters on Spiridonovka, all in the Arbat neighborhood; the men gave each one a nickname based on the color of its façade: Shchukin's former home was the Pink House, and there were also the Brown, Blue, Green, and White Houses.

AFTER GETTING MATTERS squared away in Moscow, Haskell, along with a few other men, set out for a two-week tour of the famine zone. They returned from their travels with the same opinion as Golder and Childs—namely, that the famine was much worse than they had realized and would likely require more aid and manpower than planned. Vernon Kellogg, an old friend of Hoover's and one of his special representatives in Russia, noted on October 7 that the program would have to be expanded way beyond the original number of one million children, and wrote to Hoover to encourage him to double the size of the operation. The need, he noted, was overwhelming, and a huge tragedy was unfolding before their eyes. The geographic expanse of the famine was vast, stretching 800 miles north to south, from Vyatka to Astrakhan, and 350 miles west to east, from Penza to Ufa. After hearing from Kellogg and Haskell, Hoover agreed that more had to be done and was coming around to the idea of feeding adults as well.

Haskell arrived on his inspection tour in Kazan on October 27.

Among the men traveling with him were James P. Goodrich, the former governor of Indiana, sent to Russia by Hoover to investigate the famine, and Philip Gibbs, an English journalist and writer. Two days later, the party departed Kazan for Moscow—except for Gibbs and a fellow British reporter, who wanted to get out into the countryside and see the famine for themselves. Gibbs, whom Childs called "a prince of a man," told the men in Kazan he was not convinced that the famine was as bad as characterized and that the West was being fed a good deal of anti-Russian propaganda. So Childs found an interpreter and arranged a short trip for Gibbs down the Volga to the district of Spassk to see for himself.

Gibbs returned a day later a changed man. The trauma had been so great that Childs had trouble getting him to talk about what he had seen. It was only by the second day that he had gained enough composure to describe the horrors he had witnessed in Spassk. Although Gibbs had reported on the carnage he had seen on the Western Front during the war, nothing could have prepared him for this. The condition came to be known as "famine shock," a reworking of the past war's "shell shock," and Gibbs was one of the earliest cases. Another case involved an ARA man who came upon a barn stacked with corpses in the Volga region late that summer. He began to count the bodies, but when he reached forty-eight, something inside him snapped. He couldn't go on, even though there were a good many more bodies to count. He went about the rest of the day repeating over and over "forty-eight . . . forty-eight . . . forty-eight." It was all he could say. Not until the following day was he able to go back and finish the job.

The personal letters of the ARA men are full of references to the emotional strain of their work. Nerves were frayed, strained, and at times shattered. Edgar Rickard, the ARA general director based in New York, was so concerned about the men's mental state that he recommended they be given longer vacations in Europe and shorter shifts. "This Russian job to judge from unofficial personal narratives," he wired Brown on April 7, 1922, "has developed among workers 'famine shock' such as we have not experienced in any other operations and which apparently renders otherwise superior individuals insufficient."

After he recovered and returned home to England, Gibbs published a

Bodies piled in a morgue awaiting burial after the spring thaw

fulsome tribute to the work of the American Relief Administration, whose efforts he called "the most astounding thing that has ever been done in the history of mankind." He acknowledged the work of his fellow Englishmen, but commented how "our homage is due to the magnitude and splendour of the American effort." Nothing could compare with the "untiring devotion" of the young American men risking their health and lives in the service of humanity.

ON OCTOBER 6, 1921, Childs embarked from Kazan on the large, if rather dirty, river steamer SS *Varlen* with seventy-five thousand rations for hungry villages down along the Volga. Traveling with him was the interpreter Jacobs, Rauf Sabirov, and Mikhail Skvortsov, another local Communist Party official filled with inexhaustible energy and genuine commitment to the loftiest ideals of the revolution, with whom Childs

A child dying of hunger in the streets. She no longer has the strength
to eat the scraps of food on the ground in front of her.

would become fast friends. They arrived the following day at Bogorodsk.
It was a grim sight. "A dreary, mud-besmattered Russian village," Childs
noted. Refugees lined the riverbanks. Many were dead and dying; those
with any strength left were digging shallow graves in the slime.

He was shocked to see a large pile of American food next to them on
the banks, waiting to be trucked into the interior. It sat there guarded by
only one soldier, wielding a rifle that appeared too antiquated to shoot.
The refugees stared at the food with longing, but no one made any move
for it. To Childs, the picture proved the truth about what he had heard
of Russians' passivity and fatalism, "inbred through long centuries in the
Slavic nature."

Of course, what he didn't realize was that after years of war, revolution, disease, and famine, these poor folk were too weak and defeated to
fight back any longer, whatever their Slavic nature. They had struggled
mightily for years and were now beyond resistance. Adding to the strange
nature of the scene was the fact that just a short way down the riverside
was a bazaar where peasants were selling eggs, butter, milk, and meat. The
refugees, however, had no money, and so they starved and died. Childs
could hardly believe his eyes, yet this was an inescapable fact of the fam-

ine that all ARA men soon realized: as millions perished, others around them ate. Food was to be had, but for a price, and the vendors in the markets, even if they felt sympathy for the walking skeletons in their midst, were not about to give their goods away for nothing. Golder noticed the same thing in his travels. There was food, but it was in small pockets, quite local, and the poor distribution and the villagers' lack of money meant they were starving. Urban dwellers with some sort of salary had a good chance of survival; those without did not.

The next day, they met with villagers from Laishev to organize the local feeding committee. The ARA divided the country into a number of large districts and established a headquarters run by several Americans to oversee the work in each district. The Kazan district, set up to serve the Tatar Republic, included 2,456,074 people and covered nearly forty thousand square miles. It would be enlarged in December and then again in May 1922, eventually embracing 4.5 million people and over ninety thousand square miles, roughly the size of the states of New York, New Jersey, and all of New England minus Maine, all run by only a handful of Americans out of Kazan. The enormity of the district was compounded by the horrific state of the transportation network, which made travel slow, difficult, and exhausting. At the height of the operation, thirty thousand Russian employees of the ARA were feeding two million people a day in the Kazan district alone.

Every ARA district was divided into smaller subdistricts, each overseen by an inspector, a native civilian, responsible for establishing a local ARA office and organizing relief efforts at the village level. Inspectors hired ten or so assistants, referred to as instructors, usually young Russian men with a few years of schooling and basic literacy. Instructors managed about twenty villages apiece, roughly fifteen hundred people, and typically lived in the local county seat. They were responsible for putting together an ARA committee of between six to twelve persons in each village, making certain to include the head of the village government and the local priest. It was required that at least one of the committee members be literate, and he would then serve as secretary. These committees were given two weeks to set up kitchens—most often in the schoolhouse

Childs, in a dark suit, at an ARA kitchen in the Kazan district.
His interpreter, Simson, is visible behind Childs's right shoulder.

or an abandoned peasant hut—and compile feeding lists of the neediest children. Outside every feeding station hung a large sign announcing the presence of the American Relief Administration along with the identification number for that particular kitchen. It was also the committee's job to make sure the food was going to the right people and in the right amount. The risk of theft, or at the least pilfering (think watered-down cocoa, thin grits), was a real concern, although actual recorded cases were surprisingly few.

The instructors had one of the most difficult jobs of anyone working for the ARA. It was their responsibility to travel from one remote village to the next, even in winter, often on foot, and with little to eat or to keep them warm, and make sure the food was being distributed as prescribed and to the neediest. Once the ARA woke up to the full extent of their hardships and decided to give them an American ration as well, most of the instructors didn't take the rations for themselves but gave these to their families back home. The Americans did get out into the hinterlands to inspect feeding operations, but they were never able to visit more than a small percentage of the kitchens, and so relied on the hard work and honesty of their Soviet colleagues to be certain the job was being carried out as intended.

From Laishev, the men sailed on to the village of Elabuga. Childs was struck by the beauty of the fall foliage in the area, which masked the suffering around them. The night before, he kept seeing the pitiful faces of emaciated young children in his sleep. They arrived on a Sunday and set straight to work. Childs wondered what the good people back home in Lynchburg would think of his missing church for a "secular meeting" on the Sabbath, assuming "many bigots [. . .] would condemn my action." At one time he might have agreed with them, but now he was coming to realize that such notions were nothing more than blind prejudice. Although he had been in Russia only a short time, his values had begun to shift, and he sensed he was undergoing "a radical transformation." He wrote: "It would seem to me that I am throwing off a great deal of baggage and that in the stripping of life of its inessentials [. . .] I am gaining warrant, not for the salvation of my soul, for I dislike and reject that phrase, but for the right to live."

Childs returned to Kazan on the 13th. He wrote his mother, "I never believed there could be so much misery on such a scale in the world." The surreal nature of his experience in Russia was highlighted by the fact that, despite this misery, daily life went on, somehow, as always. Just days after his return, he attended a performance of *Carmen* at the Palace of the Red Army Soldiers. "Thousands are dying of starvation, but the Soviet government must realize man does not live by bread alone." Childs had to admit that, even if the company was mediocre and the staging shabby, he enjoyed the performance more than anything he had ever seen at New York's Metropolitan Opera, since "there before us was a little make-believe tragedy which was being produced in the midst of a great living tragedy [. . .] Principals of the greater tragedy were pressing as spectators into the lesser one to forget, in the tragedy of the other, their own." He was mesmerized by the star, the Persian-born mezzo-soprano Fatma Mukhtarova, whose effect on him surpassed that of even the great Caruso. Childs invited Mukhtarova and some of the other women from the company to join him for a light meal back at the ARA house. His enchantment vanished the moment the women threw themselves ravenously at the food.

Loading supplies at the ARA warehouse in Kazan

A week later, Childs was back on the steamer, carrying food to villages along the Kama River. He fell ill with ptomaine poisoning after eating some contaminated food and had to be confined to bed for days, using the time to record his observations in a letter to an old friend. Russia, he commented, was not the chaotic mess depicted in the West, but a well-regulated country whose government enjoyed popular support. The officials he had gotten to know in Kazan were, in his opinion, all honest men, and though they may have lacked education, they made up for this with a fearless will that made all things possible. The Russians he had met exhibited a simple dignity. "We traveled some thousands of miles among the starving population, but not once were we molested or solicited to share in the food we had with us, nor was any of it stolen. In other countries, under similar conditions, we would have risked death."

Death, however, was ever present in Kazan. Around this time, Childs's Russian tutor took sick with typhus, after having just lost her brother to the disease; her sister was on the verge of death as well. Next, the maids at the ARA house came down with it, and their housekeeper, too. "Literally, people die here like flies," Childs remarked. On top of this, the Cheka was becoming more brazen. In the morning, when he arrived at work, it was obvious to him that agents had gone through all the papers in the desks. Spies planted among the personnel were reporting "our every gesture" to their superiors, infecting the work atmosphere with an air of suspicion. The agents even surveilled Childs on his trips to the bazaar. He complained to local officials, but was told it was all in his head.

Childs's concerns were in fact well founded. On October 25, the Cheka issued a special order giving all agents extraordinary powers of surveillance in the struggle against the ARA. "Based on our intelligence, the Americans are drawing anti-Soviet elements into the ARA organization, engaging in espionage to gather information on Russia, and buying up valuables." This last bit would come to spell Childs's own fate in Russia.

6

ALL OF RUSSIA
ON THE MOVE

B Y THE BEGINNING OF NOVEMBER, the ARA had established kitchens throughout the entire Volga region. Still, the famine worsened. On the 19th, a Soviet official overseeing feeding operations in Sorochinsk, on the road from Samara to Orenburg, sent his superiors a report on conditions in the area. Much of the adult population, he warned, was "doomed to die from starvation unless more help appears immediately." Bands of people were roaming the riverbanks in search of weeds and grasses, desperate to find anything to fill their stomachs. Entire families were showing up at the local soviet headquarters for some sort of help, their bellies bloated, their faces disfigured, their eyes fevered. For many, the struggle was over:

They've lost their last bit of strength, fallen, and died. Some are unable to bear the torments of the Tsar-Famine and lose all sense of reason and go mad. In our region one often sees little children refusing their ration and asking for permission to give it to their mothers. Yet there are also instances when just before the mothers die, they suffocate their young ones in order to put an end to their suffering. Open your eyes, once and for all, to the great enormity of this catastrophe, which is a hundred times worse than you realize, and know that the help you are now providing is nothing but a drop in the ocean.

Childs found himself torn with contradictory emotions. On November 6, he could write his mother of how fortunate he felt to be doing good: "It is only by being of service that one can be happy." And then, four days later, he was immersed in gloom, certain that the misery was so immense that whatever help they could provide was "pitifully inadequate." He increasingly came to believe more had to be done, especially by Americans back home. Convinced that they were ignorant of just how bad things were in Russia, what he called "this greatest of twentieth century tragedies," he sent a letter to the editor of the *Lynchburg News* in which he chastised Americans for "dickering over debts and political opinions" while twenty million people were dying of hunger. He countered the lies that aid to Russia was being misused and stolen and took on the popular notion that America had enough of its own problems and so was in no position to help. "There was never a tragedy in America to compare with this," he wrote. "To America is given a great opportunity and as an American I am deeply concerned that she will take advantage of it."

He informed readers back in Virginia of a new ARA program and encouraged them to get involved. In October, the ARA had agreed with the Soviet government to launch a program of food-relief packages to help supplement the existing feeding operations. Through the ARA offices in New York, London, and other European cities, a person could pay for the delivery of a large box of food supplies to an individual in Russia. The typical package, almost 120 pounds in weight, included 49 pounds of flour, 25 pounds of rice, 3 pounds of lard or other fats, 10 pounds of sugar, and twenty 1-pound cans of evaporated milk. Each box cost $10, over $2 more than the cost of the food, a profit that the ARA then used to help grow the original mission of feeding hungry children. The ARA had first proposed the food package program at the Riga talks, but the suspicious Soviets had rejected the idea. By the beginning of October, however, Lenin, his earlier fears about the ARA put to rest, sought to increase cooperation with the Americans and began to lobby for the program with the rest of the Soviet leadership. At a meeting of the Politburo that month, Stalin argued against the program, insisting this was not charity but in fact a form of capitalist trade, which had not been part of the original agreement. For Lenin, that was fine: "If indeed that is the goal—trade, then we ought to gain experience, for they are giving us real assistance for the starving." Lenin won the argument, but the hard-liners, men like Stalin, were not about to surrender to the Americans. This was made clear to Childs and the rest of his team in Kazan in the middle of November.

On the 11th, Childs and Wahren attended an exhibition at the Kazan Institute of Art. As they wandered the halls, their teeth chattering in the icy cold of the unheated building, Childs stopped before a canvas devoted to the famine, with images of ragged refugees shuffling across a bleak plain in a last effort to escape death. He bought the painting for 6 million rubles, less than $100. The artist was Nikolai Fechin, a native of Kazan who had studied under the great master Ilya Repin at the Imperial Academy of Arts in St. Petersburg and was now barely surviving with his family back in his hometown. Childs got word to Fechin that he would like to request a portrait and would pay him in ARA food packages. The artist was overjoyed at the commission, and soon the two were meeting daily for sittings.

While Childs was viewing art, Cheka agents were striking a blow against the ARA. That same day, they arrested three of the Russian personnel: their office manager, a man named Salomine; a Mrs. Depould, one of the ARA kitchen inspectors; and Wahren's assistant, a woman by the name of Krasilnikova. The arrests were a clear and provocative infringe-

ment of the Riga Agreement, and the Americans were outraged. Turner argued that they
should shut down the mission and leave
the next morning for Moscow; he was concerned they'd be next and was not about to
end up in a Cheka prison. Wahren, however,
managed to talk him down. He proposed
they first stop all shipments of foodstuffs,
clothing, and medical supplies throughout
the district and send a letter of complaint
to the leaders of the Tatar Republic, insisting that the ARA employees be released and
permitted to return to work immediately,
unless valid charges could be presented
against them. Wahren had the suspicion

Fechin's portrait of Childs

that the attack on the ARA had not been the work of local officials, with
whom they had good relations, but was coming from Moscow. And he
was right. There had been similar arrests at the ARA operations in Tsaritsyn and Samara.

Wahren's tactic worked, and on the afternoon of the 14th, a pale, hag-
gard Salomine appeared at the offices, having come straight from prison.
Childs thought he looked like a frightened rat terrier. Clearly shaken by
his experience, he told the Americans that the Cheka had forced him
to sign a statement admitting to harboring anti-Soviet sympathies. The
women were soon released as well. The next day, Wahren wrote to the ARA
office in Moscow to inform them that the matter had been successfully
resolved once it became clear that "we mean what we say and shall expect
them to do likewise."

Back in Moscow, Eiduk was not ready to put the matter to rest.
He wrote Haskell on the 20th, complaining that the only Russians the
ARA was hiring were from the former bourgeoisie and insisting that
these people were enemies of the state. He remarked that Salomine had
"an undoubtedly counterrevolutionary past" and described Depould as an

"ex-baroness" with "the most emphatically anti-Soviet spirit." Among her supposed crimes was appearing at the ARA kitchens covered in diamond rings and bracelets and in décolleté, an affront to Soviet morals that elicited indignation from the hungry children and their mothers. The Cheka had been left no alternative but to arrest her. Indeed, after questioning, the Cheka learned that her husband had fought for Kolchak's army; as the wife of a former White Guard officer, she should be confined to a workhouse.

The ARA pushed back. Haskell reminded Eiduk that, according to the Riga Agreement, they were free to hire anyone without regard to "race, creed, or political opinion," and they were not about to give up this right. Eiduk backed down and promised to do whatever he could to minimize arrests in the future, although he continued to maintain that among the Russian personnel were a good many criminals and political enemies. In the end, the two sides agreed that the ARA would present the Soviet government with lists of all future candidates for employment, complete with their personal histories, and if the Soviets found good cause for rejecting a candidate, the ARA would respect their wishes.

Nevertheless, suspicion remained. After observing the actions of the ARA in the Samara Province, a Soviet official wrote: "We have the impression that the ARA, upon putting together its local staff, is in fact preparing an organization capable of replacing us should the opportunity arise. There is no other way to account for the anti-Soviet elements being drawn to it. We shall remain on guard."

GOLDER, MEANWHILE, was feeling the heat as well. In early December, after returning to Moscow from yet another of his expeditions, he wrote to a colleague at Stanford that "the secret service, the so-called Che-Ka, is on my trail and after my scalp." His perfect Russian, deep knowledge of the country and its history, and extensive relationships with writers, scholars, and other intellectuals made Golder stand out from the rest of the ARA men, who were generally ignorant about Russia. All of this made the Cheka suspicious, and the agency became convinced that Golder was not who he claimed. The idea took hold that he had fought with Kolchak and had returned to Russia to carry out propaganda against the government. "I walk around as if a sword hung over me," he moaned. It was all too much, and he informed the ARA he wanted to leave Russia by the end of January 1922.

For an entire month, beginning in the early-morning hours of October 9, Golder had traveled from Moscow to Ufa, over seven hundred miles to the east as the crow flies, on the edge of the Ural Mountains, before returning west to Samara, on the Volga, then on to Penza and Saratov and from there south to Astrakhan—this last leg an especially exasperating five-day trip on a train traveling at a top speed of ten miles per hour. Everywhere he stopped, he was shadowed by Cheka agents, as welcome, in his words, "as scarlet fever," which made it difficult for Golder to speak candidly with people about the extent of the famine in the various regions and the efforts being made by the local governments.

He set off back to Moscow on a steamer at the end of October. The blackflies hovering over the Volga were so bad he had to go belowdecks, only to find there was nowhere to sit, much less to lie down for the night, since all the furniture cushions were crawling with bedbugs. He managed to locate a folding table to serve as a bed. In Saratov, the ARA sent one of its automobiles to pick him up at the wharf. Golder allowed himself the pleasure of assuming things would now go more smoothly, but it was not to be. "We rode ten minutes and then got a flat," he recorded in his diary. "The American Relief Administration is becoming Russianized quickly."

Golder was nearly as annoyed with his fellow Americans. Life at the Pink House felt at times like living in a richly decorated fraternity house. A visiting American reporter called it a "Gilded Barracks"; one of the men slept on his U.S. Army cot set up beneath a Rembrandt. The heavy-smoking Americans stubbed out their cigarettes on whatever was convenient and then tossed the butts on the floor. Golder couldn't stand to see how Sergei Shchukin's magnificent home was being trashed by this bunch of young rowdies. In the early hours of Thanksgiving Day, Golder found himself lying awake in bed, unable to sleep because of the wild partying downstairs. The Americans had invited over some ballet dancers, "and other females of that kind," Golder wrote in a letter after giving up on the prospect of sleep, and they were now all "more than half full of booze." This was no ordinary party. "The prize guest is Isadora Duncan and the woman is either drunk or crazy, perhaps both. She is half dressed and calls to the boys to pull down her chimies, I think that this is the way they are called [. . .] What may happen before morning I do not know."

Heavy drinking was endemic to the ARA operation. Lonergan, Haskell's assistant, was among the worst, drinking himself practically into a coma on a few occasions; he eventually lost his job over his problems with the bottle. Carroll, too, fell into the clutches of dipsomania, and was also sent home when things got out of hand. For some, drinking offered a release from the pressures of the job; for others, drinking, especially when meeting with Soviet officials, was a requirement of the job.

Golder had been particularly upset about the wild partying that night since he was scheduled to leave the following day on another tour, this time to Ukraine. Preparations for the trip had not been easy. Eiduk and the Soviet government had refused Golder's request for travel papers to Soviet Ukraine, insisting that there was no famine there and that all of the Americans' efforts ought to be concentrated along the Volga. What went unsaid was that parts of western Ukraine had yet to be fully subjugated following the recent peasant rebellions; there was considerable fear that an American presence might well inspire the remaining partisans to continue their resistance. The ARA reminded Eiduk that the Riga Agreement gave them the right to determine the areas served by the mission, and in the end he had no option but to relent. "There is a cry for help from the Ukraine," Golder wrote. "The granary of Russia is empty and the inhabitants are suffering from hunger and the terrors of bandit raids." He felt a sincere obligation to see for himself what the Americans could do.

The first stop was Kiev, to make arrangements for the food-relief package program, and from there to Kharkov, for meetings with top Ukrainian officials. Kharkov was then the capital of the Ukrainian Socialist Soviet Republic, independent of Russia until the formation of the Union of Soviet Socialist Republics (USSR or Soviet Union) in late 1922. There was a good deal of confusion about whether the Ukrainians would let the ARA in without a separate agreement, since the Riga accord, they insisted, did not extend to Ukraine. The Ukrainians wanted American aid, but wished to have the conditions for it spelled out in their own terms if possible. Golder returned to Moscow in early December, frustrated at the lack of a clear understanding with the Ukrainian government, although he had managed to assess in a general way the condition of the famine there. It was beyond any doubt that parts of the country were suffering as badly as the Volga, and perhaps as many as nine million people, out of a total Ukrainian population of twenty-six million, were trapped inside the famine zone. Upon reading Golder's report on Ukraine, Haskell knew the ARA had to expand operations beyond Russia. He had, however, not a single penny to help feed Ukraine.

On December 6, while riding on the train back to Moscow, a down-hearted Golder recorded in his diary: "All of Russia is on the move and in search of bread, it thinks of nothing else, it talks of nothing else [. . .] If conditions do not change for the better, the future, at least the immediate future, is really dark [. . .] Every one is asking the question, 'Where is the end?' but no one can give the answer. Many Russians insist that only America can save the country, rumors are even about that America will, but when I ask what can America do, there is nothing definite to propose." Golder kept meeting Russians who were convinced that America and Russia needed each other for their mutual survival. Many insisted that America could not get along economically without trade with Russia, and so America and Russia were bound to work together. Such notions of America's dependence on Soviet Russia infected even the high ranks of the Communist Party.

Karl Radek, a Polish Jew, member of the Russian Communist Party's Executive Committee, and prominent figure in the Communist International (Comintern), an organization dedicated to fomenting world revolution, invited Golder to the Kremlin on the 17th to talk Russo-American relations. In a mix of grammatically shaky Russian and German, Radek explained to Golder that he had sought the meeting to try to convince him that America's future lay with Russia and that it was in the United States' interest to cultivate relations with the new Soviet government. He pointed out that since the United States had had official relations with tsarist Russia, which had not been democratic, there was no good reason for America not to recognize the new government. Relations, he insisted, would be to both countries' benefit. Before Golder left, Radek offered to introduce him to other Bolsheviks who shared his views.

Golder had to admit that Radek was well informed about American politics; nonetheless, he found absurd the notion that America needed Russia, much less that it could save Russia. Russia, he kept telling people, had no money with which to buy American goods; what was more, the Russians didn't produce anything Americans wanted to buy. Still, Russians repeatedly tried to convince him the United States would be wise to make sacrifices to Soviet Russia now for the sake of trade in the future. "Russia," Golder noted, "is full of dreamers."

BUT IT WASN'T just the Russians: there were dreamers among the Americans as well. Childs wrote his mother a letter from Kazan on December 8 extolling the virtues of the Soviet government and blaming the world's problems on capitalism. He was certain that Wilson had wanted to build a socialist society in America, similar to what Lenin was creating in Russia, but the late president had been thwarted by the crafty maneuvering of American capitalists and the stupidity of the masses, who'd been unable to grasp the fact that Wilson had been working for their benefit. In Soviet Russia, he wrote, "I believe there is a sincerer desire to serve the people on the part of the ruling class of Russia today than there is in America. In a way, I have a greater faith that the true principles of democracy will be obtained in Russia than I have that they will be preserved in America." He knew that if the folks back home could hear him talk they'd take him for one of those "Bolshevists."

The following day, Childs set off on a two-week tour of the Tatar Republic, joined by Skvortsov, Simson, and two American journalists— Edwin Hullinger of the United Press and Ambrose Lambert of the *Chicago Tribune*. They took an overnight train to Sviazhsk and then climbed into several sleighs to take them to the village of Umatovo, their first stop. The trip was harrowing from the start. The men of Umatovo, "honest appearing peasants with dark brown skins and beards which seem to have taken on the color of the soil they tilled," told them that, unless they received food relief, no more than 3 percent of the village would survive the winter.

Childs spent two weeks traveling over the snow from village to village, weighed down in layers of heavy clothing, hat, and mittens, and clutching a bottle of cognac to help warm his insides and numb the bite of the icy wind. In the Tatar village of Big Bulatovo, the local ARA committee informed their party that the population had fallen from 580 to 300 in just a few months. Many had died; others had fled in search of food. Now, however, there was no more talk of leaving. It was too cold to travel, and the people were too weak from malnourishment. The draft animals that might have taken them away had long ago been killed and eaten. Many of the villagers who had left reportedly died out in the steppe. The remaining villagers had resigned themselves to fate. The secretary of the local soviet told the men that he felt it was his duty to stay on until the bitter end and help as best he could. They had food for another six weeks at the most. Once that was gone, death would come for them. They encountered a similar scene in the village of Tetiushi. Most of the people were living off the few remaining cats and dogs in the area, and Childs noticed that a good many of the villagers were beginning to show signs of bloating from hunger and poor food substitutes.

At times they traveled at night, guided by the bright light of the moon reflected off the sea of powdery white snow. On December 15, they raced along the banks of the Kama River and watched as the moon set and the sun slowly rose in the southeast. Childs found himself mesmerized by the beautiful silhouette of a Russian church against the frozen horizon. Later that day, Hullinger left them for Moscow to attend the upcoming Ninth All-Russian Congress of Soviets, and the group stopped for the night in Alexeevskaya. Their lodgings were filthy and infested with vermin. That night, Simson was bitten by a louse.

The 18th found them in the village of Mamadysh, on the Vyatka River, founded over half a millennium before by the ancient Bulgars. Throughout their trip, they had made a point of visiting the children's homes, all of which were overcrowded, dirty, grim places. The home in Mamadysh

Dining Hall No. 1 in the village of Tetiushi.
A portrait of Herbert Hoover watches over the children.

was no exception. There were no beds or blankets, and the children lay in their rags upon the floor, nestled up one against another for a bit of warmth. "They resembled," Childs wrote, "in their dirty garments and in their staring lusterless eyes, the figures of animals rather than human beings." Childs gave the director of the home 2 million rubles to buy some clothing, and they drove on to the next village.

Before they departed Mamadysh, they were warned to be on the lookout for wolves, and for bandits who had recently carried out a raid on an ARA warehouse. Childs and his party had left Kazan armed with revolvers in case of such dangers. One of Childs's sleigh drivers had told him how he had once been set upon by a pack of fifteen wolves in a deserted woods on a dark morning. He had been forced to light a ring of fires around himself and his horse to hold them off until he could make his escape. He had also heard of a schoolmistress who was being driven

Childs and the Soviet official Mikhail Skvortsov on their inspection tour

through a lonely stretch of forest when her sleigh was attacked by wolves. The driver tried to outrun them, but, no matter how hard he whipped his horse, they kept coming. Just as the wolves were about to attack, he turned, shoved the woman out into the snow, and bolted off to the sound of her screams as the beasts tore into her flesh. At one point, the men in Childs's party noticed that Simson wasn't with them. Worried, they doubled back, to find him straggling along, nearly frozen from the cold. Now safely reunited, the group pressed on through the snow.

Simson awoke the morning of the 20th suffering from excruciating pains and a high fever. It was typhus, transmitted by the louse bite several days earlier. His condition was severe, and the men knew they had to get him back to a doctor in Kazan as quickly as possible. The closest rail station was at Agryz, nearly eighty miles away, and so they piled into their sleighs and took off as fast as they could ride. They rode all day and night, stopping for fresh horses at each village. Once, when the chairman of the local soviet refused, Skvortsov threatened him with arrest if the best horses in the village were not provided within half an hour. They were on their way again in a few minutes. At one point, they halted at a peasant hut in the middle of the night to warm up and try to get some rest, only to find the walls and floors crawling with bugs. Fearful to sit, much less lie down, they stood just long enough to warm themselves and then returned to their sleighs. An exhausted Childs slept as they whisked over the snowy landscape, until he was violently tossed from the sleigh when they hit a bump; he crash-landed, headfirst, into the side of a wooden building, his heavy fur hat saving him from serious injury. They managed to reach Agryz early on the 22nd, hoping to find a train waiting to take Simson back to Kazan, only to discover it had yet to arrive. Eventually, a train appeared; later that evening, the ailing interpreter was put on board, joined by Childs and Skvortsov. Their furious race of almost forty-eight hours to Agryz had saved Simson's life, and he went on to make a full recovery.

In two weeks, Childs had traveled 470 miles by sleigh, 180 by rail; he had visited twelve of the Tatar Republic's thirteen districts, held twelve meetings with district ARA committees, fourteen meetings with county committees, eighteen with village committees, and inspected ten hospitals, thirty-three public kitchens, and thirty-six children's homes. The experience left him shattered.

On Christmas Day he wrote his mother from Kazan:

> This day of "peace on earth, goodwill toward men" broke upon me with terrible irony as I sat and surveyed in contemplation those Russian villages through which I had passed a few days previous and where all was death and desolation. I don't think I have ever suffered so profoundly as I have these past days [. . .] Has the soul of the world been destroyed since 1914? [. . .] I feel like cursing the entire world outside of Russia for its terrible heartlessness in permitting this awful tragedy to pass by without an attempt at aid on the scale which is needed.

He expected that no more than 20 percent of the population would survive the winter, so much greater was the need than what could be fulfilled by the ARA, the Soviet government, and other aid groups.

There were, nevertheless, a few sparks of human kindness left in the world. As the Americans ate their Christmas Eve dinner in Kazan, so far from home and their loved ones, the Russian women from the office sneaked into their living quarters, put up a tree complete with lights and ornaments, and left the men a few gifts and a cake, baked with the flour from their own ARA rations. The men were deeply touched by their gesture. Childs was certain none of the Americans would ever forget this Christmas or this special tree, a clear, unmistakable sign of the goodwill of the people of Kazan toward the men of the American Relief Administration.

7

THE TRADITIONS OF
RUSSIAN FRIENDSHIP

FTER THREE MONTHS IN RUSSIA, the ARA was feeding nearly
570,000 children a day in three thousand kitchens in 191 towns
and villages. Its theater of operations had spread way beyond the
central Volga region, extending east to the city of Ufa, on the edge of the
Ural Mountains, and south to Astrakhan by the Caspian Sea. The main
office in Moscow grew accordingly. There was a liaison division to manage relations with the Soviet government, an accounting division to keep
track of every penny spent, a traffic division to oversee the transport of
food and matériel by rail, a historical division to record its operations, and
a motor division to maintain the ARA's fleet of 149 vehicles, mostly Cadillac touring cars and Ford camionettes along with two types of trucks:

the Pierce-Arrow R-5 and the Standard B "Liberty," built for the U.S. Army in World War I. Top speed: fifteen miles per hour. By the time the mission was over, these vehicles had covered 1.4 million miles on some of the worst roads imaginable.

Despite the initial success of the operation, it was clear to many in the ARA, as well as to many in the Soviet government, that more help was needed. Haskell wrote to Walter Lyman Brown at the ARA's London office on December 1 that millions in Russia faced certain death before the harvest of 1922 unless additional aid from outside was forthcoming. A week later, he cabled to Hoover that as many as seven million children in Russia would die unless America did more to help. "As a Christian nation we must make greater effort to prevent this tragedy. Can you not ask those who have already assisted this organization to carry over eight million children through famine in other parts of Europe to again respond to the utmost of their ability?" he asked of The Chief. Haskell's cable had apparently been arranged ahead of time; it was not meant to convince Hoover of the need for more relief (he was already behind the idea), but was to be used by Hoover to convince the United States Congress. Hoover had for quite some time wanted to increase the size of the Russian operation. He had no interest in some large nationwide public appeal, which, given the still-weak state of the economy, might not be successful and would require him to work with all manner of groups, much to his displeasure. Instead, he set his sights on the federal government, specifically the roughly $20 million in the U.S. Grain Corporation, a successor body to the United States Food Administration created during World War I. Haskell's cable would help Hoover make his case.

Meanwhile, on December 6, President Harding recommended that Congress appropriate funds to purchase ten million bushels of corn and one million of seed grains for the ARA. In his message to Congress, Harding noted that, although the United States didn't recognize the Soviet government or tolerate its propaganda, "we don't forget the traditions of Russian friendship" and must do whatever it could to help the millions starving. Politics must be put aside and we ought to be generous, he said, in keeping with the spirit of the "Christmastide" season. "The big thing is

the call of the suffering and the dying." Harding's appeal had been orches-
trated by none other than Hoover. With agricultural prices in the United
States severely depressed because of overproduction, Hoover envisioned
a way not only to feed the hungry but also to aid American farmers:
the government would purchase their unmarketable grain, thus putting
money in their pockets that they would spend on manufactured goods,
giving a boost to the industrial sector, and so further help the country out
of the depression of 1920–21.

The Chief had other political ideas in mind as well. The very day
Harding sent his proposal to Congress, Hoover wrote to Secretary of State
Hughes that, even though the United States, unlike some other countries,
had not officially recognized Soviet Russia, "Americans are infinitely more
popular in Russia and our Government more deeply respected by even
the Bolsheviks than any other." One of the main reasons for this was the
work of the ARA, which was helping to increase respect for the United
States. Hoover let Hughes know he had no doubt that the Bolsheviks
would fall, given the inherent fallacies of their ideology, and when they
did, a new, democratic Russia would be built, led by the tens of thousands
of Russians who had fled abroad with the revolution. It was his hope that,
in light of the good feeling created by the ARA, America might be able
"to undertake the leadership in the reconstruction of Russia when the
moment arrives." Hoover made sure, however, not to broadcast this view
of the potential fruits of the ARA's mission.

Hoover, together with former Indiana governor Goodrich, who had
recently returned from a fact-finding tour of Russia, appeared before the
House Committee on Foreign Affairs on December 12 to lobby for the
appropriation. They surprised the representatives on the committee by dou-
bling Harding's initial request. "You would not want, and I should regret
to see," Goodrich told the committee, "this country start in and not do
the job right because of the lack of two or three million dollars." Hoover
addressed head-on the question of whether the country could afford
so much in foreign aid: "Well, the American public spends a billion
dollars annually on tobacco, cosmetics, and the like, and I do not think
$20,000,000 too much." Moreover, we were now feeding milk to hogs and

burning corn under boilers. Harm the economy? Too much? In fact, he remarked, this appropriation would be of great help to America's farmers. Ultimately, however, Hoover told the committee, "no other argument is needed beyond sheer humanity."

News of the bill was met largely with approval. The *New York Tribune* ran an editorial on December 8, titled "Really Helping Russia," endorsing the plan: "America is still America; her ears are not deaf to cries of human want." Yet charity didn't imply dangerous ignorance of the facts. "Give to Russia? Yes; but when giving remember that every word spoken in defense of Bolshevism tends to encoffin Russia—and increase the probability of recurrent famines." Various groups offered Hoover their support. The president of the American-Russian Chamber of Commerce, William C. Redfield, informed Hoover he would do whatever he could to pressure Congress to pass the bill, and he wrote Wyoming congressman Frank W. Mondell, the House majority leader, of the great future trade benefits of the appropriation once Russia recovered and was open to the world for business: "Nothing could be more certain to react largely and favorably upon American business than unselfishness at this moment." A lobbyist from the American Farm Bureau Federation made a similar point to the committee: "In addition to saving the lives of starving people in Russia, there will be a comeback—bread cast upon the waters has always had a tendency to come back to the giver." Support came from across the political spectrum. The liberal *New Republic*, usually a thorn in Hoover's side, called the famine appropriations "precedents of a new international order based on humanity and good will," and *The Nation* noted, "America seems to be awakening at last to the reality of the Russian famine." (This from the same publication that in September had called reports of the famine "exaggerated.")

Riding this wave of support, Hoover tried to rush the bill through the House to prevent attempts by its opponents to organize. It came up for a vote on the floor after only a week, and passed by a vote of 181 to 71, although almost 180 members registered as "not voting" rather than having to cast a vote either way, such was the politically fraught atmosphere created by the Red Scare and depression. The large number of representatives on the sidelines gave an opening to the bill's opponents in the Senate. Tom

Watson of Georgia got up on December 20 to assert that there wasn't even a food crisis in Russia, that in fact the Russians had plenty of wheat. The bill, Watson insisted, was a gift not to Russia but to Hoover and the ARA. "Charity is a business, a profession," he insisted. What Russia really needed and deserved, he informed his colleagues, was official recognition, not American intransigence over the type of government they had chosen for themselves. Senators raised a variety of objections. Some wanted government relief for the four million army veterans in dire need before doing anything for Russia. Some argued that the U.S. Constitution forbade using tax dollars for the aid of anyone other than American citizens. Some tried to make the point that American aid would only strengthen the Red Army and thus weaken America's own defenses.

The voices in favor of the bill in the Senate echoed those in the House, and the opponents were soon defeated. Having passed both chambers of Congress, the bill was signed into law by President Harding on December 22. A few weeks later, Congress approved legislation permitting the War Department and other government agencies to transfer as much as $4 million in surplus material, chiefly medical supplies, to the ARA for Russian relief.

The Ninth All-Russian Congress of Soviets opened in Moscow on December 23. Lenin informed the delegates that the Americans had committed $20 million, which he described as a great success, especially in comparison with what he characterized as the paltry help from Western Europe. He admitted that the American aid would not be enough to cover the entire disaster, but stressed that it was significant help that would go a long way toward easing the suffering of the hungry.

Lenin faced opposition from his colleagues. Just days before the congress opened, Stalin wrote in *Pravda* that the foreign aid workers operated "at the same time as the most efficient spies of the world bourgeoisie, and that, therefore, the world bourgeoisie now knows Soviet Russia, knows her strengths and weaknesses, better than at any time before, a circumstance fraught with grave danger in the event of new interventionist attacks." Grigory Zinoviev, another party leader, shared Stalin's view, as did Nikolai

An ARA warehouse in New York City with supplies
awaiting transport to Russia

Bukharin, editor of *Pravda*, who published numerous scathing denunciations of the ARA. "The Americans, like the other European capitalists, are not here to rescue the starving, to improve the conditions of the workers," asserted one piece. "Oh, no. They are preparing chains and a noose for them. Therefore, workers, be on guard [. . .] At the first attempt to slip handcuffs and a noose on us, we must do the same in return." Eiduk responded to Stalin on the pages of *Izvestiia*, defending the ARA and its work alongside the Soviet government. Yes, he admitted, the Americans now had firsthand knowledge of Soviet Russia, but this was nothing to fear: as unbiased, fair observers, they were doing much to counteract the many falsehoods prevalent in the West. Haskell had proved particularly useful in this regard, providing reliable information to the many foreign correspondents now in Moscow.

If such was Eiduk's public stance, in private he expressed a much different view of the ARA. In a "Top Secret" letter of December 21 to People's Commissar for Foreign Affairs Chicherin, Eiduk wrote that, since his appointment as plenipotentiary to the ARA, "I have tried to get to the heart of the work of Hoover's representatives," and he could now say for certain that "this organization cannot be viewed as apolitical and its work within the borders of the RSFSR* is not honest." Although the Americans followed the letter of the Riga Agreement, they looked for every opportunity "to expose the defects of the Soviet government, and I can assure you that the entire work of the ARA proves that it is not in their interests to provide serious help to us or the starving, rather the ARA is chiefly concerned with self-promotion."

The fact was, however, the Soviets needed America's help, regardless of their fears. On the 24th, Vladimir Antonov-Ovseenko, "the Bayonet," a battle-hardened Bolshevik who had helped crush peasant unrest in the Tambov region together with General Tukhachevsky and then been placed in charge of famine fighting in Samara Province, sent a report outlining the horrors unfolding in the area. There were instances in which mothers had led their children out into the steppe and left them there to die, and others, mad from hunger, had stabbed their children to death rather than have to watch them starve. And this was not all. There were reports from the district of Ramyshkovskaya that people had been eating corpses. Burials had to be carried out in secret, or else starving villagers would dig up the bodies and eat them. A guard was posted at the graveyard. The Executive Committee of Usminsky County had submitted details concerning a woman who had chopped up the body of a dead eleven-year-old boy and boiled his flesh in a large kettle.

Antonov-Ovseenko's report was corroborated three days later by an official from the Samara Cheka. The famine was driving many to suicide; parents were bringing their children into the towns and abandoning them there to fate. Examples of cannibalism, including parents killing and eat-

---

* The Russian Socialist Federative Soviet Republic—RSFSR—was the official name of the country from July 1918 until the establishment of the Union of Soviet Socialist Republics—USSR—in December 1922, which combined Russia, Ukraine, Belorussia, and Transcaucasia.

ing their own children, were on the rise. Instances of theft, robbery, and general lawlessness were becoming ever more prevalent, creating a sense of panic in the population. The mood among the working population was ugly and angry. "The feeling of the masses for the communists is hostile." They needed "immediate emergency help" to cope with the disaster.

Hoover had decided to use the congressional appropriation to force the Soviets to contribute more to the famine-relief effort. Back in late August, he had communicated to Brown that he wanted to convince the Soviets to use some of their gold reserves to help defray the expense. The Soviets had agreed to provide the ARA with $4.5 million in gold to be used to purchase American grain, at cost. Now, however, Hoover upped the figure. He informed Leonid Krasin, the people's commissar for foreign trade, that the ARA expected $10 million in Soviet gold to be used to purchase seed and grain for feeding operations in the Volga Basin. Krasin wired Moscow of Hoover's demand, and Lenin replied immediately that he should accept the new terms, so great was his desire to secure further American aid.

America had given Russia renewed cause for hope in combating the famine, but Russia showed little gratitude. When the Congress of Soviets wrapped up on the 28th, it expressed in flowery terms its thanks to Nansen and the "workers of all countries" for their aid, and condemned the world's bourgeois governments, arguing that they were still bent on using the catastrophe to orchestrate the overthrow of the Soviet government. Lenin assured the delegates that he labored under no false pretenses about the nefarious goals of the various foreign missions, and that the Cheka stood at the ready to defeat any attempts at counterrevolution. The work of the ARA over the past four months received only brief and begrudging acknowledgment.

Golder was disgusted. "In a thousand and one ways they worry us, they arrest the Russians who work for us, they block us here and side track us there," he complained in a letter to a friend back in California on the last day of the year. "I dare say that nowhere in Europe have our people suffered so many humiliations and have been appreciated so little as here. Were it not for the fact that all realize that the honor of the ARA and of

Hoover are mixed up with this work many of our men would not remain here. As it is, we all say we have got to see this thing through somehow."

Despite the challenges, the men of the ARA carried on. By the end of 1921, the famine had gotten worse—perhaps as many as thirty-six million men, women, and children now faced starvation. The question on everyone's mind as the horrific year came to an end was whether the American relief would arrive in time to save them.

1922

8

FEEDING BABIES
IN SIBERIA

H E COULD NEVER HAVE IMAGINED how horrible a trip it would be. It was Saturday, December 17, 1921, and he had been under way from Riga for a week, with Moscow still nowhere in sight. He'd been out of the filthy railcar but once in seven days, just long enough to collect some water and wood for the stove, bartered for with American cigarettes and cans of bully beef. Much of the time, the train stood motionless. He and his companion took turns tending the stove, which would go out every fifteen minutes or so if left alone, a dreadful possibility given the bitter cold. The one in charge of the stove also had to keep watch: refugees along the route kept trying to pry open the heavy door, but its weight, made all the greater by their weakness, kept them out. The night before, a violent downdraft had blown out the stove, filling the car with smoke and nearly choking them to death. They considered opening the door for fresh air, but decided they would rather risk asphyxiation than freezing. And now, just when it seemed things couldn't get much worse, their food was running out. They figured it might last until Monday, and the only thing they could do was hope that they'd reached their destination by then.

Like many of the young men of the ARA, William Kelly had hardly been able to wait to get to Russia. Now he found himself wondering why he had been in such a hurry. Kelly had come to save the starving masses, yet even before he could get started, here he was, cold, dirty, and hungry.

Kelly was born into a large family of Irish extraction in Lexington, Kentucky, in 1895. Intelligent and hardworking, he excelled in high school, and one of his teachers encouraged him to go on to college, unlike the rest of his classmates. He enrolled at Columbia University's School of Journalism, recently established by Joseph Pulitzer, then transferred, after two years, to Harvard, where he graduated in 1917 with a concentration in economics and sociology. He also went through officer training while in Cambridge, and in August was commissioned as a captain in the Military Intelligence Reserve Corps. In the first months of 1918, he was ordered to General Headquarters of the American Expeditionary Force in Chaumont, France. It was here that he met and became friends with another American officer, two years his senior, a fellow Harvard man from Virginia, the aspiring writer J. Rives Childs.

After the armistice, he was attached to the American peace delegation in Paris, again along with Childs, and then joined the executive staff of the Inter-Allied Games, held in the summer of 1919 at the newly constructed Pershing Stadium near the Bois de Vincennes, which featured over a thousand athletes—all of them former military personnel of the various Allied armies—in a variety of sporting events intended to celebrate the end of the war. That autumn, following his return to the United States, Kelly was demobilized and got a job with the Associated Press in Washington. Here he would frequently cross paths with his old army buddy Childs, but then moved up to New York, to work first as an assistant to the head of the Hoover National Republican Club, an organization of Hoover supporters seeking to convince him (unsuccessfully) to run for president in the election of 1920, and then for the American-Polish Chamber of Commerce.

In early September 1921, Major Marlborough Churchill, formerly of the general staff of the AEF in France and then head of the War Department's Military Intelligence Division, wrote a letter of recommendation to the ARA on behalf of Kelly, praising him and his "most excellent reputation" and declaring him "in every way suitable for duty with the American Relief Administration." Kelly interviewed in the New York office with George Barr Baker, head of the ARA's public-relations department, who asked him to write up "a few words about yourself." Kelly did so that same day, asking Baker to "Please set down the barrenness of style as due to the unfortunate choice of subject," words that neatly capture his dry, sardonic nature. If Childs was the ARA's idealist and Golder its realist, Kelly was its cynic. He gave Baker a rundown of his life story in a few brief, unembellished sentences, ending with these words: "Unmarried, not in love, no property, and have paid my income tax." All of this was true, except for one detail: Kelly was dating a young Vassar College graduate, Jane Seymour of New York City. It soon blossomed into a love affair and then an engagement, a fact Kelly would later use as a reason to quit his employment with the ARA in Russia well before the work there was done.

Baker hired Kelly as his assistant in early September, and by the middle of the month, his name had already been put forward as an excellent candidate for the Russian unit, in light of his experience, intelligence, capacity for hard work, and no-nonsense personality. Haskell met Kelly on a visit to New York in the autumn and concurred with this assessment, requesting that Kelly be sent over as soon as possible. At first Kelly was excited about the prospect and wrote home to his brother, J. Frank Kelly, back in Lexington on November 12 to get a copy of his birth certificate from the city clerk and "rush" it to him in New York for his passport application. The passport was processed in a few days, with the help of the Commerce Department, and sent by special courier to New York so that

William Kelly

Kelly could leave on the SS *Zeeland*, sailing for Plymouth, England, on the 19th.

In the flurry of these preparations, Kelly proposed to Jane, and she accepted. What had once seemed the prospect of a great adventure now looked like an interminable separation from the woman he loved. He went to Baker to try to talk his way out of the commitment, but his boss wouldn't hear of it. In the end, Kelly, swayed by what he later called "Baker's paternal advice," agreed to go, although only for the length of his contract—six months. His salary was the standard for most of the ARA men working the Russian job: $200 a month plus $6 per diem.

Kelly arrived in Riga on December 7. That day, he met Carl Floete, an ARA man recently sent out of Russia after serving in the Volga area and suffering from a nervous breakdown. Floete had barely survived an attack by eight hundred Cossack bandits on the village of Pugachëv that left dozens of Red Army soldiers dead in the streets. He had barricaded himself in the ARA headquarters, and although he had managed to sit out the attack unscathed, he was an emotional wreck. The sight of the quaking Floete could not have helped Kelly with his own anxiety about "going in" to Bolshevik Russia, what the men called "Bololand."

"Two innocent young men," as Kelly described himself and his fellow American Edward Bergfeld, departed Riga for Moscow on the 9th, along with a railcar of medical supplies from the Red Cross. They had been told the trip would take six days. On the 18th, still cooped up in their railcar, Kelly wrote, "Nothing that follows in Russia is likely to be more disagreeable than these last eight days," words he would soon recognize as mistaken in the extreme. Their food all but gone, the two men had little left other than two cigars, which they were saving for a celebratory smoke upon their arrival in Moscow. Finally, just as they were losing all hope, the train pulled into the capital on the 20th. They were met by Lonergan, whom Kelly knew from his days in Paris after the war, taken to the Blue House, and told to prepare to depart the next day. "I leave tomorrow for Ufa," Kelly wrote Jane, "to feed babies on the edge of Siberia." But the expected train never materialized, and so tomorrow came and went.

Kelly was still in Moscow to celebrate Christmas dinner on the afternoon of the 25th with the other Americans, a feast that included wine, champagne, and a plum pudding sent from Lexington by his mother, all consumed to the sounds of a Gypsy choir. Then he was taken to the station to catch an overnight train to Samara. Though he had moved up from a foul freight car to a wagon-lit, he had been fairly warned about the danger of lice and other vermin, and so Kelly made certain to sleep on top of his trench coat. His own cleanliness was questionable. He'd been wearing the same clothes since leaving London—twenty-five straight days—without washing them, and was in desperate need of a shampoo and haircut; but compared with the Russians on the train, he joked to Jane, "I am a Beau Brummell."

Forty-three days after leaving New York, Kelly arrived in Ufa, on the last day of the year. No one was there to meet him at the station, so he hopped into a droshky and headed for the local headquarters of the ARA, where he was warmly welcomed by Walter Bell, head of the district.

A native of Brooklyn, Bell, at forty-seven, was an entire generation older than most of the other Americans, yet, like many of them, he, too, had served in the military—first in the Spanish-American War and then in World War I, seeing action both at Verdun in 1916 and then in the Meuse-Argonne Offensive two years later. Major General John F. O'Ryan had recommended Colonel Bell to Haskell in August, when the mission was being set up, as "a very live wire"—resourceful, tireless, well liked—and although Bell had no previous experience with the ARA or any relief work, Haskell was happy to have him. Bell had reached Moscow by mid-October, and two weeks later left for Ufa with his interpreter, Boris Elperine, who was fluent in Russian, English, and French, and whose Jewish family had lived in the Russian Empire under the tsars. Both Bell and Kelly became close with the diligent, reliable, and charming Elperine, the only true friend they made there. Later, Bell would help Elperine get out of Russia and make his way to America.

Ufa—on the western edge of the Ural Mountains, the dividing line between Europe and Asia, located just about halfway between Perm to the north and Orenburg to the south—had been settled by at least the eighth century A.D. It fell under the control of the Golden Horde of the Mongols in the thirteenth century, and then Russia in the reign of Ivan the Terrible, who ordered a fortress built there in 1574. Before the Russians came, the area had long been the home of the Bashkirs, a Turkic people with their own language, akin to Tatar and Kazakh, who had converted to Islam from their traditional animist faiths during the period of the Golden Horde. But there were other ethnic groups in the region— Tatar, Chuvash, Mari, Mordvin, and Udmurt—each with its own history, language, religion, culture, and dress. In the summer of 1922, Ufa became the capital of the Bashkir Autonomous Soviet Socialist Republic.

News of the ARA's arrival spread like lightning through the city. Within days, five thousand people showed up seeking employment. One of them was a sixteen-year-old student, Aleksei Laptev. Though he knew some English, he wasn't taken on, but this didn't deter him from returning day after day to try his luck, again and again. Finally, he was hired to help out with the food-remittance program in the afternoons, after school. "That was my wonderful luck, which changed my life, and saved my family from hunger and hardships during those terrible years," he recalled decades later, after coming to America. He was paid the same as most of the other native personnel: fifty-four pounds of white flour, twenty-eight of rice, eleven each of sugar and lard, ten cans of condensed milk, and three pounds of cocoa, all of which he would pull home on his sled through the snowy streets once a month. His family couldn't believe their eyes, or their tongues, having gone years without so much as tasting sugar or white bread or chocolate. In time, Laptev became Bell's assistant, his food ration was doubled, and he earned a salary as well. When his mother came down with tuberculosis, Bell saw to it that she received free medicine from the ARA. Acts like this were typical of Bell, and he soon

ARA mascot Mischka, with Gibbes Lykes, a member of
the ARA team in Samara, and Colonel Bell

ingratiated himself to the people of Ufa. Gifts starting showing up on his
doorstep, including a bear cub the men named Mischka and decided to
keep as a sort of mascot. Bell liked nothing more than to take the playful
Mischka with him in the Ford as he made his rounds through the city.

The first train of food arrived in Ufa on November 12, 1921, and by
the end of that week, the ARA was feeding sixteen hundred children. With
time, Bell's district grew to be one of the largest, feeding at its height 1.6
million people a day. The ARA was lodged in one of the city's finest
houses, at 83 Pushkin Street. This large two-story house, with some
outbuildings and a garage, had once belonged to a wealthy landowning
family by the name of Ryazantsev, and it had plenty of space for the ARA's
offices and living quarters. The Ryazantsevs had fled Ufa for the Far East
during the civil war; after her parents died there, Yelena Ryazantseva returned and took a job as an interpreter for the ARA. Simon Baird, one

of the Americans, fell hopelessly in love with Yelena, who was by all accounts intelligent and vivacious, and she coaxed him along, only to reject
his pleading marriage proposal. Heartbroken, Baird went to pieces and had
to be sent back to Moscow.

The house boasted electricity and good heating throughout all the
rooms—far from common—and had been fitted with fine curtains,
Turkish rugs, a grand piano, and bits of decorative bric-a-brac. Bell wrote
the ARA office in London to request several phonograph records for
their Victrola—"Allah's Holiday" from the Broadway operetta *Katinka*,
"The Greenwich Village Follies," and the latest recording by the Six Brown
Brothers, the popular Canadian saxophone sextet.

Despite their fine accommodations, Ufa was a rough town. Crime was
so bad that Bell noted the Americans "have to go about dressed like Bret
Harte, with a six gun on the hip." Wartime service in France was "a summer
resort compared with our present assignment." Dealing with the various
government agencies made the Versailles peace talks "seem like a well
conducted private school."

The Colonel, as Bell liked to be called, had barely gotten the district
up and running when he was felled by typhus while out on a tour of the
republic in November. He was brought back to Ufa in a state of delirium,
and his condition worsened. There was genuine concern that he wouldn't
survive. Dr. Walter Davenport, an ARA physician, arrived in Ufa to tend
to Bell. He advised that the dying man's family back in the States be notified the end was near. But the crisis passed on December 9; miraculously,
Bell survived and slowly began to recover. He spent most of the rest of
the month in bed, weak and gaunt, a hollow look to his eyes.

Bell had recovered by the time of Kelly's arrival. He was on hand for
the small New Year's celebration the Americans organized for themselves,
as well as the larger party the night of January 2, 1922, which they threw
for two dozen Russians. Kelly found the evening a test of his endurance.
Although he didn't know a word of Russian, he did his best to communi-
cate in English and a smattering of French and German, and even danced
a feeble fox-trot with the wife of a Red Army officer. He was relieved when
the gathering broke up, around two o'clock in the morning.

The next day was Kelly's first at the office, where Bell introduced him to the staff
and he spent several hours reading the correspondence between Ufa and Moscow to
get a sense of the operation. Piet Hofstra
served as Bell's executive assistant, while
Kelly occupied the post of district supply
officer, effectively the number-three man in
the region. Kelly soon picked up on Bell's
relaxed personality and easygoing management style, which made him popular with
the Russian personnel. He approved of his
boss's approach, but found the difficulties of
trying to work in a Russian office beyond
any American's imagination. "To disinfect
and equip an office alone required an immense expenditure of time and patience," he
wrote in a report on his experiences in Ufa.
"To secure desks, a telephone, Russian type-

Colonel Bell recovering
from typhus in Ufa

writers, paper, printed forms, stoves, etc., called for incessant negotiations
with a demoralized government whose invariable answer was 'Zaftra,' tomorrow. We soon found that Zaftra in Russian is a vague word meaning
'eventually' rather than 'tomorrow.' [. . .] No American could conceiv-
ably work amid the litter and discomforts that seem not to bother a Russian Soviet department." Adding to his frustration were the official office
hours: 10:00 a.m. to 4:00 p.m., largely matching the hours of daylight.
None of the Russian employees would work when it was dark outside,
something Kelly simply could never understand or come to terms with,
especially since he and the other Americans were burning the midnight
oil to keep up with the operation.

On January 4, Kelly accompanied Bell and Mr. Ruhs—their office
manager from the Baltics, fluent in both Russian and German but unable
to speak a word of English—to inspect several ARA kitchens. He wrote
about it to Jane: "In the first kitchen I saw a tot who had been deserted by its

mother. It was standing beside the stove sticking out its tiny hands to warm them and whimpering in a soft voice. I swear the kid could not have been two and a half years old. As I stopped to look, it tottered over and clung to my coat. These Russian children rarely approach an American, contenting themselves with a fixed stare from the moment you enter the kitchen."

The sight moved Kelly, but he'd been warned not to let his emotions put him in danger. "We never think of picking up the kids or even patting them on the head for fear of infection." At the time, six of the kitchen personnel were sick with typhus.

At the next kitchen, the staff were serving the children their one meal of the day: a hundred grams of bread and a bowl of corn grits. "When we entered the kitchen there was immediate silence, just as when the school superintendent used to visit our classroom. I walked down the long line of 200 kids looking at each one closely. Not a one smiled or showed any feeling whatever. You can't imagine how stolid these kids have come to be— very, very few are heard to cry. They stand in line for their cards, move past the counter, take their food to a bench and eat every grain of it without uttering a sound." Despite the waifs' "foul rags," Kelly admitted that many of them have "bright, intelligent faces that cannot but appeal to us."

Like many of his American colleagues, Kelly noticed a curious passivity in the Russian people. In an article for the *New York Evening Post*, he wrote:

> The Bolsheviki have given Russia a name for violence. And yet
> there is no more peaceable, harmless people than the peasants,
> who make up nine-tenths of the population. Themselves starving,
> they would stand and watch others eat without a murmur. I never
> saw or heard of a food riot or demonstration in a Russian city.
> Uncomplaining, they bore their lot, reasoning little as to the causes
> of their plight and feeling no great resentment against anybody.

Comments such as these revealed less about the nature of the Russian masses than the ignorance of American aid workers. Had Kelly been better informed of the violence that had racked the Russian land since

1914, not to mention the widespread peasant jacquerie in the revolutionary years of 1905–6 or the sporadic yet bloody rebellions that had erupted in the eighteenth and nineteenth centuries—the Pugachëv Rebellion of 1773–75, which shook the very foundations of Catherine the Great's empire, being the most famous example—he would have realized that what lay before him was not the living embodiment of the Russian soul, but the pitiful remains of a defeated and dying people.

On the 7th, the Russian Orthodox Christmas, Kelly, Bell, and Elperine drove out to a poor hovel to visit a mother and her four children, all stricken with typhus. They had read about them in a newspaper article, and Bell, unusually moved by the story, had sent the family special rations from an ARA kitchen. The men found the family living in a single room in the back of a courtyard. The children, barely clothed and sluggish from hunger, were doing their best to play with a few scraps of colored paper. They were pretty children, Kelly noticed, but "so white and expressionless—not a move from them while we were there. They simply stared at us." The mother was in rags. Crying, she told them she had sold her clothes for food and burned all the furniture to keep warm. Her husband was in the hospital with typhus. They'd been cold and hungry for days now.

Kelly described the scene in a letter to Jane:

> When all hope was gone, they had prayed, as the little girl had assured her [the mother] that God would hear their prayers. Then the American food had come with the promise that it would continue until the children were well enough to come to the kitchen. We comforted her as best we could and tonight have sent down sweaters, blankets and socks from our small stock of Red Cross supplies as a Xmas gift. The poor woman twice dropped to her knees and tried to kiss Bell's feet. This is only one case in thousands that happened to come to our attention.

Although he had been on the job but five days, Kelly had been utterly swept up in the importance of what he had earlier scoffed at as baby-feeding.

"Do you wonder that I am becoming so attached to this work that I would revolt if they tried to pull me back to Moscow to do headquarters work?" Seeing such things made their hearts "ache to be able to help these people. In all this great district with 3,000,000 people there is no source of help except the A.R.A. We four Americans are the only contact they have with the rest of the world."

The ARA eventually opened about two thousand kitchens in the Ufa district, and Kelly visited fifty or so of them during his time there—a small fraction, he admitted, but more than any other ARA man managed to inspect. For him, nothing in Russia could compare with these visits. "To enter a village kitchen and watch these starving kids devouring our food made all the worries, and the strain and discomforts of our everyday life seem trivial." When the aggravation of dealing with Soviet officials got him down, he would "drop everything and wander out to the nearest ARA kitchen just to look at the children and get back my confidence that it was worthwhile trying to help them after all."

The night of the 7th, they were invited to Christmas dinner at the apartment of Mr. Ruhs. One of the guests was the new Bashkir representative to the ARA. He and Kelly had a good talk, and the man promised to supply Kelly with loads of excellent data about Bashkiria that he felt certain would be most appreciated by the people of America. "Has anyone ever heard of Bashkiria?" Kelly asked Jane. "I hadn't. These Bashkirs are most friendly to us and when I go to their capital I expect to be given the country. Maybe we will compromise on a few of their quaint hand towels, full of colors and strange designs." As time passed, Kelly's estimation of the Bashkirs grew. "The Bash," as Kelly liked to call them, were much easier to work with than the Russians, perhaps, he wondered, since they seemed "much more mentally alert." For their part, the Bashkirs got along well with the Americans and held them in high regard, in part because at their first meeting Bell had drunk the president of the Bashkir Republic under the table. No small feat.

Not everyone in Ufa, however, was so keen to help the Americans. A few days later, a fire broke out in the hall outside Kelly's room while he was asleep. An attentive servant saw the blaze and quickly put it out. Once the smoke had cleared, they noticed a drum of kerosene; it had been arson. "Some kind and grateful Russian tried to set fire to our house tonight," Kelly joked sarcastically. He and Elperine went to report the incident to the Cheka, and they offered to provide a permanent guard outside the ARA house on Pushkin Street. The idea seemed like a good one, but when the man appeared, the Americans took one look at the rough fellow and decided they'd be safer on their own, and so they sent him home. The decision had most likely been too hasty: that week, the house was burgled four times. The men were at a loss for what to do. "We could get a military guard," Kelly remarked, "but they would be as likely to steal as anyone else."

Word that big changes were afoot had arrived in Ufa on the 4th, when the men received a telegram informing them that President Harding had tasked the ARA with distributing twenty million bushels of wheat in Russia. The news was vague and far from complete. "We have no details," Kelly commented at the time. "We are only told to 'prepare for big things.'" The prospect was at once exciting and frightening. Kelly and Bell sat up late the night of the 6th, discussing the news. They were thrilled at the idea that more food would be coming from America to help the needy, but they had no idea just how it would ever get distributed. The expectation was for 350 tons of wheat—they had still not heard that it was to be corn instead—to be shipped to Ufa over the course of the coming six months, an increase from two railcars a day to twenty. Given what he had seen of Russia's rail system, Kelly felt certain there was simply no way it could handle so much freight and was likely to collapse under the strain. What was more, even if the railroads could handle the load and deliver all the grain to the railheads, there simply weren't enough healthy horses to convey it out to the villages, many of which lay buried in snow a hundred miles from the closest rail line. The task, in Kelly's estimation, was "appalling."

In the meantime, reports of mass starvation east of the Urals—near Chelyabinsk, along the Trans-Siberian Railway—had been coming in to the ARA headquarters. Haskell, back in Moscow, ordered that the team in Ufa should increase the number of children on the feeding rolls in the district to 150,000, and that Bell and Kelly should go investigate the situation in Siberia. "We are both eager to get away and conquer new worlds," an excited Kelly informed Jane. He boasted they were to be the first ARA men to enter Asia.

9

FAMINE'S HORRORS

I N 1924, AN ÉMIGRÉ RUSSIAN SCHOLAR arrived in Minneapolis
to accept a teaching position at the University of Minnesota. Pitirim
Sorokin, who would go on to become one of the great sociologists
of the twentieth century, had been born into a peasant family in Russia's
Far North. He made his way as a young man to the capital, where he entered the university and joined the revolutionary movement. He rejected
the Bolshevik coup as an act of counterrevolution and was arrested—and
nearly executed—more than once by the new regime before finally being
freed and allowed to return to academic life in Petrograd.

In the winter of 1921–22, Sorokin and a few of his colleagues decided
to visit the provinces of Samara and Saratov for the purpose, as he called

it, of making "a scientific investigation of starvation." They failed in their investigation, but the experience was far from wasted.

> I saw a famine; I know now what it means. What I learned
> in those awful provinces was far more than any investigation
> could have given me. My nervous system, accustomed to many
> horrors in the years of Revolution, broke down completely before
> the spectacle of the actual starvation of millions in my ravaged
> country. If I came out less an investigator, I do not think I came
> out less a man.

What he called "the village of N." in Samara Province was particularly harrowing. The homes were deserted; there was nothing left alive. An unnerving silence hung over the village. "This place was as though dead," he wrote in *Leaves from a Russian Diary*. Then they heard the creaky sound of a sleigh. Slowly, it came into view. Two men and a woman were pulling the body of a dead boy, and then collapsed, exhausted, onto the snow. Sorokin and the others approached. "I had seen starving faces in the cities, but such living skeletons as these three people I had never seen." They were shaking from the cold and draped in rags; their faces were not white but "blue, dark blue with yellow spots."

"God help you," Sorokin said to them, not sure what else to say.

"God?" one of them replied. "We forgot God and He forgot us."

They were taking the boy's body to the corncrib to place it among a dozen or so other frozen corpses. When they had finished, the strongest of the party locked the door and said in a whisper, "It is necessary to lock . . . they steal." Sorokin and the others didn't understand. Steal? Steal what?

The man answered: "Yes, to eat. That is what we have come to. In the villages they guard the cemetery not to let the bodies be taken from the graves." And then he proceeded to tell them gruesome tales of peasants who killed one another for food, even of a mother who killed her child to eat.

Later in the day, as it was growing dark, they came upon a deranged man, shaking his long hair and beard and frenziedly waving his arms before an abandoned church: "Ring the bell," he cried in a hoarse voice. "Ring the bell. They will hear! They will hear!"

"Mad," said the man who had been pulling the sleigh. "He is always ringing the bell of the chapel. He thinks the bell will wake up the world and make it come to save us. But nobody will hear, even God," he said mournfully. Yet the madman set to ringing the bells. It shook Sorokin to the core, and he began to weep.

Ding-dong! Ding-dong! Slow and mournful as a funeral knell. Ding-dong! Ding-dong! For almost an hour it beat on our brains, our hearts. Then dead silence fell again [. . .]

This S.O.S of a mad peasant in the far interior of the land was heard. It crossed the ocean and beat on the hearts of the Great American nation and brought relief that saved from cruel death at least ten million men, women, and children. God will forever remember that deed. God will forever bless that generous people.

Sorokin and his small party traveled from village to village, each a site of death and misery. They encountered parents who were trying to give away their children, for they had no way of feeding them; people lying in their homes waiting to die; women and girls ready to sell themselves for a bit of bread; and refugees by the thousands fleeing to they knew not where—just to escape. And they encountered indisputable proof of cannibalism. "The Revolution promised to save the people from despotism. The Bolsheviki promised to give food to everyone. If they did not keep those vows, at least they gave the people the Communion of human sacrifice, human flesh and blood."

The scenes brought to mind God's punishments for those who fail to obey in Deuteronomy 28: "Cursed shalt thou be in the city, and cursed shalt thou be in the field . . . Cursed shall be the fruit of thy body, and the fruit of thy land, the increase of thy kine, and the flocks of thy sheep . . . The fruit of thy land, and all thy labors, shall a nation which thou knowest not eat up; . . . And thou shalt eat the fruit of thine own body, the flesh of thy sons and of thy daughters."

For twenty days, as Sorokin wandered through the famine zone, his mind kept returning to this ancient curse. The memory of what he saw never left him. "Many and great have been the sins of the Russian people, but in these years of famine, suffering, and death, through all the punishments of God, the nation has expiated, has paid in full for all its offenses."

Lenin's Russia had little patience for men and women with ideas like Sorokin's. In 1922, Lenin personally directed the banishment from Russia of several dozen of the country's best minds—philosophers, scientists, writers, and scholars, the cream of the old Russian intelligentsia, what Gorky called "the creators of Russian science and culture" (and Lenin called "shit"). Herded along with their families onto two steamers that would become known collectively as the "Philosophers' Ship," they sailed off from Petrograd for Europe. Sorokin was among the exiles. When he left Moscow in September of that year to join his compatriots in the former capital awaiting expulsion, he was wearing a suit that had been given to him by the ARA, with $50 in his pocket.

While Sorokin was traveling through the famine zone, Evelyn Sharp, an aid worker from the English Society of Friends, was busy administering relief in the county of Buzuluk, southeast of Samara. An entry from her diary echoes the horrors witnessed by Sorokin. "As we left the house this morning we saw the body of a man lying face downwards in the snow. Before the day was out I came to think he was the happiest thing I had seen." Sharp was forced to behold so much misery that day, in numerous "receiving-houses" overflowing with starving and diseased children, all at death's door, that it was in fact pleasant finally to reach the cemetery: "The sight of the silent dead in the cemetery was shorn of much of its tragedy. A great pile of some four hundred bodies stood awaiting burial in the frozen ground—men, women and children, many half naked, all emaciated and frozen stiff so that at a little distance they looked like bundles of faggots. One's first feeling was one, not of horror or repulsion, but of relief that their sufferings were over."

A report dated January 15 from the chairman of the Pugachëv County Executive Committee to Vladimir Antonov-Ovseenko detailed numerous cases of "CANNIBALISM" (as in the original) in the area. The peasants were now simply too weak from hunger to bury the dead and had been forced just to pile them up in barns, sheds, and stables. The unfortunate corpses left on the street were frequently picked up by the starving and taken home to eat. In the village of Kamenka, a woman by the name of Zhigunova, together with her elder daughter and a woman named Pyshkina, ate two of her dead children. Next, the three women killed and ate two adult women: one Fofanova from their village, and an unidentified seventy-year-old. Once all this meat was gone, mother and daughter Zhigunova killed and ate Pyshkina. Many similar gruesome stories were being reported from the villages of Semyonovka, Pestravka, Bartenevka, Ivanovka, Bolshaya Glushitsa, Porubezhka, and Talovoe. Based on interviews with the cannibals, the authorities had learned that the brains and "the soft femoral parts of the body" were especially sought after. In a rare moment of confession, the district chairman admitted that simply having to work on such horrendous cases "was destroying his nerves," and he worried that the full extent of the situation was not fully appreciated by officials in the larger towns. "Such nightmarish facts force us to scream from every crossing and corner of the need to deliver immediate emergency aid to the population, which is trying to survive until spring with every last bit of strength and by any means possible. Yet these nightmarish horrors have yet to fully penetrate to the Center." The district officials demanded clear and direct orders on "just what measures they should take against CANNIBALS."

By the end of the month, officials of Pugachëv County were still awaiting instructions. The number of cannibals being arrested kept growing, and the authorities didn't know what to do with them. Clearly, they'd broken some sort of law, but what exactly? And how should they be punished? When asked during interrogation why they'd done it, they all gave the same answer: "I want to eat."

That cannibalism had appeared with such ferocity in the county of

Pugachëv should not have been surprising. By January 1922, of the district's 357,125 inhabitants, all but 4,700 of them were starving. Given the hundreds of thousands staring death in the face, it's surprising there weren't in fact more cases of cannibalism.

KELLY, BELL, ELPERINE, and Dr. Francis Rollins, their district physician, had planned to depart Ufa for Siberia on January 14, but as of the 15th they still had no train to take them. "We may propose, the railways dispose," Kelly remarked. Finally, a train arrived, and the men left late on the 16th, to arrive in the town of Zlatoust, in the Ural Mountains, the following afternoon. They surveyed the situation there, joined by the local ARA Russian staff, who kept the men up late that night drinking. "Vodka, incidentally, is what the wildcats drink as eyeopeners," a hungover Kelly noted. Their train reached Chelyabinsk on the morning of Thursday, January 19. They were now in Asia, although it turned out they were not the first ARA men to venture so far east: the Americans stationed in Orenburg had in fact beaten them to it. The cold here was so intense it made Kelly's eyebrows hurt when he got off the train.

The conditions in Chelyabinsk were beyond belief. On Friday, Kelly and Rollins toured the city. Still shaking from the experience, he wrote about it the next day:

> I would not try to describe what these hospitals look like. You
> will never see anything like them or the people in them. No
> blankets nor bedclothes, no clothes, wretched food, little heat,
> improvised buildings, everything worse than you can imagine. It
> would be much better to put them all out of their misery at once.
> In all this district with more than 2,000,000 inhabitants, there
> are only 56 doctors. Never have I seen such frightful looking
> specimens of humanity as I saw yesterday in these hospitals. Only
> the children look human. Dr. Rollins was so disgusted at the
> sight that he objected to walking through the wards.

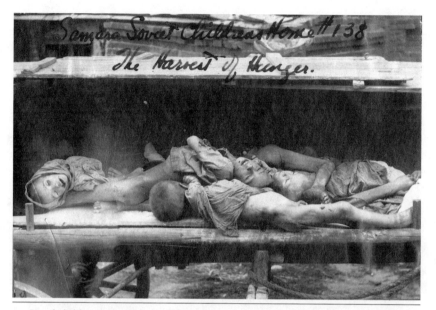

Dead children being carted off from an orphanage. The handwritten text reads:
"Samara Soviet Children's Home [Image] #138. The Harvest of Hunger."

From there, they went to a children's home, another grim shelter filled with children picked up from the railroad station and off the streets. Kelly didn't see how any of them would survive until spring. "There is just enough food and heat to make their death a slow one."

Kelly and an interpreter headed off next to the Bashkir town of Argayash, a hundred or so wooden huts scattered alongside the railroad on a wide, empty plain. The suffering was more than Kelly could bear.

> I have been to Argayash and back. The discomfort of the trip, the
> makeshift meals, the extreme cold, and above all the constant
> presence of human misery, worse than which I cannot imagine,
> has wearied me. I am heartily glad that Bell has thought it best
> to send me direct to Ufa while he and the Doctor branch off and
> go down a narrow gauge road into another Bashkir canton. I
> have lost all curiosity to explore further in this region. I can tell
> in advance what I would see if I went down into Bashkiria. There

seems to be no boundaries to the famine area. Were we to travel
as far as China, I doubt if we should see any great difference in
the condition of the people.

Almost everyone he saw in Argayash was living on hunger bread.
Kelly admired the local ARA staff, who were working incredibly hard
despite terrible conditions, but after visiting a few kitchens he had to stop,
regardless of his guides' desire that they carry on. No, Kelly insisted, he'd
seen enough. On the train back to Chelyabinsk, he wrote to Jane:

> I often think now of how people in New York told me how they
> envied me the opportunity of seeing so many interesting things.
> Yes, interesting, that's the word. Yes, it's very interesting to move
> among people who a glance tells you would be better off dead
> than alive. There is no escape, even in this car, for men and
> women come to the door begging for bread and children can
> be heard whining beneath the car window whenever the light is
> showing.

As soon as the extreme nature of the crisis in and around Chelyabinsk
became clear, Bell sent a telegram to the ARA in Moscow to ask for immediate assistance, but there was little available to offer. Permission was
given to increase the number of children's rations to fifty thousand once
they were available. By the end of August 1922, the ARA had managed
to feed 11,625 children and 273,000 adults in Chelyabinsk Province. "It
is impossible to describe the sufferings and misery that presented itself on
every side," Bell lamented. "The people who were still alive looked more
like skeletons than human beings."

Kelly returned to Ufa at the end of January. Emotionally drained and
overwhelmed at the extent of the famine, he found it difficult to get back
to work. He wondered just how much death their efforts could really prevent. If nothing else, however, he realized he could make a difference in
the lives of their Russian staff, and so he made sure everyone in the office
would henceforth be paid in American food, rather than Soviet rubles.

They were overjoyed when he told them the news. He was a bit worried about the decision, since he had not received Moscow's approval, but ultimately he didn't care. Even if he was reprimanded and forced to go back to the previous arrangement, in the meantime their employees would be getting something to eat.

CHILDS WROTE HIS mother from Kazan on January 4 with news of the impending increase in their operation. He admitted it would be a staggering task, but told her they were up to the challenge. Fechin had completed his portrait—his colleagues thought it made him look too serious, but he disagreed—and his language lessons were coming along nicely. He was now able to speak "a sort of pigeon [sic] Russian." Lastly, he told her how delighted he was that "my dear old friend Kelly," whose career had been almost identical to his since 1917, was also now with the ARA in Russia.

On January 9, Childs boarded a train to Moscow to report to Haskell on his last inspection tour. The trip was long—sixty hours to go 350 miles—and he arrived on a bitter-cold day, the thermometer straining to reach minus twenty degrees Fahrenheit. Speeding along in a sleigh through the city streets, Childs was amazed at how Moscow had changed in the four months since his last visit. All the busted and boarded-up shops had been repaired, renovated, restocked. Everywhere was "life and movement . . . It was such a sight as to make one rub one's eyes and to wonder how otherwise than in the rubbing of the genie's lamp by an Aladdin this transformation had been so suddenly effected."

He had been scheduled to leave on the 15th, but again there was no train. After the ARA complained to the Cheka, one quickly appeared. "There is no doubt that in Russia," Childs wrote in his diary, "there is one absolutely dependable organization of the government and that is the Extraordinary Commission." The car was unheated, and he was unable to keep warm. After a day on the train, he became listless and unusually fatigued. He began experiencing pains in the back of his head; then his eyes refused to focus. He found a stove, but couldn't shake the cold that had permeated his body, even though he was raging with fever. He barely made it back to Kazan, where, on the night of the 17th, he had to be put straight to bed.

Childs had come down with spotted typhus. He became delirious. Part of the time, he was unconscious; the rest of the time, he suffered from frightening hallucinations. Dr. Davenport was summoned to Kazan. For two days, Childs hovered between life and death. A group of Russian women organized a special service in a local church to pray for his recovery, and news of his illness was published in the American press. The crisis had passed by the first week of February, but it wasn't until the middle of the month that he was able to get out of bed. His legs had become useless, and it took him two weeks just to learn how to walk again, with the aid of his nurses. Haskell ordered a three-week leave, and Childs traveled with Walter Duranty from Moscow through Riga to Berlin, where he checked in to the fashionable Hotel Adlon. Even though he was still wobbly on his feet, Childs hated being away from Russia and wished to return. "I am so anxious to get back to Kazan where my heart is," he wrote his mother. "The Russian experience is the richest I have ever had; I wouldn't take anything for it." Remarkable words about a country that had nearly cost him his life.

10

THE BURNING
HOTEL

D ESPITE THE ARA'S UNDENIABLE SUCCESS after only a few months, Hoover and his organization continued to be the target of attacks. In the United States, *Soviet Russia*—published by the Friends of Soviet Russia, a communist front organization—ran articles denigrating the work of the ARA and other "bourgeois" relief efforts. *Soviet Russia* advertised what it dubbed "the working-class appeal" and encouraged Americans: "Give not only to feed the starving but to save the Russian workers' revolution. Give without imposing imperialist and reactionary conditions as do Hoover and others." They raised money, but it was never clear how this was used. It appears that most of it went to what the Friends called "relief propaganda" rather than actual hunger relief.

The crusading Minnesota journalist Walter Liggett organized a group known as the American Committee for Russian Famine Relief that included among its supporters a number of Catholic bishops, state governors, and U.S. congressmen, most notably Senator Joseph France of Maryland, a foe of Hoover and leading voice for official recognition of Soviet Russia by the United States government. In Hoover's eyes, Liggett's ACRFR was just another Red front organization, which it most definitely was not, and he used his authority as secretary of commerce to convince the Justice Department's Bureau of Investigation (forerunner of the FBI) to investigate it for possible ties to the Soviet government. Liggett, a fearless muckraker who never backed down in a fight, repaid Hoover's unfair treatment with a scathing biography of him during the presidential campaign of 1932, which he lost to Franklin D. Roosevelt. As for Liggett, his life came to a violent end three years later when he was gunned down in front of his wife and daughter by the notorious Minneapolis mobster Isadore Blumenfeld (aka Kid Cann), bloody payback for Liggett's investigations into ties between organized crime and the state's Democratic-Farmer-Labor Party.

Some Americans, such as Ralph M. Easley—chairman of New York's Executive Council of the National Civic Federation, established to manage disputes between business and labor—remained convinced that the recent congressional appropriation of funds for the ARA had nothing to do with famine relief and was at base a "shrewd scheme" hatched by South Dakota agricultural leaders to put money into the pockets of Midwestern farmers sitting on mountains of surplus grain.

Hoover bemoaned ever having gotten involved in Russia. "You will realize," he wrote in February to Rufus Jones, head of the American Quakers, "that I went into the Russian situation with great unwillingness, under pressure that I was not doing the right thing unless I lent my influence to it [. . .] From a personal point of view, I have every reason to regret that I ever touched a situation that is so pregnant with mud and personal vilification from all sides as this appears to be." Hoover was not being honest. He had never been dragged into Russia, but embraced the operation from the beginning, both for humanitarian reasons and out of the hope that the example of the ARA might bring about political change in Soviet Russia. Moreover, Hoover never did understand that by insisting on complete control over the relief effort, to the point of discouraging a broad appeal to the American people and refusing to accept well-meaning and serious offers of support, he was opening himself, and the ARA, up for understandable criticism. Even if much of the negative publicity was unfair, Hoover bore some responsibility for it.

Soviet officials continued to be perplexed by Hoover as well. In light of the ARA's excellent work and its apolitical nature, some of the country's leaders hoped this might mark a warming between Soviet Russia and the United States, and the establishment of official relations between the two countries. They found it baffling that no overtures were forthcoming from the American government. People's Commissar for Foreign Affairs Chicherin, confused, penned an article for *Izvestiia* in January in which he confessed, "America is a riddle." He was at a loss to explain American behavior toward the Soviet state, ultimately coming to the (mistaken) conclusion that U.S. policy was being held hostage by reactionary émigrés from tsarist Russia.

Although Chicherin and a few other top Soviet officials looked favorably on the ARA, this view was far from universal. The Cheka, for instance, had always been suspicious and had grown increasingly convinced over time that the ARA represented a serious threat to the Soviet state. According to an internal memo dated January 26, surveillance of the ARA had proved that the majority of its American staff had been drawn from the ranks of the military and intelligence services and that many of them knew the Russian language (not true), having spent time in the country before the revolution or fought in one of the White armies during the civil war (also not true). It claimed that Golder had been observed instigating anti-Soviet conversations with peasants; Hofstra in Ufa had been heard making toasts to the good old days; and a certain Thompson was caught ripping up portraits of Lenin and Trotsky in an ARA kitchen. The memo highlighted the fact that the ARA had been establishing operations in cities along the country's borders (Petrograd, Vitebsk, Minsk, Kiev, Odessa, Kharkov, Ufa), which it presented as proof that the Americans were encircling them and creating a series of bases that would be easy to supply with matériel in the event of a counterrevolution. (Needless to say, the Americans had been asked to set up feeding operations in these locations, and most of their efforts were nevertheless concentrated in the Volga region, the very heart of Russia.) The Russian personnel, the memo warned, were all drawn from the old tsarist elite and so were by definition hostile to the Soviet regime. They had been supplying their American masters with information on politics, the economy, and daily life that would be vital in organizing revolts against the government. It was clear that "measures must be taken immediately that, without harming the battle against the famine, might remove everything from that organization that threatens the interests of the RSFSR."

Concrete actions soon followed. On February 11, the State Political Directorate (known by its Russian acronym, GPU), the successor to the Cheka,* issued an order to its agents: "Take all measures to purge the ARA organization of undesirable elements." Arrests of Russian personnel on political charges were made in Tsaritsyn, Samara, and Pugachëv County. An angry Haskell wrote to complain to Eiduk that these actions were undermining the work of the ARA, since their native employees now "live in terror of threatened arrests which are liable to take place at any time of day or night." Haskell's concerns were brushed aside. The pressure on the thousands of Russians working for the ARA increased.

DESPITE THE WAVE of horrifying reports documenting the extent of the famine that had been reaching Moscow for months, the government continued its punitive treatment of the country's peasants. Requisitioning had ended, but brutal tactics had not. In late 1921, Felix Dzerzhinsky, the

---

* The Cheka was abolished on February 6, 1922, and replaced with the State Political Directorate (GPU) within the People's Commissariat for Internal Affairs.

An ARA transport column passing through Tsaritsyn

first director of the Cheka and later head of the GPU, was dispatched to Siberia as an extraordinary plenipotentiary to see that all the grain taxes were being paid. He created "flying revolutionary courts" to go about the villages and send peasants guilty of failing to pay their taxes to prison or labor camps. The abuses of power reached such a level that an inquiry was opened. There were reports that peasants were being locked up in unheated barns, whipped, and threatened with execution. Some were stripped, bound, and forced to run naked through the streets—in winter. Many women had been beaten unconscious and then tossed naked into holes in the snow. In some areas, the grain taxes were so high as to practically guarantee starvation. According to a secret-police report from the autumn of 1922, "Peasants are killing themselves en masse because they can neither pay their taxes nor rebel, since all their arms have been confiscated."

With America now saving the country from collapse, Lenin realized that the time was ripe for attacking another of the state's main enemies: the church. On February 23, 1922, the Central Executive Committee ordered the mass expropriation of the valuables of the Russian Orthodox Church for famine relief. As Trotsky put it, "Turn gold into bread!" If there was ever any confusion about the true purpose of the campaign—to help famine victims or to destroy the church—Lenin made their goal unmistakably clear in a top-secret letter to Vyacheslav Molotov dated March 19: "It is precisely now and only now, when in the famine regions people are eating human flesh, and the roads are littered with hundreds if not thousands of corpses, that we can (and therefore must) carry out the confiscation of church valuables with the most savage and merciless energy, not stopping [short of] crushing any resistance." With the peasants starving, he reasoned, they might just side with the regime against the church; but even if they didn't, they were at last too weak to fight back.

Or so Lenin thought. Patriarch Tikhon denounced the campaign as a "sacrilege" and threatened to excommunicate anyone who took part in it. The government responded by labeling Tikhon, and other prelates who spoke out, enemies of the people. Violent clashes erupted between GPU agents and peasants defending their local churches—more than fourteen hundred by the middle of May. On March 15, in the town of Shuia, two hundred miles northeast of Moscow, GPU troops turned their machine guns on protesters, killing five people. Lenin, enraged by the people's willingness to resist, ordered several dozen arrested and executed by firing squad, to make it clear to the populace that the government would stop at nothing. "The greater number of representatives of the reactionary clergy and reactionary bourgeoisie we succeed in executing for this reason, the better," he insisted.

The campaign raged for much of the year and brought in over twelve tons of gold, silver, diamonds, pearls, and other precious stones. A public show trial, the first in Soviet history, was put on for resisters in April. Over twelve hundred clergymen were found guilty and put to death. It is estimated that, all told, at least eight thousand people were executed or died defending their places of worship. The church's expropriated wealth ended up in Gokhran—the State Treasury of Valuables. How much of this gold was turned into bread is unknown.

ON FEBRUARY 6, THE SS *Winnebago*—the first ship carrying American corn purchased with the congressional appropriation of December 1921—arrived at the Black Sea port of Novorossiisk, where it was greeted by a brass band, a Red Army company, and speeches by local officials and representatives of the ARA. Soon ships began to dock with their cargo at Odessa and Baltic Sea ports, too—Petrograd, Reval (now Tallinn), Windau, and Libau. To help with communications and coordination of the effort, the U.S. Navy dispatched several destroyers to the region under the command of Rear Admiral Mark Bristol, the high commissioner to Constantinople. One destroyer was kept in port at Odessa at all times, to pass information back and forth to the ARA's London office by wireless. At the same time, the navy took advantage of its location to monitor Soviet radio communications, including diplomatic traffic, which it recorded and sent along to Washington. The Soviet government was aware of this, but there was little they could do to stop it, and they accepted it as a small price to pay for American aid. Nonetheless, the GPU remained forever vigilant. Within weeks after the arrival of the American ships, Iosif Unshlikht, Dzerzhinsky's deputy, issued a directive on the urgent need to prepare for a likely intervention that spring led by the ARA, which was intending to land troops at ports both on the Black Sea and in Finland with orders to march on Petrograd. "I must point out yet again," he noted, "that the ARA is a wicked organization."

Hoover was uncomfortable with the navy's overstepping its role. Back in September, an American officer of the USS *Gilmer* had taken it upon himself to write a detailed report of what he had seen after walking around in Novorossiisk, including details on the placement of guns and minefields. He claimed to have obtained from "an informer" a plan for the city's defenses and sent all of this information back to the U.S. Naval Department. When word of this reached Hoover, he ordered an immediate stop to

The SS *Winneconne* being unloaded in Odessa. This steamer carried
22,500 cases of milk, 3,000 tons of flour, and 350 tons of sugar from America.

such activities, since they were at odds with the ARA's mission. He also
requested that, as soon as the ships were no longer required, the navy be
ordered to stay away from all Black Sea ports; their evacuation was begun
that autumn.

The first ship to dock at Odessa was the SS *Deepwater*, carrying 10,234
tons of bulk corn and 132,000 feet of lumber. Huge amounts of grain had
been shipped from Odessa before the revolution, when Ukraine served
as the breadbasket of Europe. The *Deepwater*, however, had come not to
export but to import, and none of the equipment at the dock was capable
of unloading such a massive cargo. Since most of the corn had been trans-
ported loose in the hull, a call for sacks had gone out across all of Ukraine,
and before the grain could be unloaded and transferred to railcars, tons
of it had to be bagged by hand.

Simbirsk and the railway bridge over the Volga

Despite their weakened state, the stevedores worked quickly to complete the task as soon as possible. The lumber sent from America was put
to use repairing the railcars, a necessary step before the corn could be sent
off into the interior, since the cars were in horrible condition after years
of war and neglect. Once loaded, each railcar was locked and affixed with
two seals—one of the ARA, one of the Soviet government—and a large
poster was attached to the side, usually an image of an American ship
bearing grain to the famine-stricken of Russia. The ARA wanted everyone who might see these trains as they snaked their way across the vast
country to know who had come to their aid.

The logistics involved were enormous. The Soviet government had
promised to supply the ports with four hundred empty railcars a day but
were only able to come up with around sixty. Besides the problems associated with damaged rolling stock, tracks, and roadbeds, fuel was constantly in short supply. When coal ordered from England failed to arrive
because of ice in the Baltic, frozen logs had to be used to power the lo-
comotives. Everything moved slowly over the rails. It took the first train
leaving Odessa for Simbirsk an entire month to reach its destination, a
distance of some fifteen hundred miles. And a great many trains—over a

third of them by the end of January 1923—sent east never even made it
to their destinations, getting lost, accidentally diverted, or commandeered
by any number of groups along the way.

Things went so terribly wrong that first month that the ARA almost had to stop all operations. The ARA began to get matters under
control and everything appeared to be running smoothly, until an even
greater railroad crisis erupted in March, very nearly putting an end to the
entire ARA mission and taking the intervention of Dzerzhinsky himself
to solve.

Golder arrived at Novorossiisk the same day as the *Winnebago*, February 6. An ARA man told him there had been trouble from the start. A
group of local Greeks had gotten wind of the cargo and showed up with
baskets, expecting to help themselves to the corn. When they were sent
away, they became indignant, grumbling to the Americans that the corn
had been sent from overseas specifically for them. Others were already
making similar demands. The railroad men let it be known that they intended to take a share for their efforts. It seemed, according to the local
ARA representative, that the list of those entitled to shares was "endless."

The next day, Golder went down to the docks to watch the unloading
of "the golden grain." He wrote:

> The American Relief Administration has tackled the biggest and
> hardest job in its history, and we shall breathe a sigh of relief
> when it is done. It is working against insurmountable obstacles;
> against a government that is suspicious; against railway officials
> and employees who are thinking of themselves only; against a
> transportation system that is on its last legs; against dishonesty,
> trickery, demoralization, incompetence, apathy, famine,
> typhus, etc.

His despair over the plight of the country of his birth was growing ever
worse.

When Golder was in Moscow at the end of January, he learned that
his report on conditions in Ukraine had been important in the decision

to begin aid there; on the 10th of that month, Haskell signed a separate treaty with the Ukrainian authorities that essentially copied the provisions laid out in the Riga treaty with Russia. The size of the ARA's job had grown enormously, adding eighty-five thousand square miles and ten million people. The relief was desperately needed: by April, an entire third of the Ukrainian population was facing starvation.

Hoover now wanted Golder to travel to the Caucasus and investigate the situation there. Golder couldn't think of anything he'd rather avoid. He was still hoping to leave Russia for Stanford by the end of March, having finished collecting materials for the Hoover War Library—fifty large crates of books, periodicals, and documents—but his sense of loyalty to The Chief and his concern for the reputation of the ARA overrode his personal wishes, as they had in the past and would continue to do. Typhus was raging, and a rumor was going about that three of the Americans had gone missing, most likely victims of merciless highwaymen; still, despite the risks, Golder prepared for his trip. "Life in Russia," he wrote philosophically, "is not dull." There were the usual difficulties of arranging transportation, but a gift of three packs of Lucky Strikes to a technical engineer at the station in Moscow did the trick, and on February 2, Golder pulled out of the station in a horrible blizzard, joined by his frequent travel companion Lincoln Hutchinson, a Harvard-trained economist known to the men as "The Professor." The car's bumper was crowded with poor souls, covered in ice and snow, leaving the city, and the two men opened their door to as many as they could to save them from a likely death during the night.

They awoke the next morning to find that the train had become snowbound. The heat had gone out in their car, and they sat bundled up until they were able to make contact with the nearest stationmaster, who brought them wood in return for coffee, aspirin, a bit of sugar, and some American cigarettes. He told the Americans that the bodies of as many as thirty refugees were being taken off the trains as they passed through his station every day, all dead from hunger, typhus, or exposure. By February 5, they had passed through Rostov-on-Don and then tracked farther south, to Krasnodar, before turning westward toward Novorossiisk.

Spring had come early here, and the surrounding fields were seas of icy slush and mud.

After a few days in Novorossiisk, Golder and Hutchinson embarked on an American destroyer and motored through heavy seas to the Georgian port of Batumi, and from there by automobile to the capital, Tiflis (now Tbilisi). They spent the next month traveling through the mountains of Georgia, Armenia, and Azerbaijan, either by rail or in one of the two Fords brought along for the journey. To cover their expenses, Golder carried a beat-up old suitcase stuffed with 50 million rubles, as well as tens of millions in the local currencies of Transcaucasia, much of which, Golder noted, "is no longer legal," given that the governments that had issued them no longer existed. Everywhere they went, it was the same story. "We heard the old tale of woe—no food, no work, no money." Officials everywhere sought American aid, but Golder didn't see signs of famine comparable to what he'd witnessed in Russia and Ukraine. Part of the trouble was a lack of reliable information, which no one seemed to possess, making it difficult to assess with any accuracy just how bad things were. In Baku, the minister of agriculture painted for the two men a picture of misery that sounded much like what they had heard, and witnessed, in so many other places. "Everywhere one turns, he sees hands outstretched, hears voices pleading for food, for seed, for implements, for machinery, for clothing, and above all for capitalists," Golder remarked.

Heading back north into Russia, they saw that the trains passing in the opposite direction were covered with refugees. Most had no idea where they were heading. Some talked of finding food in the Caucasus or Turkestan or even Persia, where bread was supposed to be cheap. Golder didn't have the heart to tell the desperate travelers that, even if they were to make it to Persia, their rubles would be worthless there. Most of them were surviving on what they called *makukha*—the sticky remnants of the sunflower seed after it's been pressed for oil; some ate the pulp and cracked shells on their own or mixed with a bit of flour or tree bark. At one station, they saw an ARA train carrying corn on its way to the Volga. The well-armed soldiers guarding the train kept the refugees back with an occasional warning shot.

Russian soldiers guarding a food transport train

Nonetheless, a few managed to sneak up under the cars, cut holes in the floor, and make off with some of the grain. One Russian man asked Golder why the Americans were helping them. When told it was purely for humanitarian reasons, he replied, "Of course, we will pay you back as soon as we can." Golder couldn't imagine such a possibility; the situation was too hopeless, the despair too widespread and deep. Still, the ARA was vital if things were ever to improve, for it gave the Russians hope. "The only thing," he wrote at the time, "that seems to put courage and fight into these people is the thought that foreigners are coming to their rescue."

The men reached Rostov-on-Don on March 10. Golder was disgusted to see store shelves filled with the best food and luxuries for "the Red rich," while outside huddled "cadaverous human beings with outstretched bony hands and beseeching voices, begging for bread in the name of Christ." The markets here, just as in much of the famine area, were full of food, but the prices were so high almost no one could buy. "In present-day Russia three classes of people have enough to eat—the thieves, the grafters, and the speculators; and they usually work together." It broke Golder's heart:

> Parts of Russia are returning not only to a primitive but to an animal state [. . .] In daytime human beings fight with dogs over the garbage piles or work in gangs making raids on the food markets, and at night prowl around like beasts looking for prey. After a certain hour of the night it is not safe to be out alone in any of the large cities [. . .] With scenes like these before them, educated and intelligent Russians are struggling with all their might against the fate which they think awaits them unless help comes from somewhere, and they have little hope of that. They are like guests caught at night in a burning hotel, running here and there to find an outlet where none exists. The Soviet will not let them out and foreign governments will not let them in, and so they must lose their reason and die. History has few such tragedies as Russia.

11

KELLY CALLS
IT QUITS

THE FIRST WEEK OF FEBRUARY FOUND KELLY, back from
Siberia, in Ufa, struggling mightily to run the district on his own.
Hofstra was sick in bed, and Bell and Elperine had left to inspect
the town of Sterlitamak, capital of the Bashkir Republic, eighty miles south
of Ufa, on the Belaya River. With Elperine gone, there was only one Russian employee in the office who spoke English, a Mr. Willig, without
whom Kelly was useless. "I can't read two words of Russian," he admitted with some embarrassment. This situation would have been stressful
under normal conditions, but Kelly had just learned that they should soon
expect to receive twelve thousand tons of corn arriving by train from the

Black Sea. On top of this, he had been given no instructions on how they were supposed to store, transport, or deliver all this grain.

Hofstra was soon well again, and the two were joined in the office by Harold Blandy, another of the Ufa team just returned from a trip out into the province. Blandy had grown up in New York City, the son of a respected attorney, graduated from Yale, and then enlisted in the British Royal Flying Corps during the war. He remained in England, throwing himself headlong into the London nightlife and piling up debts faster than he could pay them. It was apparently the need to escape his creditors that led Blandy to the offices of the ARA and a job in Russia. The men in Moscow didn't take to Blandy and soon noticed his vulnerability to the temptations of the big city, and so they sent him off to Ufa to be rid of him, thinking he would have a much harder time getting into trouble way out on the edge of the Urals. They were wrong.

He liked to sleep in and arrived late at the office, well after Kelly and the others. He frequently complained of being ill and unable to work. One Russian employee called him nothing but "a dead weight." He had a weakness for Russian women, and there were rumors he was trading food for sex. Kelly couldn't stand Blandy, and he made no effort to hide it. "My busy days have come," he wrote to Jane on February 19. "My mind is in a whirl from thinking of a thousand matters to attend to. Bell is away, Blandy is worse than useless in the office. That leaves only Hofstra and myself to keep the shop."

One of Kelly's main criticisms of Blandy was his overly emotional response to their work. One night that month, a practically hysterical Blandy telephoned Kelly from the station to tell him that six children were about to be sent off without enough rations to survive their four-day journey and begged for whatever extra food was in the house. Kelly scrounged up three loaves of bread and some cookies, but he couldn't see the point of such acts. "Haphazard handouts, whenever our eyes fall on a pitiful sight, are pathetic in their futility. Poor Blandy, I am sure, has the satisfaction of thinking he is accomplishing something, whereas such incidents are depressing to me. I see in them only a diversion of food from one starving kid to another."

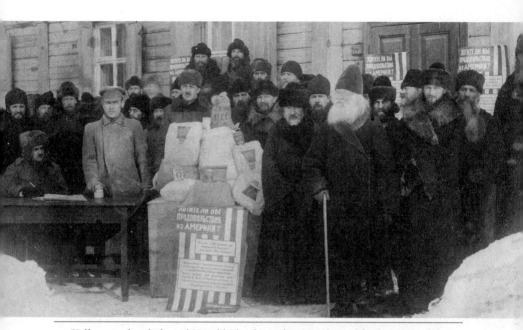

Kelly, seated at desk, and Harold Blandy, with mustache and fur hat, to his left,
taking orders for food-relief packages from the United States. The poster reads,
"Would you like foodstuffs from America?" Among the items on display are
rice, Van Camp's evaporated milk, and bags of "fancy bacon bellies."

On the night of the 15th, William Garner, a member of the ARA's
publicity division, arrived with the news photographer Floyd Traynham.
Kelly took them on a tour of the city's hospitals, kitchens, and children's
homes the next day. The newcomers saw plenty. "They sought local color
and found it, I think," Kelly wrote with a hint of wickedness. "One poor
wretch dropped at their feet and had to be hauled off to a hospital in our
Ford. Later we passed two frozen corpses in a sleigh. The sights in the refugee home were too much for the photographer. He fled from the building.
Well, at any rate, they saw the worst and got some pictures including me
talking to a picturesque Soviet official." The experience was apparently
more than either Garner or Traynham could handle, and they didn't
bother to return to the ARA offices the following day. On the 17th, they
showed up to photograph Kelly and Hofstra meeting with three Tatar

Piet Hofstra (left) and Kelly receiving three clerics at the ARA office in Ufa

Muslim clerics in their ecclesiastical robes and then filmed Kelly and the mullahs outside their home, in the snow, showing off their Koran, said to be over a thousand years old.

By the 23rd, Willig, the interpreter, was beginning to crack under the strain. Mentally exhausted, he wasn't able to do a whole day's work, and Kelly kept having to let him go home early. Kelly feared the poor man was on the verge of a nervous breakdown, and he couldn't blame him, for the picture before them was utterly bleak. Things were looking bad for the coming summer, and who was to say what might follow. "And next winter, what?" Kelly wondered. "When twenty or thirty or forty million people have died there may be an improvement."

Three days later, a beleaguered old French couple wandered into the office. They had just arrived in Ufa from Central Asia and had had no idea the famine had reached this area. Out of food and money, they begged Kelly for some help of any kind. Taking pity on the couple, he gave the husband a job. Although he couldn't admit it to others, deep down Kelly must have recognized that Blandy wasn't the only one practicing haphazard relief.

That afternoon, he waited around to see when the rest of the staff prepared to head home for the day. No one wanted to be the last to leave. Walking the dark streets of Ufa alone was a dangerous proposition. Twelve people had been murdered within sight of the ARA offices. Bell had brought up the matter with the police, but they simply shrugged, admitting they had lost control of the city and that there was little they could do, except present to the Americans a large pile of guns to choose from to defend themselves. Before leaving for the night, every ARA man made sure to pat his coat pocket to see that he had his revolver with him. Kelly wrote that day at the office, before heading home:

> I shall keep my right hand firmly on my Colt 45 during my entire stroll. Ufa may once have had street lights, but I see no evidence of them. The moon and the snow provide such illumination as there is at present. Reports of holdups are so unpleasantly frequent that I strongly favor the middle of the street where no citizen, no matter how empty his cupboards, can head my way without courting a serious shock. If he survives, someone else may ask him in his own lingo what it was that he wanted. I must admit that so far the few pedestrians I have passed in the night seemed desirous of keeping as far away from me as possible. Doubtless they were not prepared for trouble or did not carry the comforting immunity from all molestation and arrest that reposes in my pocket.

Kelly spent the first week of March preparing for the arrival of the corn, typically working till midnight every day. Although exhausted, and overwhelmed by the enormity of the job before him, what with roughly five hundred thousand rations of corn expected to arrive that month, Kelly could still joke about the situation to Jane: "Now, do you think I know what a day's work is?" he teased her. The first train from Novorossiisk pulled into Ufa on the 7th. Only after it had arrived did Kelly and the rest of the men learn what they were dealing with. Up until then, they didn't know whether to expect wheat or corn, whether it was to be shipped in bulk or in sacks, and, if the former, who was to grind it and where were they to store it, since the Soviet government had as yet failed to provide them with any additional warehouses. The detachment of Red Army soldiers guarding the train told Kelly it had taken them several weeks to reach Ufa, the train having gotten lost on its way east to the Urals. The soldiers had not eaten in days, so he gave them 2 million rubles to buy themselves a few dozen pounds of black bread. He found he liked the soldiers and the dramatic stories they told about their journey. Hoping to save future trains from lengthy detours on their trips to Ufa, Kelly cabled Novorossiisk to be sure to equip all future convoys "with a map of the world and a compass." Little good this did: it took two whole months for his telegram to arrive.

After many hurried meetings with local officials, Kelly and Bell had managed to secure warehouse space for the corn, and just in time: within days, they received 113 railcars. They could barely keep up with the shipments; everything became a mad scramble. Their work slogan had been "catch as catch can," but now even that was no longer possible. They put up a large organization chart on the office wall, thinking that if they could visualize the entire operation they might see ways to streamline it, to cut out unnecessary steps and create efficiencies. This proved a pointless exercise, however, for they were too busy to spend any time consulting it. If nothing else, Kelly liked to think, the chart gave the office some dignity.

Kelly found his brain was buzzing from the work, and it was impossible to turn it off at the end of the day. The pressure was becoming more than he could handle. To make matters worse, his wisdom teeth were coming in, causing a constant ache in his mouth. He wrote to Jane:

> In recent days I find myself inquiring: "Is it really true that I am
> a conscientious cuss?" I couldn't tell you why I have worked as I
> have these last few days. I don't expect any credit—no one except
> possibly my interpreter will know what the strain has been. I am
> utterly void of enthusiasm, as I know we are only prolonging
> the lives of people whose doom is sealed. I care nothing for the

opinion or gratitude of the Russians [. . .] Theodore* has orders
not to read me any letters of thanks from persons to whom I have
allocated food packages. And yet there is something driving me
to give everything I have to my job. I wonder if I imbibed more
of the idea of military discipline in the army than I suspected.

Adding to their troubles, the ARA office was notified soon after the
corn shipments began arriving that the GPU had arrested the head of
the central warehouse for stealing. He wasn't the only one. A worker was
caught pilfering flour and replacing it with substitutes at one of the Ufa
kitchens that month, and there were reports of Russians selling the ARA
corn allotment in the local markets. Bell asked the GPU to arrest the
kitchen worker and, if he was found guilty, to put the person in jail and
establish surveillance at the markets to stop the illegal trade. He thanked
them for all their help in the past and stated that he looked forward to
their "future cooperation." The warehouse manager, a man by the name of
Linhart, came by the ARA house in tears, pleading for mercy and begging
to have his job back. He told Kelly that he and his wife were hungry and
asked that he at least be given his ration for the past month. Kelly, however, would hear nothing of it. So Linhart changed tactics. He stopped
crying, dried his tears, and told Kelly he knew of others who were stealing from the warehouse, much more than he did, and he was ready to
name names. Kelly didn't bite. To keep Linhart on or show him any
mercy would only encourage more petty theft, and that would mean less
food for the truly needy.

"His life or his wife's life are nothing to me when I stack them against
the lives of a score of children that might have been saved, or prolonged,
with the food he stole," Kelly wrote to Jane. "What would you do?" he
asked, as if seeking her approval of his actions. "The man makes a personal appeal, the children don't. They are huddled in the corner of an
orphans' house . . . dumb." The Linhart incident changed Kelly for good.
He was done with the Russians, he was done trying to make friends with

---

* Theodore Kushnarëv, another translator working for the ARA in Ufa.

them, he was done taking them at their word. "From now on I trust no one." He stopped socializing with the Russian personnel and was prepared to be disliked by everyone. If this was what it would take to be free to hire and fire as he saw fit in order to get the job done, then so be it.

The ever-growing ranks of the hungry meant the ARA could ill afford to have its own employees helping themselves when no one was looking. An appeal for relief came in from the Kirghiz Republic, and the bighearted Bell found it impossible to say no. With only seven Americans in the entire district, Kelly pressed Moscow repeatedly for more personnel, but got no response. In just eight months, the Ufa district had grown from 50,000 to over 1.15 million. As of April, an entire third of the population of the Bashkir Republic was relying on ARA rations. By September, the Americans in Ufa were managing 30,000 Russian personnel and feeding 1.6 million people in 2,750 kitchens.

The snow kept falling throughout March, and there was no hint of winter's end. The drifts around the ARA's house stood a full twelve feet high. Scurrying along the paths cut like canyons into the snow, Kelly couldn't help thinking that if only snow were edible their problems would be solved. He had seen enough of Russia. "Can you find some way to support us in Florida or the Riviera," he asked Jane, "where I shall never have to look at any more snow?" On the 27th, he sent her a cable to say he planned to start for home come June. Two days later, he gave notice that he would be quitting his service by May 1.

Bell was not about to lose his best man without a fight, and his attachment to Kelly was shared by the rest of the office. He pulled Kelly aside, praising his work, letting him know their operations would have collapsed without him, and asking him to reconsider. But Kelly stood firm. He feared the famine was worsening, and he didn't care to see any more than he had already; the sight of so much misery on the streets of Ufa had become too much for him. "I walk with my eyes on the ground," he confessed to Jane, "partly to pick my step but mainly to avoid seeing the passersby."

12

CANNIBALS

DURING HIS STAY IN UFA, the PR man William Garner pushed Kelly for information on a subject of particular interest: cannibalism. He said he was hoping to get a chance to sit down with a cannibal for an interview before heading home. This wasn't just morbid curiosity on his part; rather, he had been directed by his bosses to find solid, incontrovertible evidence of cannibalism. The ARA had received Soviet reports on the problem but wanted its own proof. "We have 'em," Kelly told Garner, "but they won't talk for publication."

Kelly had heard plenty of stories since arriving in Russia. He was convinced there had been thousands of cases of cannibalism that winter, but it was difficult to get precise details. Few Soviet officials were willing to talk to the Americans about this most horrifying aspect of the famine, largely out of a sense of shame and embarrassment for what they felt it said about their country. Nonetheless, a few had shared with Kelly what they knew, telling him that cannibals were dealt with forcefully when caught—put on trial and punished, some of the guilty even sentenced to death for their crimes. Once, Kelly saw the trial records of a case, complete with a photograph of the accused and a boiled human head. The official policy of the ARA was to soft-pedal such "horror stuff," in Kelly's words, in order to avoid accusations that the Americans had been exaggerating for cheap publicity. In early February, the Moscow office wired London to say that "any implication that the American Relief Administration vouches for the existence of cannibalism should be carefully avoided."

"There are continual rumors about cannibalism around here," Henry Wolfe, the high-school history teacher from Ohio, wrote from Samara on February 12 to his little brother Eddie, a student at Phillips Academy back in Massachusetts. "It is said there are cases where starving people have been eating dead bodies. I have heard some weird stories, but don't know whether they are true." He left soon after for the village of Melekess, a journey of some two hundred fifty miles. Wolfe wrote Eddie again from there on March 5, describing his trip: "At nearly every village we visited we heard of cannibalism. The stories were told to me by reliable persons and their accounts were corroborated by everyone in the village [. . .] There is a woman in prison here in this town who ate her child. (Keep this on the quiet.) I'm going to see her today. You can't imagine the terrible straits the peasants in the famine zone are in."

Wolfe had wanted to join the ARA from the moment he learned of the negotiations in Riga. He traveled to New York in August 1921 to hand in his application in person even before the treaty had been signed. A member of the staff told him they might be in touch later, but they'd already received five hundred applications and couldn't make any promises. He waited around for several days, hoping to hear something. "The more I think of this Russian proposition the better I like it and the more I hope they will need me," he wrote to his mother. But nothing came through, so Wolfe headed back to Ohio to prepare for another year of teaching history to the kids in the public schools of Coshocton County. This was a far cry from his days as a volunteer ambulance driver during the war, first with the American Field Service in France and then the Red Cross in Italy, where he crossed paths with Hemingway and Dos Passos. Like Childs and Kelly and many others of their generation, Wolfe missed the thrill he had experienced in Europe. He sent letter after letter to the ARA that autumn, but still there were no openings for him. Finally, in December, he received word that they could use him if he could be ready to sail from New York on January 7. The office made sure to instruct him to bring heavy underwear, high boots, galoshes, and his sleeping bag.

When he arrived in Moscow at the end of the month, he was shocked to discover that his war service had not prepared him for Russia. The stench of the railroad station was beyond description, as was the mass of ragged humanity lurking in the darkness. Two days later, on the ride from the station in Samara to the ARA house, he passed two dogs fighting in the street over a partially eaten corpse. Wolfe looked at his driver in horror, but the man paid no heed. Such things had become commonplace. On a short walk after dinner, he counted fourteen dead bodies lying in the streets around the personnel house.

Wolfe spent most of his time as the lone American in the village of Melekess (now Dimitrovgrad) in northern Samara Province. Touring the villages in the area, he encountered the same hardships witnessed by other ARA men—the frozen corpses stacked like cordwood in locked warehouses, awaiting burial in the spring; the fetid hospitals lacking beds, blankets, aspirin, and soap; the walking dead, their eyes sunken and dull, dragging one heavy foot after the other through the snowy streets before collapsing from exhaustion. He had a particular curiosity about what he called "the infernal crimes" that hunger could drive people to. In village after village, he met peasants who admitted to eating human flesh, whether corpses they had found or victims they had killed for food. It became something of an obsession for Wolfe, and he spent several weeks "on the trail of the cannibal," as he wrote in a letter to a fellow ARA man, William Shafroth, in early March, aided by "definitive information concerning cannibals" from local officials. Just to be safe, he made sure to carry a revolver with him on his travels. Hearing the stories of cannibals was one thing, but to be able to catch them in the act was another. "If it can be seen, perhaps it would be valuable information to the ARA." Not long after this, Wolfe found what he had been looking for, and he posed alongside his Soviet helpers for a photograph with his find, a mission-accomplished look on his face. The ARA had its proof. He sent the photograph on to his superiors in Moscow. Unfortunately, the details of the image—where it was taken, the names of the men and women surrounding Wolfe, and the facts behind the discovery of the body parts—have been lost.

According to official Soviet reports, the first instances of cannibalism appeared in late summer 1921.* The government was, not surprisingly, alarmed by the reports; nonetheless, it permitted articles about them to be published in the leading newspapers—*Pravda* and *Izvestiia*. By the spring of 1922, however, some officials felt the press had gone too far. In March, People's Commissar for Public Health Nikolai Semashko complained in the pages of *Izvestiia* that the press had begun to treat the matter as some sort of "boulevard sensation." Secondhand stories were being reported as facts, and reporters were increasingly prone to unwarranted speculation and exaggeration.

The medical doctor and amateur poet Lev Vasilevsky was prompted by Semashko's criticism to conduct his own study of cannibalism. In Vasilevsky's opinion, the problem was too important to be swept under the rug or left to unscrupulous reporters. The truth needed to be known, and the guilty punished or, if proved to be psychologically ill, institutionalized. So he set out to undertake a serious investigation, interviewing medical workers and state and local officials, and consulting the materials that had been collected by the city of Samara's "Famine Museum," which had been created by two local academics both to document the horrors of the famine and to educate the public. Among the museum's collections were a series of gruesome photographs of cannibals, typically shown alongside the body parts that had been found with them at the time of their arrest.

---

* Russians distinguish two forms of anthropophagy: *liudoedstvo* (literally, "people-eating" or "man-eating") and *trupoedstvo* ("corpse-eating"). Since English typically makes no such distinction, all forms of anthropophagy, including necrophagy, are labeled here "cannibalism."

Three women arrested for cannibalism, photographed with the evidence of their crime

Photographs of starving peasants and cannibals were also displayed at various state-backed exhibitions intended to enlighten people on the horrors of the famine.*

In 1922, Vasilevsky published a brochure based on his research, *A Horrifying Chronicle of the Famine: Suicide and Anthropophagy*. In sparse, unadorned prose, Vasilevsky compiled a chilling catalogue of murder, violence, insanity, and ineffable suffering. He quoted a Bashkir edition of *Izvestiia*: "In the cantons are very many cases of people consuming human flesh. Driven wild by hunger, they are cutting up their children and eating them. In the grip of starvation, they are eating the bodies of the dead." Vasilevsky also quoted a provincial official from the village of Bolshaya Glushitsa, in Pugachëv County, who warned that they were being "threatened with the danger of mass cannibalism."

---

* A second Samara museum dedicated to the famine opened sometime later in 1922. It had its own medical research group, which, among other things, gathered the corpses of famine victims to study the impact of starvation on the human body.

According to Vasilevsky, there had been hundreds of cases of cannibalism, and he predicted that the numbers were certain to grow as the famine worsened and the taboo against eating human flesh weakened. Indeed, it was the fear of "psychological infection" that prompted Vasilevsky to publish his research with a warning on the title page stating that this work was not to be distributed within the famine zone: readers, he worried, might draw the wrong conclusions from his work. Among the cases recounted in *A Horrifying Chronicle* was that of a group of three adolescents from Ufa Province. Before they were caught, they had lured little children to a remote hut, strangled them, chopped them up, then boiled and eaten their remains. The authorities never did manage to determine the exact number of their victims. The three youths were sent off to a special facility for juvenile criminal offenders, yet the overseers made certain to separate them, concerned that they might try to continue their crimes from inside the institution.

Vasilevsky spoke to the investigating medical doctor. He found the case particularly disturbing. It turned out that the three inmates had had plenty of food at home and had apparently ventured into this grisly business out of sheer curiosity. In their interrogations, they had appeared normal, quiet, and even respectful, but he had no doubt that their "derangement had reached an extreme stage from which there was no hope of recovery."

Their case reminded Vasilevsky of something he had read in a Kursk newspaper: "People are no longer people. Human feelings have died out, the beast, devoid of all reason and pity, has awakened." Although Vasilevsky had to agree, he insisted that this had nothing to do with the Russian character but was quite simply the logical result of years of misery and suffering. In this, Vasilevsky was correct. Acts of cannibalism have been recorded during famines throughout history in other parts of the world, such as Ireland during the Confederate Wars of the seventeenth century and China during the Great Leap under Mao.

Around the time Vasilevsky's brochure appeared, the Samara State Publishing House released *The Book of the Famine*, a much larger work, filled with official documents—telegrams, letters, interrogation records, police reports, and photographs—describing in grisly fashion many cases of murder, suicide, and cannibalism.

One of the most complete records concerned a fifty-six-year-old illiterate peasant from the village of Yefimovka in Buzuluk County by the name of Pyotr Mukhin. On January 12, 1922, he testified before Balter, an investigator for the Samara Province Revolutionary Tribunal, that his family had not had any bread since Easter of the previous year.

At first they lived off grass, horsemeat, and then dogs and cats. After that, they were reduced to gathering bones and grinding them into an edible paste. But then this, too, ran out, along with all the animals in the village.

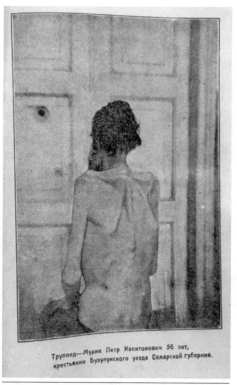

Трупоед—Мухин Петр Капитонович 56 лет, крестьянин Бузулукского уезда Самарской губернии.

The Russian caption reads: "Corpse-eater—Mukhin Pyotr Kapitonovich, 56 years old, peasant from Buzuluk County, Samara Province."

All over our region and in our own village a great number of corpses lie about in the streets and are piled up in the public warehouse. I, Mukhin, early one evening stole into the warehouse and took the corpse of a boy around the age of seven. I had heard that some people of our village were eating human flesh. I took him home on a sleigh, chopped up the corpse into small pieces, and set about to boil it that same evening. Then we woke the children—Natalya, 16 years old, Fyodor, 12, and Afanasy, 7—and we ate it. We ate the entire body in one day, all that was left were the bones.

Soon after, a man from the village soviet came and asked Mukhin whether the rumor that they had eaten human flesh was true. Mukhin said yes, it was—many did it in the village, although they hid the fact. The man took him to the soviet for questioning. "We don't remember what human flesh tasted like, we were in a mad frenzy when we ate it. We never killed somebody to eat them. We've got plenty of corpses and so it never crossed our minds to kill someone. There's nothing more I can tell you . . ."

That same day, Balter questioned Mukhin's twenty-eight-year-old son-in-law, Prokofy, a former Red Army soldier. He told Balter that, a week before he began eating human flesh, he had had to bury his grandfather, father, and mother in the course of just ten days. All of them had starved to death. Earlier, in the spring of 1921, he had buried his only son, aged two, also dead from hunger. A week before Christmas, his pregnant wife, Stepanida, brought home some boiled human flesh from her father, Pyotr Mukhin, and they ate this together with Prokofy's sister Yefrosinya. The three of them were arrested and taken to the village soviet, along with some human flesh found in their home.

They were held for three days with no food, and then conveyed to Buzuluk, a journey of four days. Given nothing to eat along the way, they asked one of the accompanying officials whether they might eat the pieces of flesh. He told them no: it had been entered into the police files as evidence. They ignored him and ate it anyway.

Mukhin, his daughter, and his son-in-law were all held in the Buzuluk House of Forced Labor, where they were examined by a psychiatrist from the faculty of Samara University in the middle of January. It was his judgment that none of them displayed any signs of "delirium, delusion of the emotions (hallucinations or illusions), maniacal agitation, condition of melancholy or similar signs of emotional disturbance." They were neither mad nor insane, but in their right minds. It was hunger that had made them resort to cannibalism, and they presented no danger of committing violence against the community. "They present as typical normal subjects who have been placed in exceptional circumstances that have forced them to commit acts of an anti-human nature, at odds with the normal expression of human nature." The subsequent fate of Mukhin, his daughter, and his son-in-law is unknown.

The matter-of-fact tone in which these flesh-eaters described their actions was typical. According to the report of the ARA inspector in Pugachëv County, a man by the name of Svorikin, once the starving had eaten human flesh, they no longer considered it a crime. The corpse, devoid of any human soul, was food, either for them or for "the worms in the ground." He noted: "They speak of these things with a curious kind of passiveness and quietness, as if the question were not of eating a person but simply a herring." The practice became so common in this district that the peasants approached state officials to request the government to permit it. That this took place in Pugachëv County in Samara Province is not surprising. This part of the Volga region, which included Buzuluk, home of the Mukhins, suffered like nowhere else. By July 1922, the population had fallen from 491,000 to 179,000 in just two years: over 100,000 had perished from starvation and disease, 142,000 had been evacuated by the state and various relief agencies, and roughly 70,000 people had simply vanished without a trace. Pugachëv County was particularly remote: cut off from the rail lines, isolated from the outside world, left to survive on its own. It was precisely in such places that the most desperate victims of the famine resorted to cannibalism.

But not all peasants were willing to accept their fate and take to eating the dead. On the morning of December 8, 1921, in the village of Pokrov-Tananyk in Buzuluk County, a group of almost fifty angry peasants dragging the body of a brutally murdered man on a sleigh arrived at the home of Comrade Golovchëv, the county chairman. They pounded on his door until he came out, and demanded he give them food or else they would come back and eat the man instead. They threw the bloody corpse on the doorstep and departed. Golovachëv's response is not known, nor is it known whether the mob made good on its threat. The policeman who reported this incident added, "Crimes of cannibalism are becoming more and more prevalent."

EVEN IF THE ARA wanted to play down cannibalism in its publicity, the subject was too explosive to keep out of the Western press, which had a tendency to treat it with the same tawdry sensationalism that had so angered Commissar Semashko. In April 1922, Reuters reported that during a riot in Samara a member of the ARA staff had been killed and eaten. That same month, a story appeared in a Parisian newspaper stating that the American boss of the ARA in Samara had been murdered, cooked, and eaten by the locals. A bemused Wolfe wrote to his brother in mid-May to say he was sure Eddie had read of the reports that an American had been killed and eaten in Samara, and that the likely victim had been none other than Henry himself, but there was no cause for alarm: this was an old rumor that had been going around for months, and he was safe and sound.

On May 29, *The New York Times* carried a story on cannibalism that made reference to an exhibition of gruesome photographs recently set up in the Kremlin, only a few doors down from Lenin's office. The article questioned the reason for the exhibition, surmising that the terrifying images and stories were part of the government's strategy to wring more aid out of the West. Many of the photographs had been taken by GPU agents to be used as evidence in criminal cases. Although the article gave a vivid, and horrifying, description of the images, the *Times* refused to publish some of the details, substituting in brackets the words "Here follow details too revolting for publication."

By the autumn of 1922, Wolfe had had enough of Russia. On November 9, he wrote a letter to Haskell informing him that he was beset by "a depression and nervous tension which make it impossible for me to work as I would." Given what he had seen, no one could blame him. He had gone to Moscow on leave for a time, hoping this would help his mental state, but as soon as he returned to the famine zone, he felt stricken once again with famine shock. The only thing for him to do was resign and go home. The comfortable normality of his native Ohio had never looked so good.

13

SAVED AT THE EDGE
OF THE GRAVE

S HE WAS SITTING AT AN OPEN CUBICLE when he entered. Her brown eyes caught his attention, and then he noticed her smile. He was smitten from the start.

Childs had returned to Russia from his convalescence in Germany on March 24. The next day, he stopped by the Petrograd ARA offices to say hello to Herschel Walker, the local director, before catching the train to Moscow. The young woman busy at her desk was striking. He asked Walker for an introduction.

Georgina de Brylkine-Klokachëva had been born into wealth and privilege. Pavel Brylkine, her nobleman father, served as an officer in the Imperial Navy, as had his ancestors since the days of Peter the Great. Her mother, Mathilde Blanc-Garin, was born in Paris. Theirs wasn't a happy marriage, and Mathilde left her husband when Georgina was still a little girl; mother and daughter spent many years living abroad. Georgina attended boarding schools in England and Germany and then returned to Russia with her mother sometime before the outbreak of World War I. By then, Georgina's father had died. With the revolution, the Bolshevik government dispossessed the family of everything it owned. Having lost their home, they found shelter in two small rooms on the Moika River. Georgina married a young officer, but ten days later he was killed, fighting against the Red Army in the civil war. To support them, Georgina sold matches on the streets of Petrograd.

That evening, a few hours after meeting her, Childs attended the opera with several ARA employees, including Georgina, her mother, and several of their aristocratic friends. It was Childs's first real exposure to the old tsarist elite, now designated "former people" by the new regime. He was struck by what had become of them: "They are broken in spirit as well as in body [. . .] Their morale is gone and their spirit is crushed so that one must give credit to the Bolshevik government for having very effectually achieved at least one of its aims, that of stamping out the bourgeois element of society in Russia [. . .] Never was the spirit of any class of people any more completely subdued."

He couldn't take his eyes off Georgina. He marveled at how, though she was only twenty-four years old, her hair was already streaked with gray. The next day, he visited mother and daughter for tea; listening to their tales of woe, he understood how someone so young could have already begun to gray. Mathilde, once a great beauty and still physically stunning at forty-two, had been shattered by the experiences of the revolution, her nerves destroyed beyond repair. Georgina, however, had somehow managed to survive. She was animated, intelligent, bubbling with life. Childs left them for the station and could think of nothing else but Georgina on the trip to Moscow before returning to Kazan. As soon as he arrived in the capital, he wrote a letter to tell her that she had made an impact on him as no one ever had before. His life had been thrown upside down. He was certain there was something momentous about their meeting. He couldn't begin to think about work, and now there was only one thing that mattered—his desire to please her.

Georgina wrote back to thank him for his letter. "I do wish I could follow you in your beautiful dreams and superstitions," she told him, "but life has struck upon me too hard to allow my mind to follow them." Nevertheless, she encouraged his infatuation, teasing Childs that she hoped the pretty girls of Kazan would leave him some time to write to her and wondering whether he would keep his promise and come back to visit her again soon. This was all the encouragement the lovesick Childs needed. She filled his dreams at night, he confessed to her, and he began to scheme about how to have her transferred to Kazan. He wrote to say that he kept repeating her name over and over—Georgie, Georgie, Georgie—for it surely was "the prettiest name in the whole calendar of feminine nomenclature." He gushed that only with the help of the great writers, men such as Baudelaire, Byron, and Goethe, could he hope to express his feelings for her. To convey his longing, he quoted from Matthew Arnold's "The Buried Life": "I feel a nameless sadness o'er me roll."

Besotted though he was, Childs was too busy to moon about all day thinking of Georgie. The first shipment of corn—thirty-seven railcars from Odessa—had arrived in Kazan on April 2, a few days before Childs's return, and everyone was scrambling to get it sent out into the villages. Ivar Wahren, Childs's superior in Kazan, was away in Moscow, thus making Childs the temporary head of operations for the entire district. The crush of the corn effort lasted the entire month. "I'm working myself to a frazzle," he wrote his mother, but he couldn't imagine being any happier. "I have reached the point where I do not think I would ever be satisfied with living anywhere except in Russia. Old timers say the Russian bug is a disease and that when it gets into your veins you are hopeless; that there is nothing like the Russian nostalgia." He was living a life of service, just as his parents had taught him, he wrote, and no other work, and no other country, could give him such profound satisfaction. "I believe my future lies here."

Of course, it was more than the good he was doing for his fellow man on the other side of the globe that had made Childs so happy. Not one to keep things from his mother, he told her he had met a girl. He told her of Georgina's beauty, of "her spirit of heroism and character," of her being "an aristocrat of aristocrats." And he told her he was thinking of marrying her. "Yes," Childs confessed, "your son has lost his heart." His mother and father back in Lynchburg were none too pleased.

THE ARA MEN throughout the districts had been frantically working to manage the sudden arrival of tons of corn when, suddenly and inexplicably, the trains stopped arriving. What had been a tidal wave of grain slowed to a trickle. Just as many of the Americans had feared, the Russian railroad system was too damaged to handle so much freight: only about 20 percent of the prewar rolling stock was still in service, and the country was dotted with so-called locomotive graveyards, where rusting hulks sat idle. Trains began to break down en route to the famine regions, blocking the line and causing the entire network to seize up. Soon nothing was moving. As much as sixty thousand tons of American food and medicine sat in storage for lack of transport.

The problem lay not just with the sorry state of the rail system, however. The state had fallen months behind in paying the rail workers' salaries, and some decided to take matters into their own hands. At Kozlov (now Michurinsk), sixty miles west of Tambov, the railroad men began breaking the seals on the idled ARA cars, unloading the grain, and placing it in their own warehouses, over the objections of the Americans, one of whom was arrested by the GPU after he attempted to intervene. In other areas, empty freight cars intended for the use of the ARA were being seized to ship seed purchased by the Soviet government for the spring planting. The situation was critical. If the corn did not make it soon to the railheads, where it had to be milled and bagged, and then sent out to the villages, often hundreds of miles away across primitive roads, the entire operation would fail. Everything now depended on the weather. If the spring thaw came soon, the melting snow would turn the roads into mud so deep no one and nothing could get through. The infamous *rasputitsa*—the season of bad roads, a time when Russia's rural villages became islands unto themselves—would keep the corn from reaching the hungry. Months of hard work would have been in vain, and millions more would die of starvation. Everyone in the ARA prayed for a long winter.

Back in Moscow, Haskell was frantically trying to understand just what had gone wrong. Eiduk insisted he had the situation under control and would get things straightened out, but Haskell was losing faith. As a start, he agreed to allow some of the railroad workers to help themselves to American grain if this would get them back to work. Eiduk took advantage of Haskell's offer, and soon the seizures of ARA supplies went way beyond anything Haskell had agreed to. When he tried to get a meeting with Kamenev, he was rebuffed. Haskell was becoming convinced that the crisis was not the result of circumstances, but that some in the government were in fact carrying out a secret campaign to sabotage the ARA's mission.

Just as the rail crisis was reaching its height, a gathering of over thirty nations was taking place in Italy to address questions surrounding the economic reconstruction of Central and Eastern Europe, still suffering from the ravages of the war. Key to the discussions was the status of Soviet Russia. The Genoa Conference opened on April 10, and Lenin had great hopes that the talks would result in major Allied investments and the import of Western technical knowledge and skill, all of which were desperately needed to rebuild the country. The Russians were going to Genoa "not as communists, but as merchants," Lenin wrote in *Pravda*. But his hopes were dashed by disagreements between the Soviets and the Allies over matters of Russia's foreign debts and compensation to foreigners who had lost property in Russia. Still, the talks were not a complete bust. The Soviets had been secretly meeting with the German delegation, with the goal of coming to a bilateral agreement to bind the two pariah states together in defiance of the Allies. The Treaty of Rapallo, signed on April 16 a few miles from Genoa, on the Italian Riviera, normalized relations and confirmed a shared commitment to furthering "the economic needs of both countries." More important, though not included in the official public treaty, was a secret arrangement to permit Germany, in violation of the Treaty of Versailles, to set up military and armament facilities on Soviet territory in return for German help in developing the Soviet armed forces. The ferocious German Wehrmacht that invaded the Soviet Union in the summer of 1941 owed much of its early development to Lenin's backdoor diplomacy at Rapallo.

The United States did not participate in the Genoa Conference, and there was a perception among the Americans that their refusal to negotiate with, much less recognize, the Soviet government lay behind the transportation crisis. At a meeting with Kamenev around this time, Quinn, Haskell's chief deputy since March, was told that since the United States did not officially recognize Soviet Russia, it was only to be expected that the ARA's freedom of action would be limited. The trouble, in other words, lay with the Americans, not the Russians. Frantic to get the Russians to do something, Haskell sent Hoover a telegram on April 10 (the same day talks began in Genoa) en clair recommending that all food purchases back in the United States, as well as all grain shipments to Russia, be halted until the Soviet government proved beyond any doubt that they wanted the relief mission to continue. Just as he had intended, Haskell's uncoded telegram was intercepted and read by the Soviets, and almost immediately Eiduk telephoned him to arrange a meeting for the next day.

On one side of the table sat Haskell and Quinn; on the other, Kamenev and Eiduk. It was clear from the start that Kamenev was prepared to do anything not to lose America's help. He admitted that the requisitioning of supplies was "criminal" and promised it would stop that instant. He also promised to stop the arrests of ARA employees without prior consent of the Americans, and to fire any officials in his office guilty of obstructing the work of the ARA. He assured Haskell that ARA rail freight would be given the same priority as that of the Soviet government. Throughout the meeting, Kamenev berated Eiduk for his poor work as plenipotentiary and for not bringing this matter to his attention sooner. Before the meeting adjourned, Kamenev let Haskell know that his government was well aware that no one but the Americans could handle the current crisis facing the country.

Kamenev arranged a follow-up meeting the next day to include

Haskell, Eiduk, and Felix Dzerzhinsky, now
both head of the GPU and people's commissar for transportation, and thus the man responsible for Russia's railroads. Haskell was
taken aback by the sight of the feared "Iron
Felix." His manner was gentle and polite—
attentive, even—his eyes a soft blue.

Dzerzhinsky asked what had gone
wrong, and Haskell gave a long list of the
troubles he'd been experiencing with Eiduk.
For every complaint Eiduk had an excuse,
and for every excuse Haskell had a letter or
telegram or some other document to refute
Eiduk's lies. Dzerzhinsky became irate at his
subordinate. With a tone of voice Haskell
had never heard before in his life and, as

Felix Dzerzhinsky

he recalled, "a look in his eyes calculated to inspire fear," Dzerzhinsky
remarked, "Comrade Eiduk, you have been deceiving me all through
this conference." Eiduk began to quake, then froze in his chair, unable
to speak. Now certain where the fault lay, Dzerzhinsky told Haskell
he would see that the railcars would start moving again, and they did:
within two weeks, the worst of the crisis had passed.

Eiduk lost Dzerzhinsky's favor, and in June he was replaced by another GPU agent, fellow Latvian Karl Lander, a longtime Bolshevik and
hardened revolutionary remembered for unleashing a reign of terror in
the northern Caucasus during the civil war that included the execution of
thousands of Cossacks.

Haskell was convinced that Dzerzhinsky's methods to get the trains
moving again must have included the arrest, imprisonment, and even execution of railroad officials. The methods were horrible by the ARA's standards, but he figured the lives saved so far outnumbered the lives taken
that in the end it had been justified. "I don't care about his past record,"
Haskell stated. "Dzerzhinsky is all right in this country—he gets things
done." In the middle of April, a grateful Kamenev wrote Haskell: "The

Karl Lander

government and Russian nation will never forget the generous help that was offered [. . .] the more so because this country is not in a position to cope with the national calamity, prostrated as it is by the World War and Civil War."

THE MEN IN KAZAN scrambled to get the corn out. In a mere ten days, they managed to bag and distribute 145,795 rations to seventy-three hundred men who had come to the city with their horses and sleighs to take the food back to their villages. Another twelve thousand men and women carried the corn home on their backs. But there were troubles along the way. The village of Spassk prepared 3,250 sleighs to send to Kazan, but only 110 made it because of a thaw that flooded the low areas. More than a dozen peasants drowned trying to ford swollen rivers on their journey.

Henry Wolfe was in the village of Melekess when the first corn arrived on April 19. The news spread quickly, and starving peasants began to swarm into the village. As the local mill ground the corn into meal throughout the day and night, the people—Russians, Tatars, Kalmyks, and Mordvins—waited patiently. By the next morning, the roads were choked with horses and wagons. The wagons were carefully loaded, one by one, and there was no sense of hurry or panic. Wolfe noticed how the people took their sacks "as a mother handles a baby [. . .] No miser ever guarded his gold with more care than these famished peasants watched over their flour." Some had come on foot from villages miles away. They hoisted the sacks up onto their backs—small ones for the children and old people, large ones for the able-bodied men—and trudged off toward home.

On the 23rd, the chairman of the local committee of Novo-Maina visited Wolfe to thank him for the corn, which had saved the lives of fifteen thousand people in his county. "When the wagons came into sight of the village all the people able to walk went out to meet them," he told Wolfe. "People so weak from hunger that they could not walk dragged themselves after the others. The people knelt on the ground crossing themselves and thanking God and America for this delivery from the grave. Many of the people were crying." Before leaving, he pulled out a piece of paper with a poem he had written:

TO THE AMERICAN PEOPLE,
Great Land, Great People,
Greetings to you from the edge of the grave;
Only in you we found our Savior,
And at the edge of the grave you saved us.

Wolfe was profoundly moved by the experience. He wrote:

The importance of the arrival of the corn cannot be over-emphasized. The situation in this district had become terrible beyond description. Cannibalism had become commonplace. People brought their children into the town of Melekess and abandoned them there. Personally I have seen people eating horse manure and other horrible stuff. In one day recently in the village of Moiseevka thirty people died. Without help from the outside the whole countryside would have been depopulated. The arrival

Children kneel in gratitude at the arrival of American corn in the
Samara village of Vasilevka on April 10, 1922.

of the corn has changed all this. All over the county the people
are once more, after many months, eating something good. From
a land of sadness and death this county is becoming a place of
life and happiness.

The arrival of American corn elicited universal gratitude across Russia
that spring. "You saved our children from a profound abyss and opened
their closed eyes," wrote the peasants of one Tatar village. "Long live the
American government and the A.R.A.!" The people of Matushkino also
wrote a letter: "The American help is for us the manna from the Heav-
ens! [. . .] The help given by the Americans can never be forgotten, and
the story of their glorious exploit will be told by grandfathers to their
grand-children, from one generation to another."

Much of the corn reached the villages during the Easter season, thus
linking American aid with the celebration of Christ's resurrection. Church

bells rang that year to mark not one but two miracles, for that is how many viewed the unexpected appearance of food after years of misery. Russians frequently called the ARA men "messengers from heaven." And it wasn't just peasants, steeped in traditional Orthodox culture, who viewed the appearance of food through the lens of Christian faith. In Petrograd, the noted artist Alexander Benois remarked to one member of the ARA that an American food package "seemed like a miraculous manifestation of Providence." Several ARA men later recalled that Russians stopped them to bow at their feet in thanks. A group of old men once forced their way into Wolfe's room during dinner, fell on their knees, and began making the sign of the cross, tears streaming down their cheeks. They told Wolfe that they had come to worship the representative of the ARA because he was the only man with the power to save them. America acquired an aura of the holy land. One aid worker was besieged by a group of refugees outside Saratov who wanted to know how they might go to America. It was a question put to many of the men in the ARA.

There were, however, problems that accompanied the arrival of the corn. Russians had no experience with this American staple, and some didn't know what they were supposed to do with it. In some instances, peasants ate it raw and became terribly ill; a few even died. Indeed, most of the food sent from America struck the Russians as strange. *Izvestiia* noted that mothers and their children didn't initially like the ARA menu. The kasha and cocoa were so sweet that they felt sick. The peasants found American food inferior to their traditional diet of cabbage and other simple, hearty fare. Mikhail Kalinin brought up the matter with Haskell once, acknowledging their gratitude for America's help but pointing out that Russians were used to eating black bread and fish. What the Americans were offering was too fancy and in nutritional terms amounted to nothing more than "a box of candy." One foreign aid worker lectured an ARA man on the advantages of using whole-wheat flour: it was healthier, more in keeping with the Russian diet, and, at a third the cost of white flour, would allow the Americans to feed that many more children for the same amount of money. The American didn't know what to say to this, mumbling simply that the ARA shipped only the best possible food products.

Whatever the shortcomings of American food, the corn campaign proved a huge success. It saved the peasants not only by filling their empty stomachs and giving them the strength to go back to working their fields, but also kept them from eating the seed grain imported by the Soviet government, which had to be planted that spring to ensure a decent harvest come summer. Russians never did develop a taste for corn, but it put an end to the worst of the famine. And the campaign had a number of other beneficial effects. The need to move all that grain forced Russia to make improvements to its transportation system and seaports. The appearance of dozens of tons of imported grain lowered food prices over all, and also helped to stem the tide of refugees to the cities. It even encouraged the cleaning up of towns and cities. The ARA created so-called corn gangs, typically groups of refugees organized into work brigades to repair roads, bridges, buildings, and railroads in return for a salary paid in corn. Intended to fight the filth that bred disease, work in the corn gangs also lifted the Russians' spirits. One ARA man, Harold Buckley, commented on the new life in the Russian city Orsk:

> The effects of the corn have been to change Orsk from a dead
> city, and one with a mourning appearance, to a city of happy
> people who live in the natural way of natural people, who sing as
> they stroll in the evening in little groups through the streets, who
> dance in the park on the nights when the band plays, who, in
> short, do everything they did in better days.

Along with death, the famine had brought silence to the villages. The sounds of rural life produced by the abundance of animals—wild and domesticated—and people—women singing in the fields, men hitching up their wagons, children at play, church bells calling the faithful to pray—had disappeared. Now, with the arrival of the corn, life and its joyful noise had returned.

Within the ARA, there was a sense that the worst of the crisis was over. That April, Hoover decided they should plan to end the mission within six months. In May, the New York office received reports from the various district supervisors supporting Hoover's decision. Assuming a good harvest that year, Russia would be able to see its way clear of the famine, and no further American aid would be necessary. The Russian job was all but done. Or so it seemed.

CHILDS LEFT KAZAN by boat on April 28 to oversee the distribution of corn in the district. He watched as grain was loaded onto the vessel on a warm, sunny afternoon, amazed that just ten days earlier the river had been filled with ice. All around were hungry people. "They hover like birds of prey around the cars and boats, kneeling in the dust and dirt to pick up from the ground the grains of corn which fall from the sacks as they

The office of the ARA committee in Tetiushi

are borne on the backs of laborers." When they got too close, a crack from the army man's rifle shooed them away, for a time. Only after they had departed did Childs bother to check his own food supplies—two boxes of nothing but cereal (Quaker Oats, Shredded Wheat, Grape-Nuts, and Corn Flakes), packed for him by the Russian housekeeper. He was crestfallen: "I particularly detest that typical American institution, breakfast food."

For two weeks, he traveled throughout the territory. On the 30th, they docked at Tetiushi to inspect the warehouses in the shadow of the tall cliffs along the river. Crowds had assembled to collect their share of corn and bring it home. At a meeting with the chairman of the Tetiushi relief committee, he was told that the local people there would never forget how the Americans had saved their lives.

May 5 found him and the interpreter Simson stuck in Spassk with no transportation. It was Karl Marx's birthday, and so everyone had the day off. He used the time to record his thoughts on what he had seen of late.

"The famine, as if to mock the Soviet government, has awakened the most individualistic instincts of man. There seems very little desire on the part of the more fortunate inhabitants of the villages to assist those who are in greatest distress." He had heard instances of families not helping the weakest members. "Those who are dying from hunger can hope to receive no assistance even from members of their family. When one is compelled to take to bed from weakness due to hunger, he is left undisturbed and unaided." Now, with the warm weather, he was seeing the sick leave home and take to the roads, where they'd lie down in the hope that "some Good Samaritan" might come along and render help. But no one ever did. They just lay out there, dying, "all swollen from hunger and with skins the color of yellow parchment."

As the body starves, it first turns to its stores of glucose for energy. Once those have been depleted, it turns to its fats, then its proteins. The hungry organism begins to devour itself from the inside out. The skin loses its healthy color and thins. Kwashiorkor, a severe form of edema caused by a lack of protein, leads to swelling of the hands, feet, and belly. One's hair and teeth fall out; the skin erupts with a variety of infections, breaks open, and emits a foul-smelling liquid. The eyes take on a sickly hue, and some victims begin to suffer from night blindness. Drained of all energy, the mind slowly dimming, the victim eventually stops moving altogether and dies.

As they traveled through the villages, the ARA men learned to read the thatched roofs for signs of the severity of the famine. Where the roofs were still largely intact, the people had suffered little. Where the barn roofs had been stripped but the cottage roofs not touched, the people had suffered from real famine. Where the thatch on both the barns and the cottages had been stripped, the people had suffered from extreme hunger. The peasants would first feed the thatch to their animals to keep them alive. Once they had eaten all their animals, they ate the thatch—mixed with clay or *lebeda*—to keep themselves alive. First they ate the thatch off the barn; next, off the cottage. If they were fortunate enough to have two rooms, the peasants tried to resist eating that last bit of thatch over one of the rooms to maintain some sort of shelter from the snow and rain.

In village after village, the people crowded around Childs to thank him and America for its help. Even government officials joined in and abandoned the formal reserve he had encountered on his earlier tours, going so far as to give public thanks not only to the American people but to the government as well. In the village of Buinsk, one grateful official insisted that should the Americans ever find themselves facing a national disaster, they could count on the sympathy and practical support of the Russian people.

Georgina was forever on Childs's mind, and he wrote to her often. "I wish I were in Petrograd," he told her again and again, and spoke of his wish to come see her in June. He confessed everything in his letters—his anguish at failing to become a writer, his dream to trek across Central Asia, the tragic death of his older brother, who had been his parents' much-beloved favorite son, his fondness for the bottle, his views on God, politics, and the meaning of life. Humans, he wrote, are "like so many million leaves which bud and wither and fall. I believe that the only paradise is the one which we may be able to create on this world, that the only hell is the one through which we are living now." It was man's duty to try to make this world a bit better than it had been when he came into it. "That is my religion and I have the conceit to believe that if it were the religion of the world that we would very soon attain our paradise—here on this earth. That explains why I am a socialist, why I am a cynic, why I love irony [. . .] and why above all else I feel I would be unworthy of existence if I passed out of it without having contributed my share to the forward march of humanity." At times he feared he went too far and she must consider him "a sentimental maudlin fool."

Georgina encouraged Childs to open his soul to her, although his belief in socialism and admiration for the Soviet project did not meet with her approval, for obvious reasons. She wrote that it was clear to her he simply couldn't understand how her family and others like them had suffered— "for us who have been through ruin and still deeper sorrows—it sounds strange to hear you being so fond of 'present Russia,' whereas for us it has ceased to be a home—our constant wish and longing are to get out of it some day and our great sorrow is that we cannot find any combination allowing us to do so!" From her letters, it's clear Georgina's affection for Childs was genuine, but there are hints of doubt as well: How honest were her suitor's expressions of love and how true were his motives? Could she trust him, and what would life with Childs mean? Did she even dare to imagine he might be her ticket out of Russia to a better life in the West?

As the weeks passed, Childs's obsession with Georgina grew. He spent hours staring at her picture and could think of nothing but the idea of seeing her again. He wrote that he had to keep asking himself if she was truly real, or, "as Poe said, 'only a dream within a dream.'" With each new letter from her, he fell deeper under her spell. "Are you some goddess in human flesh? I am fast disposed to believe so for surely I never believed your like existed in this sorry world." Before the end of May, he informed his mother that he planned to propose to Georgina the next time he saw her, and if she refused him he would remain a bachelor the rest of his days. He hoped they could marry that summer, and then he would be able to get her out of Russia. Childs wrote to Haskell to request leave so he could travel to Petrograd. As of June 1, he was still waiting for his boss's reply.

14

A DEATH IN UFA

L ATE ON THE NIGHT OF APRIL 5, three sleighs glided out of Ufa, carrying Kelly, Boris Elperine, an ARA accountant, several guides and drivers, and weeks' worth of supplies. They were heading for the town of Sterlitamak. The ARA office there had been engaging in suspicious activities, and millions of rubles had gone missing. There was a suspicion that Hofstra was in part to blame, for he was the one who'd set up the office and hired the unscrupulous employees. The local Bashkir government was not at all happy with how things were being run. This had led to friction back in Ufa among Bell, Kelly, and Hofstra, and now Bell was sending Kelly to straighten things out. "I depart on a secret mission with plenipotentiary powers to clean house and conciliate the government. If I am successful, Moscow will never hear a breath of the scandal." Kelly was ready for a break from Ufa and excited by the challenge of the task at hand.

It was a miserable two-day trip over bumpy roads in bitter cold temperatures. They'd been warned about wolves and bandits along the route. Kelly had his suspicions about their unsavory-looking drivers, too; he'd finger the Colt pistol in his pocket whenever one of them got too close. Kelly had reason to be edgy: he was carrying 200 million rubles with him. So lawless was the territory that the Bashkir government, fearing highwaymen, had refused to transfer 50 million rubles from Ufa to Sterlitamak.

They arrived safely on the 7th. The town was a dreary outpost of mud and squalor. By the end of the next day, Kelly was wishing he could leave. "Already I sigh for the flesh pots of Ufa! May you never know this queer feeling of being at the edge of the world," he wrote to a friend back home. Had he known at the time he'd be trapped there for three weeks, Kelly might well have gone mad.

The Bashkirs were glad to welcome Kelly, and they threw a large party in his honor. "It was a scream and I confess a scandal," he wrote once his hangover had lifted. "My intentions were the best, but little did I guess the potency of Bashkir hooch. Tonight, twenty hours later, I am good as new. In fact my tooth aches less than before the debauch. It makes my head spin to think of it. Call it by any name it was virtually straight alcohol." A drunk Kelly got up to deliver toasts and opine on the shortcomings of the Soviet economic system, which Elperine dutifully translated for their hosts, who listened politely. "We parted the best of friends. Boris tells me they are delighted with me. My memory is not a good guide to the last part of the evening. I am charged with singing, but I don't remember it. I do remember falling out of the cart. I also remember firing my automatic once in the market place and again outside my door. I had some reasons but I don't remember what they were."

It didn't take long for Kelly to complete his secret mission and set things right at the local office. He also made sure to visit a few of the children's homes. It was not easy. Kelly had been devastated by the suffering he'd been exposed to and had lost the belief they could do much

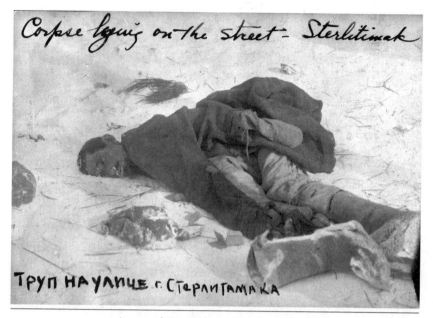

Corpse lying on the street - Sterlitamak

ТРУП НА УЛИЦЕ г. СТерлитамака

A corpse lying in the snow in Sterlitamak

to help, or that things would soon get any better. He acted as if he had become hard and unfeeling, in part as a way of coping, but from beneath his gallows humor his anguish creeps through. "My immunization is progressing. Today I passed two corpses lying on the street. I scarcely gave them a second glance."

The situation in the Bashkir Republic was indeed horrific. Of its 1,269,000 inhabitants, as many as 999,600 were starving. Officials in Sterlitamak had been sending telegrams for weeks to People's Commissar for Nationalities Stalin, seeking more help from the ARA. Now they informed Kelly that in some Bashkir villages up to half of the population had died, and some villages had completely died out "and vanished from the earth."

The men had planned to head out into the district on an inspection trip, but the ice had not fully melted on the Belaya River, so they remained stuck in Sterlitamak. Kelly felt like "a prisoner of mud." Though the friendly Bashkirs kept inviting him to parties, he begged off, using his sore wisdom teeth as an excuse. Finally, on the 17th, he gave in and accepted an invitation to a gathering at the apartment of the Bashkir people's commissar for transportation. As he and Elperine were leaving their quarters, they stumbled upon the body of a dead child lying in the mud. Dogs had gotten to it, tearing off the ragged clothes and chewing up much of the bony little body. The two men stepped around it and continued on their way.

Again, the hooch was flowing. An old phonograph was playing some sort of waltz. Men and women sat around smoking and drinking. "With the first toast the fight was on, they fighting to get me drunk and I determined to stay on deck." Instead of draining his glass with each toast—as was the custom, especially for men—Kelly carefully sipped his drink. The women found his behavior insulting, and a clear indictment of his masculinity. Kelly swore back at them in English. As for Elperine, he had abandoned his job as interpreter, gotten drunk, and slipped off somewhere with one of the women. The two men left the party early in the morning. Shots rang out in the dark on the way home, and they both kept a hand on their pistols. When they went out the next morning, they passed a pile of human brains splattered in the road. A dozen corpses were being picked up from the town's streets every day.

With nothing to do and no way to return to Ufa because of the *rasputitsa*, Kelly whiled away the days in the local ARA office. He killed time by writing to Jane and friends back home. In one long letter, he offered his pessimistic views on Russia and its future. "Is the government conducted efficiently? The Board of Aldermen of any Dakota town could be counted on to administer the Gubernias I have come in contact with or this Bashkir Republic better than their present executives [. . .] With rare exceptions they are incompetent to conduct the affairs of a small town grocery store." He admitted he knew nothing of the men who ran the central government, but, given the personnel in the provinces, there was little the men back in Moscow could accomplish even if they had the talents of a Herbert Hoover. As far as he could tell, the Russians had no word for "initiative." Of the higher-ranking Russian personnel he'd met, "Tired, timid men they are, the best that the country affords, but woefully inadequate for the jobs they hold [. . .] Utterly without ambition, they are not however without fear that after the ARA leaves the enemies they have made in the performance of their duties will do them harm." Though it was true that a good crop would relieve the current suffering, it would do nothing to help "check the decline into barbarism that is inevitable as the capital equipment of the country wears out." They needed investment, but since they had tried so hard to discredit capitalism and the West as evil, it was impossible to see where this would come from.

As the rain came down day after day and the men sat about waiting for a boat to appear from Ufa to take them home, Kelly leafed through old copies of *The Saturday Evening Post*. The colorful food advertisements didn't help his flagging morale. The enforced tedium had brought him to "the verge of insanity. For days now I've been in a state of coma," he complained in one of his letters. None of them wanted to go out: every walk meant encountering corpses lying facedown in the mud. Eventually, they managed to persuade some Tatar drivers to attempt the trip on the morning of April 30 despite the horrendous roads, flooded plains, and seas of mud. After a thirty-six-hour slog, the men finally reached Ufa. Bell was so happy to see Kelly again, he fell upon his neck.

Bell not only had missed Kelly, but was frantic for an additional set of hands around the office. Sixteen of the staff had fallen ill with typhus, including Hofstra, which meant Kelly was now the number-two man in the district. Their excellent translator, Willig, had died of the disease while Kelly was away. Short though they were of manpower, one of the first things Kelly did was dispatch Blandy to Sterlitamak, in part to oversee corn shipments in the area but also to get him out of the way. Blandy didn't last long there, having come down with a horrible fever that, upon his return to Ufa, proved to be typhus. He died within a week, on the 17th. Kelly didn't mourn, although he did worry about his own health: he had been around Blandy during his illness. The ARA office in Ufa closed for only a day to recognize the loss of one of its own. The Russian personnel found this cold and strange, but Kelly didn't "give a hang" what they thought. "For one who craves a ceremonious funeral, Ufa is no place to die. With us it is necessarily let the dead bury the dead."

Blandy's body was sent to the local undertaker for embalming, but

Funeral of H. F. Blandy

Blandy's funeral in Moscow

he botched the job and it had to be redone. Kelly, together with the other
Americans, took the flag-draped coffin to the station for the journey back
to Moscow. On the way, a swarm of children ran alongside the truck to
say their goodbyes to the kind Mr. Blandy, who had visited their school
to teach them magic tricks. Blandy's body lay in state and was accorded
an elaborate public funeral procession through the streets of the capital,
complete with pallbearers in white top hats and tails and six elaborately
caparisoned horses, the coffin bedecked with a mound of lilies, before his
remains were shipped back home to America.

As an acknowledgment of Blandy's service to the Russian people, the
Soviet government paid for the entire ceremony. Back in Ufa, the ARA re-
furbished the main hospital with new medical and surgical equipment and
christened it the Harold Blandy Memorial Hospital. The city fathers erected
a monument to Blandy in the main square, and one of the children's homes
adopted his name as well. It seemed his name would live on there forever as
a symbol of one American's sacrifice to the people of Russia.

Blandy was not the only American to die there. Clayton Kratz had been working for the American Mennonite Relief Unit in Ukraine when he was arrested as a spy by the Red Army in the autumn of 1920. He was never seen again, and the cause of his death remains unknown. And then there was the case of Philip Shield, who disappeared without a trace from the streets of Simbirsk one evening in October 1922. There was talk that he had committed suicide, despondent over a love affair with a married woman, or been murdered by a gang caught stealing sugar from an ARA warehouse, or was just another victim of random violence. Despite a thorough investigation, the truth behind his mysterious vanishing was never discovered, and his body was never found.

The trial of those long days in Sterlitamak convinced Kelly that he really had had enough of Russia; when he returned to Ufa, he informed Bell that he intended to quit service no later than June 20. Bell was, not surprisingly, unhappy with this decision. "We are all alone, Kel, and the job must be done," he told him. Kelly had been "a life saver" to Bell, who couldn't imagine carrying on without him. The American unit was tiny at the moment—with Hofstra out and Blandy dead, they were down to only five men, although more help was expected from Moscow—all while they were trying to feed over four hundred thousand children and eight hundred thousand adults. In addition, they were setting up a "City Improvement Committee" in Ufa and five other towns, to engage in a variety of construction projects, from building roads and bridges to digging wells and repairing hospitals. In the town of Zlatoust, they oversaw the building of 270 automobile bridges, repaired 160 old ones, installed ninety-four drinking fountains, restored two large schools, and constructed an eight-hundred-meter-long drainage canal, a project that had been in the planning stage for over seventy years but was completed only with American support.

Kelly had been prepared for Bell's begging him to stay on longer, and he recognized that there was still much work to be done, but he'd had enough. He wrote to Haskell on May 20 to request permission to quit in thirty days, exactly six months since he had arrived in Moscow. He hoped this would provide Haskell with enough time to send a replacement, whom Kelly could help train. He was sorry to leave, he said, but needed to, owing to "the most urgent of personal reasons." What these were he didn't bother to say.

ON MAY 15, Hoover delivered an address to the International Chamber of Commerce in Washington in which he spoke of the situation in Soviet Russia. He told those gathered that the overthrow of the tsarist regime, which for centuries had practiced what he called "misgovernment," had been a blessing, but now "a great nation is suffering agonies the world has not known since the Dark Ages." The pendulum had swung too far in the direction of destruction, and the Russian people were slowly dying, not from external causes but from internal ones. Although the Bolsheviks' extreme form of communism had been abandoned the previous year for a milder version of socialism, the current economic system stifled all productivity and was doomed to failure. If that was the model the Russians chose for themselves, that was their decision. Through the help of the United States, more than ten million Russian lives had been saved, yet the ultimate fate of the nation lay with the Russian people, not foreigners.

He recognized that voices could now be heard insisting that the establishment of official diplomatic relations with the United States was crucial to the revival of the Russian economy, an idea Hoover dismissed—quite correctly—as mistaken. First, Russia was broke and had no money for trade. Second, as long as the legal system offered no real security for investment, foreign capital would avoid Russia. And third, even before the First World War, during a more favorable economic and political period, American trade with Russia had been negligible. The American people never abandoned Russia and had provided great charity, but charity could not be the solution to Russia's problems.

Hoover's speech came just as the Genoa Conference was about to end in failure. That was fine with him and Secretary of State Charles Evans Hughes, neither of whom wanted American relief to be the opening to official recognition of the Soviet government. Talks were renewed in June at The Hague, but again the United States chose not to attend, and again the conference ended with no resolution to the questions of Russia's foreign debts or diplomatic recognition by the Allies.*

Hoover's special emissary Golder had grown ever more pessimistic about U.S.-Soviet relations in recent months and supported his boss's views. "Six months ago I regarded the Bolo leaders as real statesmen," he wrote in April, "but today I see in them cheap east side politicians and shopkeepers. They think they can buy the American people by tempting with the pig bristle trade; they think they can bully us until we are ready to buy them off by offer of a loan or recognition." In meetings with Kamenev, it became clear to Golder that the government was making life difficult for the ARA as a tactic to force the United States to agree to establish official relations. Trying to do business with the Bolsheviks, he remarked in disgust, was like trying to deal with "a white slaver." Governor Goodrich, another of Hoover's eyes-and-ears on the ground, disagreed with Golder, however, and that same month recommended to Hoover that the United States recognize Soviet Russia as the best way to help moderate the government, which might well even lead to its replacement.

Although the United States sat out the meetings in The Hague, Hoover wanted to maintain a dialogue with Soviet officials in the hope that relations could be improved. He tasked Golder and Goodrich with the job. Beginning in June, the two men initiated meetings with their Russian counterparts that Golder would report on in regular letters to Christian Herter, Hoover's assistant and future secretary of state. President Harding was supportive of this back-channel diplomacy and had met with Goodrich before his return to Russia that year to give him instructions on feeling out the Soviet leadership concerning matters of trade and political relations.

On the night of June 8, Golder and Goodrich were driven to the Kremlin for a conversation with the high-ranking communist official Karl Radek, resuming the talks Golder and Radek had started back in December. Radek was furious at Hoover's speech, denouncing the United States as Russia's "bitterest enemy" and insisting to his stunned guests that

---

* The Anglo-Soviet Trade Agreement of March 1921 did not establish official relations between Great Britain and Soviet Russia, although the Soviets considered the pact de facto recognition.

America would never be prosperous without trade with Russia. Concerns about the protection of private property were, in Radek's words, a mere "academic question." They were building up their army and cultivating the Japanese, and once those developments were completed, the Americans would change their tune and wish they had accepted the Russians' offer of good relations.

As these discussions were going on, the ARA was trying to decide just how much longer it should stay in Russia. Back in April, Hoover had made the decision to end the mission within six months, both out of a conviction the worst was over and a desire to be rid of the headache of trying to work in Soviet Russia. To get a sense of what conditions were like out in the countryside, which would be necessary for any final decision about pulling out of Russia, Haskell called the district supervisors to Moscow in mid-June for an update on the status in their territories. Golder remarked at the meeting that the men were exhausted after the corn campaign and many of them wanted to head home. Several of the supervisors expressed the view that the campaign had been an enormous success and that the next harvest would be adequate to see the Russians through without further American help. Indeed, Soviet officials at the Hague conference had stated that the famine was over and the country no longer required relief aid. The Soviet press began publishing optimistic reports that spring about the coming harvest in the autumn. Based on what he had heard, Haskell, over the objections of some of the district supervisors who remained convinced that the famine had not been defeated, decided that the ARA should end the mission as soon as possible. Haskell passed this conclusion on to Hoover and proposed stopping all relief work by the middle of October, with a final withdrawal by December. "The great famine in Russia," he informed his boss, "is over with the present harvest." Haskell had effectively endorsed Hoover's earlier decision to wrap up the operation before the end of the year.

Kelly had to wait for Bell to return to Ufa from the ARA conference in Moscow before he could leave. He was itching to start packing and be on his way. Finally, Bell arrived on June 24, and the two sat up talking late into the night about the future of the operation. Bell told him that

Haskell was fed up with the Soviets' obstructionism and was ready to end the job. The office put on a small farewell ceremony for Kelly on the 26th and presented him with a silver cup engraved with a Russian inscription of thanks. There were several speeches in his honor. Kelly noted in a letter how he couldn't help blushing, the first and only time he had done so while in Russia. Everyone accompanied him to the station, and he said his last goodbyes. Saying farewell to Boris Elperine was the hardest. Elperine was the only Russian friend he had made, and he was certain he'd never see him again. After the train pulled out, Bell cabled Haskell to praise Kelly's exceptional character and work effort. They all regretted his departure immensely.

Kelly had planned to leave Moscow on the morning of July 4, but a crash on the line meant he would be delayed. So he joined the other ARA men for a traditional American-style Independence Day celebration, held out in the park of an old noble country estate, complete with a picnic and a baseball game. Some English-speaking Russian girls were invited along—"to make it seem natural," as the sardonic Kelly put it. The game between the Blue House and The Outlaws attracted a curious crowd of locals, who watched from the edge of the field and nibbled on sunflower seeds. The game almost ended in a brawl after a questionable call by the umpire, but cooler heads managed to calm everyone down and keep play going. The Outlaws eked out a win in the end: final score thirteen to twelve. Kelly didn't stick around for the last out. As soon as he heard that the wreck had been cleared and traffic restored, he dropped his glove and headed for the station. "Out of Russia!" he wrote to Jane a few days later from Riga. "Very dirty, disreputable looking and all that, but all here!" From there it was on to London and then New York.

Other baseball games were played around Russia that day, including one between the ARA men of Kazan-Simbirsk and Samara. On the mound for the Kazan-Simbirsk club was J. Rives Childs.

Childs and six others left Kazan on the morning of July 2 aboard the beautifully appointed steamer *Pecherets* for Simbirsk, some 140 miles to the south, where they picked up three Americans and continued on toward Samara.

Aboard the *Pecherets*. Left to right: Childs, in white Russian-style tunic; Henry Wolfe; and Alvin Blomquist, attached to the ARA in Simbirsk

This was the most beautiful stretch of the river, and the men sat out all evening on the deck, watching the play of colors on the water and the rising moon. When they arrived in Samara on the 4th, they unloaded the Cadillac at the wharf and drove over to the ARA offices. After everyone had gotten acquainted and had a bite to eat, they piled into their automobiles and headed out to a vacant lot on the edge of the city to execute their duty as Americans, according to Childs's diary. Samara was defeated, twelve to seven, on the superior pitching of Childs, or so he at least liked to think. He took great pride in having "given proof of our patriotism" and in the fact that he and his fellow Americans had introduced the national pastime "upon the steppes of Russia and within the shadows of the Urals."

Childs was ebullient that summer. Everything seemed to be going his way. He was seeing ever more evidence of a growing friendly spirit toward America on the part of the Soviet government, and he was hopeful this would lead to an official diplomatic understanding between the

ARA men in Simbirsk playing a game of baseball behind their personnel house.
A Russian local watches the strange goings-on from behind the fence at left.

two countries. He had heard talk that once the relief effort was finished a new body—the American Reconstruction Administration—was to be created to assist in the economic revival of the country. The best of the ARA men would be chosen to remain in Russia, and he had it on good authority he would be among them. Even more encouraging, in late June, Hoover's assistant Christian Herter passed through Kazan with a delegation including Haskell, Goodrich, Brown, and Edgar Rickard, the ARA's general director in New York. Herter pulled Childs aside and told him that not only Hoover, but even President Harding himself had been reading Childs's reports, and both men found them most impressive. He also confided that Russia might well open up to the West, and when it did, Childs would be offered a trade-commissionership. Childs could hardly imagine better news.

And then there was Georgina. On June 7, Childs received Haskell's approval for his request of leave to travel to Petrograd. He wrote Georgina to let her know he was on his way and told her to prepare herself for a surprise. He decided to keep his plan to propose a secret. Though he had already told his mother, he now wrote her again, making her promise not to tell the townsfolk about Georgina's background. He assured her he was marrying Georgina *despite* her being an aristocrat. Neither of them was a snob, he told his mother, and should anyone ask about his views, she should repeat his words: "I am a SOCIALIST." If they didn't like it, "they may lump it."

His train arrived in Petrograd on the morning of June 13, and Childs went straight to the ARA office to see Georgina. Herschel Walker, her boss, gave her the afternoon off, and they walked to a local park, where Childs asked her to marry him. She was stunned. It was all so sudden, they hardly knew each other, she told him before insisting they ought to go speak to her mother first. Mathilde was even more stunned by Childs's proposal. He spent the entire evening trying to convince them of his sincerity and the correctness of his thinking. He left after dinner, saying he'd return the following day for Georgina's answer.

When he arrived the next morning, Mathilde was still as adamant as the day before that Childs was rushing things, but Georgina had come around. After a long argument, Mathilde finally gave in. Childs managed to assure her that once they were married and his work with the ARA was completed, he would see to it that she and Georgina got out of the country. No doubt this had some influence on Mathilde's decision.

After a visit to the Revolutionary Tribunal to arrange the paperwork, the two were married in a brief civil ceremony on June 16. That evening, Georgina and Mathilde went to see Childs off at the station. He promised to return in August, when they could have a proper wedding ceremony in St. Isaac's Cathedral. He was also going to do whatever was possible to have his new bride transferred to Kazan. On the train, he wrote a letter home: "Dearest Mother, I cannot write you how happy I am." It seems she kept the news from Childs's father, who didn't approve of the union; he learned about it only after coming across an announcement of the marriage in *The New York Times* on the 28th. After that, he never wrote to his son again.

15

"AHRA!"

T HE SUMMER OF 1922 saw the peak of what could be called ARA celebrityhood. According to one American at the time, the ARA had become "the most popular institution in all of Soviet Russia." Dr. Babayeff, a member of the ARA staff in Odessa, remarked how "the word 'American' has acquired a fascination and a weight in all classes of the population [. . .] The remembrance of the American Relief Administration will live for a long time in everybody's mind." The writer Korney Chukovsky recalled:

> Soon in the children's language there cropped up the new word "Americanitsa," meaning stuffed full. Children returning home

panted, "I am stuffed full by the Americans today." When they
had thoroughly mastered their lessons they would say, "We know
our lessons the American way." One lad marveling at the muscle
of his play fellow, described it as "a real American wrist" [. . .]
Is it any wonder that hungry fathers grew envious of quickly
fattening children? We were proletariats [sic] but our offspring
were becoming bourgeois, who would return and boast, "You
munch cucumbers and potatoes but to-day we had hot macaroni
and cocoa."

Russian children yelled out "Ahra!" when they saw the Americans in
the streets. Instead of pronouncing it as a three-letter acronym—A-R-A—
Russians shouted a two-syllable cheer, a subtle reworking of "Oohra!,"
the Russian for "Hurrah!" Neologisms sprang up signifying the cultural
influence of the Americans. The ARA men were called "Aravtsy" or "Ari-
itsy" or "Arovtsy." References to the ARA appeared in theatrical works and
literature by such writers as Vladimir Mayakovsky, Velimir Khlebnikov,
and Mikhail Bulgakov. A group of medical students at a Moscow benefit
concert staged a skit titled "ARA Gruel":

We sing to thee, oh ARA gruel,
Our joy, our life, our daily fuel.

The fascination with America reflected just how far the activities of
the ARA had spread throughout Soviet Russia. Beyond food relief, the
Americans were now active on a number of fronts.

The ARA was busy that July organizing a massive inoculation campaign against cholera, typhus, and smallpox, intended for all children
and adults receiving American food as well as anyone else who requested
an injection. The vaccines were being specially prepared by the Pasteur
Institute in Paris, and sent weekly to the ARA in Moscow by courier,
and from there out to the districts. By the middle of the summer, the
ARA had ordered seven million doses, half of which had already been
delivered.

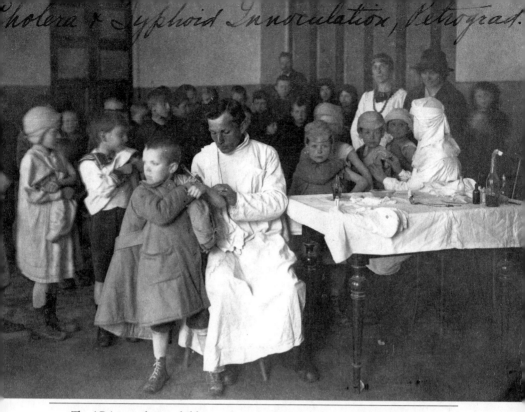

The ARA inoculating children in Petrograd against cholera and typhoid fever

The initial response to the campaign had been so overwhelmingly popular that the Americans decided to try to vaccinate as many people as they could get medicine for from Paris. To encourage local doctors to leave the cities for the famine districts, where the need for vaccination was particularly acute, the ARA offered food packages, an incentive that proved effective. When malaria broke out in the Volga region that summer, the ARA shipped 120,000 hypodermic doses of quinine, along with five hundred thousand quinine tablets and three hundred pounds of the compound in bulk form. By the end of the year, the ARA had imported ninety-one million units of diphtheria antitoxin, eight million of tetanus antitoxin, and four and a half million doses of smallpox vaccine.

The most basic medical supplies were still lacking. Dr. Mark D. Godfrey, stationed in Simbirsk, remarked how one town in the district had not seen medical gauze in four years. A doctor's assistant walked thirty miles to get a supply of gauze from Godfrey's dispensary. Before leaving, he told Godfrey that, taking no chances of being robbed of his treasure, he planned to avoid the main road and cut through the forests on the way home.

The ARA outfitted a train with medical supplies—twenty-two railcars crammed with all kinds of medicine, equipment, blankets, bedding, and disinfectants. "Sanitary Train No. 1" carried with it a full staff of nurses and orderlies under the direction of a medical doctor from the ARA as it traveled across Russia, stopping in Tula, Kursk, Orël, Ryazan, and other cities. Roughly five thousand hospitals and clinics received American medical supplies.

In Petrograd, the ARA purified the water system, using 250 tons of lime chloride, and inoculated seventy-five thousand persons against a cholera outbreak. In Samara, the ARA donated a Wallace and Tiernan Chlorine Control Apparatus, along with a six-month supply of chlorine gas, to provide pure water for two hundred thousand people. Chlorine gas was also provided to the town of Orenburg. The ARA's medical division was asked by a local board of health in the Mari Autonomous Region to help construct a new water-supply system. The Americans set up a dental clinic inside the ARA dispensary in Moscow, staffed by volunteers. Russians could bring in whatever gold they had—tsarist rubles, jewelry, medals—and the dentists would melt it down and use it to repair old crowns and fillings. The less fortunate received an older, more rudimentary procedure—teeth pulling, albeit for free. Across Russia, the ARA sterilized vermin-infested clothing, handed out soap, dispensed drugs to the needy, opened a venereal-disease clinic, funded public baths, and sponsored a sanatorium for tubercular children.

Mission creep became widespread. In May 1922, the doctors of a Kiev hospital wrote a letter to the ARA requesting that it overtake the administration of the facility, since they had lost all confidence in the Commissariat for Public Health. Such requests became increasingly common. Russians asked for help setting up and reorganizing children's shelters, hospitals, mobile clinics, ambulance services, and dormitories. The ARA also distributed well over half a million pounds of clothing and shoes donated by a number of American organizations.

Officials in Moscow suspected the Americans might well be dumping

Three children in Odessa with new shoes from America and
clothes made from grain sacks, courtesy of the ARA

cheap goods on them, confident that the Russians would be grateful for
anything, and so they carried out a series of tests on some sample clothing
items, submitting them to repeated washings to see how well they held up.
They were stunned by the results. With each successive washing, instead
of coming apart, the material actually became, in the words of their report, "even softer and whiter. After the fourth washing, the muslin was as
white as snow, moreover so soft, smooth, and thick that none of us could
find the slightest defect." One Soviet official had a suit made for himself
out of some American fabric. The cloth was so warm and well made that
he found he could sit comfortably in his office, even rolling up his sleeves,
while his co-workers sat shivering in their cheap suits and overcoats.

The ARA helped administer relief to Russia's scholars, academics,
students, and artists, including a gift of $1.1 million from the Rocke-
feller Foundation, directed to schoolteachers. Cut off from research in

Among the scholars and scientists who received support from the ARA was the
Nobel Prize–winning physiologist Ivan Pavlov. A group of men from the
ARA took this photograph during a visit to his Petrograd laboratory.

the West, Russian physicians begged the Americans for the latest specialist
literature, and so the ARA found a way to distribute subscriptions for
twenty-seven different medical journals to universities across Russia. The
ARA organized the shipment of twenty-eight thousand pounds of scientific literature to Russia donated by the Smithsonian Institution, the
American Society of Mechanical Engineers, the Carnegie Institute, and
other groups. In Moscow, a program was created to feed over four thousand students, some of them training to be medical doctors.

The ARA administered a gift from the YMCA's Students' Friendship
Fund that fed ten thousand students in Moscow, Petrograd, Kiev, Yekate-
rinoslav, and Odessa. In late June, three hundred ballet dancers came to
the ARA kitchen housed in Moscow's legendary former Hermitage Restaurant to collect food parcels paid for by the great prima ballerina Anna
Pavlova. When Morris Gest, the New York theatrical producer who would
bring Konstantin Stanislavsky and the Moscow Art Theater to America in
1923, wanted to send 250 food parcels to support the actors of Odessa, the

ARA made sure his wish was carried out. Over two hundred Americans trapped in Russia since the revolution with no way to leave were repatriated with the help of John Lehrs, chief of the ARA's liaison division.

In the middle of July, Hoover wrote an interim report on the mission for President Harding. So far, the ARA had distributed 637,000 tons of cereals for seed and food; 55,111 tons of evaporated and condensed milk; 25,000 tons of sugar and fats; 3,400 tons of cocoa; and 29,721 tons of medical supplies, clothing, and sundries. The ARA now employed about two hundred Americans in Russia and the United States, and eighty thousand Russians in charge of 15,700 kitchens feeding 8.5 million people. It was impossible to know just how many lives had been saved. The Americans' enormous efforts had generated much goodwill. "There is a deep feeling of gratitude in the minds of the Russian people and the results will, I am sure, be of lasting satisfaction to the American people."

Days later, *Izvestiia* stated that an even higher number of people were being fed by the ARA—nine million—and pointed out that it was preparing to add another 1.2 million in Ukraine. The same article contrasted these figures with those of the other foreign missions: the Quakers, twenty-eight thousand; the Italian and Swiss Red Cross, ninety-four thousand; the International Workers' Committee for Aid to the Starving in Russia (*Mezhrabpomgol*), one hundred thousand. The operation led by the Norwegian Fridtjof Nansen provided relief for just over one million people. By August, at the height of the mission, the number being fed daily by the ARA reached almost 10.5 million, a figure that amounted to about a quarter of all the men, women, and children in the famine zone. This was ten times what the ARA had originally envisioned feeding, and more than the combined population of sixteen U.S. states—Nevada, Wyoming, Delaware, Arizona, Vermont, New Mexico, Idaho, New Hampshire, Utah, Montana, Rhode Island, North Dakota, South Dakota, Maine, Oregon, Colorado—plus the District of Columbia.

DESPITE THE ARA'S enormous efforts on behalf of the people of Russia, the secret police refused to acknowledge the reality of its work and maintained that relief was really just a cover for the Americans' nefarious intentions, as an internal report from the summer of 1922 reveals:

> Observation of the work of the Russian division of the ARA over the past several months has allowed the GPU to establish the true character of its activities. From the materials now in the possession of the GPU it is clear that besides its help to the starving of Russia, the ARA is working toward different goals that have nothing to do with humanitarian ideals or philanthropy. The staff of the ARA, those having arrived in Russia from America, has been selected with the involvement of conservative, patriotic American clubs under the influence of Bakhmeteff, the former Russian consul in the United States [. . .] Almost all the men of the ARA are in the military. The majority of them are either officers in America's espionage and counterrevolutionary agencies or men who served in the White or other belligerent armies. Finally, some of these men worked with the ARA in Hungary when it overthrew Soviet power in that country. Colonel William Haskell, head of the ARA in Russia, was at one time the Supreme Commissar in the Caucasus. He was well known at the time as an irreconcilable foe of Soviet Russia, a figure who worked to turn Georgia, Azerbaijan, and Armenia against us. He spread all sorts of lies about the Bolsheviks in the press.

Plots were seen everywhere. Comrade Karklin, the plenipotentiary to the ARA in Samara and also an assistant to Stalin in his role as people's commissar for nationalities, had sent a secret letter in May to the Central Executive Committee warning that Jews in Ukraine had been using the ARA as cover to establish contact with bourgeois Jewish and Zionist organizations in the West. That American Jews had been responsible for sending many of the food parcels to family and friends in Ukraine fueled the authorities' suspicion. Viewed through the lens of anti-Semitism, connections between Western and Soviet Jews suggested some sort of international Jewish conspiracy. According to Karklin, something had to be done. In the eyes of the secret police, attempts by Soviet Jews to establish their own relief committees in cooperation with foreign organizations amounted to an act of sabotage, and all such committees were to be immediately uncovered and disbanded.

Most Russians, however, did not share the GPU's cynical distrust. Upon hearing that Hoover planned to send relief packages to Russian scientists and scholars, Maxim Gorky wrote to him on July 30:

> Your generous assistance is worthy of the greatest praise.
> Nevertheless permit me to express my feelings of gratitude
> to all citizens of the United States of America and complete
> satisfaction with the humanitarian work of the American Relief
> Administration, of which you are chairman. In the past year
> you have saved from death three and one-half million children,
> five and one-half million adults, fifteen thousand students, and
> have now added two hundred or more Russians of the learned
> professions. I am informed that this charity cost America fifty-
> nine million dollars, figures which are sufficiently eloquent.
> In all the history of human suffering I know of nothing more
> trying to the souls of men than the events through which the
> Russian people are passing, and in the history of practical
> humanitarianism I know of no accomplishment which in terms
> of magnitude and generosity can be compared to the relief that
> you have accomplished [. . .] The generosity of the American
> people resuscitates the dream of fraternity among people at a
> time when humanity greatly needs charity and compassion.
> Your help will be inscribed in history as a unique and gigantic
> accomplishment worthy of the greatest glory and will long
> remain in the memory of millions of Russian children whom you
> saved from death.

The same day Gorky wrote this letter, a special meeting of ARA officials, including Hoover, Rickard, Goodrich, Brown, and Herter, was held at the ARA headquarters in New York to discuss the future of the mission. Despite Haskell's recommendation from the previous month to withdraw from Russia by December, a recommendation that essentially supported Hoover's earlier wish back in April to leave Russia by October, a new plan emerged. The ARA, Hoover and the others now decided, would continue the mission through the harvest of 1923, albeit on a reduced level: adult feeding would be halted after September 1, and programs aimed at children would be limited to the areas of greatest need, especially the big cities, where the Soviet government had been encountering difficulties. The program of food-relief packages would also continue. Although the Soviets had stated that the famine was over and the situation now largely under control, the ARA was not entirely convinced. Reports on conditions in the country were often contradictory and difficult to verify, a problem that went on well into the autumn. Just ten days before the ARA meeting of July 30, Nansen had publicly warned that the last harvest had been a failure and the famine was far from over. The ARA office in Moscow had, in fact, been receiving reports from its men in the field confirming this assessment. Moreover, most Americans were of the opinion that the famine was still a grave danger, and Hoover was worried about a public-relations disaster if the ARA was seen as pulling out while Russia continued to starve. In the end, Haskell's recommendation following the June Moscow conference was overturned. The Russian job was not over.

MANY OF THE ARA men were glad to know the mission had been granted an extension, perhaps no one more so than Harold Fleming, who had been trying to get to Russia since he first learned of the Riga talks the previous August. Fleming was then a member of the ARA mission in Prague, compiling reports for the London office on the feeding operations and general economic conditions in Czechoslovakia. Fleming had been born in Salem, Massachusetts, in 1900, and attended Brown University. He participated in the Student Army Training Corps and was preparing to head off to fight in Europe just as the war ended, dashing his hopes of foreign adventure. He transferred to Harvard to study economics, received his

B.A. in 1920, and then went to work for the YMCA in London for the rest of the year. After that, having saved up a bit of money, he took off to travel across the continent, ended up in Prague, and signed on with the ARA.

Within days of writing Walter Lyman Brown at the ARA headquarters in London in August 1921 that he wished to apply for the Russian job, Fleming fell ill with a kidney ailment. His condition worsened over the coming weeks, and in October he had to be moved to the university hospital in Vienna. The doctors feared they'd have to operate. His family back in Massachusetts was notified. Fleming was still recuperating in the hospital as late as December. The ARA had decided to send him back to the States as soon as he was well enough, despite Fleming's insistence that he wanted to stay in Europe with the ARA once he was better. Captain Arthur C. Ringland, his boss in Prague, had nothing but praise for Fleming's work and character, but stood firm. Finally, by mid-December, Fleming was well enough to leave the hospital, but by that point he had nowhere to go: Ringland informed him the Prague mission was winding down its work and the Russian mission didn't need him. He visited Italy for a while, and then returned to the Austrian capital in the hope of being hired by the local ARA office there, only to be told there was no place for him. Dejected, Fleming returned to the States.

Nevertheless, he didn't give up. He kept writing to the ARA in New York, and to every letter he got the same negative response. Then, finally, his luck changed. On May 15, 1922, only four days after yet another rejection letter, London sent a cable to the New York office stating that they needed Fleming to start for Russia immediately to take up a position in the statistical-historical division. "Speed is of the essence," the telegram read. Fleming was overjoyed. His dream had at last come true.

Five days later, he sailed from New York for England on the SS *Ryndam* of the Holland America Line. He made his way to the ARA headquarters on Belgravia's Eaton Square to complete his paperwork: pay, $200 per month plus $6 per diem; he was officially warned that, should there be "any engagement on your part in any political or commercial activities of any nature what-soever," he would be terminated forthwith and forced to pay his own passage home. Before leaving for Russia on June 5,

Harold Fleming

Fleming found time to visit Selfridges department store for one last chance to stock up on provisions.

He arrived in Moscow on the 10th. The first order of business was getting inoculated against typhoid, paratyphoid, and cholera and then setting to work on drafting a large map showing the expanse of the ARA work operations across the country. He wrote his parents back in Beverly, Massachusetts, that he was feeling much better than before he left, largely since he was getting so much fresh air and exercise: fearful of contracting typhus in the crowded streetcars, he walked everywhere. "Moscow is a cross between modern London and ancient Pompeii," he wrote. There was life on the streets, goods in the stores, people crowding the restaurants and cafés, yet all was not as it first appeared. Passing by the large department store of the Moscow Soviet, opposite the Bolshoi Theater, he caught sight of a display window stacked with boxes of Kodak film. Surprised, he stopped and approached for a closer look: "Develop before February 1, 1918," the boxes read. His initial excitement at being in Russia wore off quickly. He found the city "the most defunct and moribund metropolis that I have ever cast eyes upon." Work was fine, but his evenings were unbearable. He had nothing to read and the theaters bored him, and so he spent his free hours after work alone, strolling through the parks, looking longingly at the pretty Russian women.

And then everything changed. Her name was Paulina Zhirnova. They met toward the end of July; she was his Russian-language instructor. "Dear Folks," he wrote, suddenly an altogether different man. "Just to let you know first off that I am having the time of my life; feel happy as the day is long; in the best of health and seem to be always feeling ready to start something." He informed them, "I have found a very pretty dictionary who can't speak anything but Russian and, I think, likes me as much as I like her, which is quite a bit I can tell you." He saw to it she was given regular food packages from the remittance program.

Harold and Paulina were soon inseparable; they spent every free moment together. On the weekends, they visited the many parks in and around Moscow to picnic, swim, and go for boat rides. Nights were spent at parties with "former countesses or princesses or something of the sort," he wrote. They stayed up until the early hours of the morning, talking and drinking tea, or going to the ballet and then gathering with friends at someone's apartment and getting drunk. Fleming found the late nights exhausting: "These Russkies have got me by the tail on being night-hawks." He was also exploring his love of photography, and bought himself two new cameras—a VPK, Vest Pocket Autographic Kodak, hugely popular with soldiers during the war, and a German Atom camera with a Carl Zeiss lens. He was fast becoming fond of Moscow, he told his parents in early August, and was going to be heartbroken when it was time to leave.

There was one aspect to life in Moscow he didn't care for: Russian work habits. Soon after arriving, he hired a draftsman and told him he was expected to show up every day for work promptly at 9:00 a.m. "Ah, yes," the man replied, "it is the capitalist method of exploiting us." Not surprisingly, he didn't work out; a few weeks later, Fleming had to fire him. "I am going to install new methods of checking up on my typists now," he told his parents. "Of all the slow, dawdling, poking, meandering, mooning crews they are the worst. Somebody comes to the door, and every machine stops; you start to give one of them a mild hauling over the coals, or describe some new work you want her to do, and every machine in the whole outfit stops automatically [. . .] They seem to think the office is family and office hours a picnic." It didn't take him long, however, to put together a small team of two draftsmen and four typists "who tremble at my slightest whisper." Now he could get things done. His personal and professional lives were in harmony. "I should be content to stay here in Russia for a couple of years, I believe [. . .] Everything is going splendidly, and I've never had a better time in my life."

16

A WEDDING
IN ST. ISAAC'S

C HILDS WAS NOT BACK IN KAZAN LONG before he left again on an inspection tour of two new territories—the Votyak Autonomous Region* and the province of Perm—that expanded the Kazan district to approximately four and a half million people and ninety thousand square miles. Together with Simson and Anatoly, their chauffeur, he set off in the Cadillac on the afternoon of July 19. "Like untraveled roads in the west of America, the one over which we passed was sometimes hardly distinguishable so thick was it overgrown with grass and

---

* Now the Udmurt Republic.

weeds," he noted in his diary. "More frequently the line of the telegraph poles proved a better guide than the marks left by previous travelers."

Two days later, they stopped in the village of Karakulino, on the Kama River in Perm Province. Childs met with a young man, apparently the secretary of the county soviet, and asked him about the food situation and how well the relief operation was being carried out. He wanted to know whether the peasants knew exactly who was helping them and where all the food had been coming from. But the official informed Childs that it didn't really matter whether or not they told the peasants the food had come from America, because they simply had no concept of America or any other place outside their narrow little world. His words confirmed what Childs himself had come to believe:

> I am sure from my contact with the Russian peasants that I have been given an understanding of the darkness of mind of the average Russian, but I doubt exceedingly if it is possible for one who had never been in Russia to measure fully the profundity of this darkness. One sometimes feels after conversation with them that they are little better than animals, and yet again they give manifestations of so much human feeling that one is inevitably led to the conclusion that given only the chance which human beings merit and which has been denied the Russians for so long, they will prove themselves.

A backhanded compliment if ever there was one.

Most Soviet officials were convinced the peasants knew where the relief was coming from and who had saved them, a fact that made them anxious that the peasants might start to think too highly of their distant benefactors. In a statement that had obviously been put together by the authorities, the villagers of Bolshaya Glushitsa in Samara Province sent a letter that summer to the Provincial Central Executive Committee: "Our Soviet rulers gave us winter and spring seed, and our national government called on the Americans for help. We are grateful to our dear leaders for the invitation they made and promise that here, on our Soviet land, we shall in the future get by without the help of the foreign bourgeoisie and we ask that you convey this message to Comrade Lenin."

Soviet authorities sent large numbers of factory workers who belonged to the Communist Party out into the countryside, wherever the ARA was active, both to assess the political mood of the peasants and to counteract any signs of gratitude toward the Americans. There was a feeling that the Americans weren't content just to feed the hungry, but insisted on brainwashing them, too. "Advertising, so natural an element of the American character, does not surprise me," wrote a Soviet official in the Tatar Republic to Karl Lander, "but advertising for the sake of advertising, that's something altogether different. I personally am sick to death of their story that the aid is a gift of the American people and that first among all others due thanks for this aid is Mr. Hoover. Not for no reason did they bring 3,000 portraits of Mr. Hoover here from Moscow to be handed out. It's obvious they made a conscious decision to bring these instead of bringing full rations, but they're mistaken in thinking that the starving children will somehow get full just by looking at portraits, even if they are of Mr. Hoover."

From Karakulino Childs motored down the Kama River to Sarapul. The people here, he soon learned, were in "a very desperate plight." Of the town's 236,000 inhabitants, nearly 75,000 were receiving some kind of aid, either from the ARA or, to a lesser extent, from the Soviet government. But this still wasn't nearly enough: more than 45,000 children were experiencing acute need for which no aid was available. These unfortunate ones were left to starve and die. The local Russian ARA committee chairman, who was also the chairman of the district soviet, made a special plea to Childs that at least some of Sarapul's adults be fed through the autumn. Childs heard the same thing in other places on his trip, and each time he had to give the people the same answer: the ARA was ending adult feeding after August 31. To Childs's regret, "I could promise him nothing."

From Sarapul they traveled overland to the east, leaving behind the open expanses near the river for the foothills of the Ural Mountains. The

villages here reminded him of towns he'd seen in the American Rock-
ies, and the majesty of the vast stretches of virgin pine and fir lifted his
spirits. On July 23, he reached the city of Perm. After a meeting with officials and ARA representatives, Childs and Simson enjoyed a fine dinner
at one of the city's restaurants: soup, veal, white and black bread, a bottle
of wine, and ice cream. The bill came to 18 million rubles, a little less
than $5 at the time. After dinner, they went for a stroll, ending up in a
small park where a band was performing classical music. This pleased the
snobbish Childs, who found it "far better music" than you'd likely hear
in a similar American town, "where some clangy ragtime, if such might
be called music, was being beaten out upon the helpless winds."

The tour convinced Childs that, although the famine had been brought
under control in the Tatar Republic, conditions in the two newly acquired
territories were horrific, far worse than what he had ever seen before in
the Tatar lands. There simply wasn't enough aid to go around. Much of the
seed intended for planting had, from what they could tell, been eaten
instead, which did not bode well for the coming winter. Things were
going to get much worse before they got better. Despite this gloomy
picture, Childs wrote to his mother from the steamer *Pecherets* on the
29th that he so loved these tours, which, despite the physical discomfort,
were always "fascinating" and loaded with "revelations." They fulfilled his
wanderlust. "I have become such a nomad and gypsy in fact that I do not
know how I shall ever bring myself to settle in one place." And for nearly
the rest of his long life, he never did.

Childs was in Kazan just long enough to write up a report of his tour
and have his clothes washed before he was on his way to Georgina in
Petrograd. He sent her a cable from Moscow on the night of August 10,
telling her to expect him at the station the next morning at eleven o'clock.
"Dearest love and kisses Rives." On the train that night, he wrote to his
mother, still defending his decision. For four years, Georgina and her
mother had been experiencing "a pleasant little hell on earth," he told
her, and the depth of his fiancée's feelings for him, and the courageous
nature of her character, could be judged by the risk she was taking in not

turning her back on their relationship. The threat of an "inquisition" by the GPU was quite real given her desire to marry him, and worse punishments could not be ruled out.

Georgina was waiting at the station with a cousin when Childs arrived. From there they went to fetch Mathilde, and then off to dine at Donon, once one of the most fashionable restaurants in the imperial capital, which had reopened during the NEP years. Last-minute arrangements were discussed in advance of the ceremony, planned for Sunday. Childs could hardly contain himself, he was so excited.

He arrived at the imposing, golden-domed St. Isaac's Cathedral early Sunday afternoon, August 13, wearing a cutaway ordered from London especially for the occasion. The church choir sang a hymn as Georgina appeared, dressed in blue silk. With her were her two witnesses—a cousin on her father's side by the name of Klokatcheff and a Mr. Duchesne, formerly an official in the Imperial Ministry of Finance. Childs was served by Wahren, his superior from Kazan, and Major Philip H. Matthews, head of the ARA transport division. The service was brief, and by three o'clock it was over. Georgina's wedding ring was a large diamond solitaire, a gift from her mother.

The party piled into three automobiles and drove off to the ARA house for a reception. Childs found himself particularly taken with his new mother-in-law's friends, a few charming elderly ladies "who seemed to have stepped out of the pages of some romance of a lost age." He sat all evening entranced by their stories of old St. Petersburg. At the table next to Wahren sat a young Princess Chegodaeva, a member of an ancient Russian noble clan, the descendants, according to a fanciful legend, of Genghis Khan. Chegodaeva worked for the ARA in Moscow, where she had caught Wahren's eye. A romance quickly followed, and he had invited her along to Petrograd to be his date. Seeing the happy face of his colleague Childs, Wahren began making his own plans to marry.

The next day, the newlyweds boarded a train for Moscow. Childs and Georgina moved into new rooms in the ARA house in Kazan, sharing part of a floor with Wahren and Princess Chegodaeva. Their first weeks together were blissful. Georgina played the piano, read, and in the morn-

ings went to sit for Fechin, whom Childs had commissioned to paint his
bride's portrait. On his days off, they rode out to a dacha overlooking the
Volga River at Shelengar that the ARA had rented for the summer, or
paid a call to the Fechins' home, located in a tranquil pine grove outside
the city. "I continue to love Rives more and more (if that is possible),"
Georgina wrote to Childs's mother. "He is so sweet, so attentive and so
tender in his manners towards me." In the evening, Georgina typed the
manuscript of the book Childs had been writing, called *Red Days in Russia*. Childs had great hopes for it. The journalist Arthur Ruhl had read
it and offered high praise, telling him it really was just the sort of book
about Russia that was needed at the time. His plan was to send it off to
Macmillan Publishers in the United States, since they had expressed interest in his query letter. He confessed he now felt he truly was "on the
road to literary success."

IN LATE SEPTEMBER, Wahren was transferred to Moscow and he, together with Chegodaeva, now his fiancée, left Kazan. Wahren had been
one of the best friends Childs had ever had, and he was sorry to see him
go, even if it meant that he would now be the new district supervisor. From
what he could tell, it appeared that the mission would last another eight
months or so, which was fine with him, since he was having such a pleasant time in Russia. He and Georgina began making plans for the future,
including a trip to Turkestan in the spring. Childs took Georgina with
him on a short inspection tour in October. He was impressed by her
enthusiasm and curiosity, and how she attended every meeting, stay-
ing up to listen to the end no matter how late they dragged on. Based on
what he was seeing in their district, Childs was confident they had turned
the corner on the famine and the worst was now behind them. Few of his
American colleagues shared his optimism, but he didn't care. He was in
awe of the resiliency of the Russians and had complete faith in them. "One
must have great praise for the extraordinary recuperative powers of the Russian peasant," he informed his mother. "Nothing seems to be able to daunt
him [. . .] In the moment of greatest trial you will hear the Russian exclaim

Fechin's portrait of Georgina

in his characteristic expression: 'Nitchevo' or 'it doesn't matter.'"

He envisioned great things for Russia. "If nothing interferes with the program of practical socialism which Russia is today working out I believe her recovery will be much more accelerated than that of many other European nations." He instructed his mother to read H. G. Wells's *New Worlds for Old*, his popular 1908 defense of socialism, insisting that nothing would make clearer to her the desirability of a socialist program and the dangers of excessive individualism and private ownership of property. Childs noted that the average American had no idea what socialism really was, since he'd been duped into misunderstanding by mass "hysteria." For him, socialism simply meant "anything that promotes the general welfare, that contributes to the greater good of the greatest number." President Lincoln had been a socialist, in his estimation, in that he fought for a government of, for, and by the people, not a particular class. For now, however, Childs sadly concluded, men were nothing but "slaves under the yoke of capital."

On October 28, as a heavy snow fell in Kazan, Fechin delivered his portrait of Georgina. Childs extolled it and considered this work superior to his own portrait by the artist. Childs was in love. He felt blessed. "She is the sweetest wife a man ever had," he told his mother.

17

UNITED NATIONS

AN EXHAUSTED GOLDER was granted leave in October and left Russia by way of Riga for Paris and then London. He had spent part of August and September on the road on yet another investigation tour. Conditions on the railroads had improved, yet challenges remained. Before he left Moscow on that tour with Harold Fisher, official historian of the ARA's Russian mission, the GPU warned them to be on guard against thieves on the line. Several ARA men had been robbed down to their underwear during the night, so Golder and Fisher made sure to barricade their door and block the window before bunking down. They slept with their clothes safely tucked under their pillows.

They passed through Bryansk on the way to Ukraine. At one stop, they managed to buy a tough roast chicken for 3.5 million rubles. Golder's contacts in Kiev told him the food situation had improved since his last visit and everyone was grateful for American relief, which had also had a secondary effect of forcing the speculators to lower their prices. Next, they headed south to Odessa. The city lay in ruins and lacked any signs of the kind of renewal they had seen in Kiev. Broken-down cars and engines clogged the railroad tracks, every last tree in the city had been chopped down, and once-beautiful homes had been stripped bare for firewood. The two men joined the crowd of spectators for a military parade on September 1. As they watched, one of the "flying machines" fell from the sky and crashed, killing a number of people on the ground, including several children. Later that day, Colonel William R. Grove took them on an inspection tour. He informed them that banditry was rampant in the area, although the outlaws never stole from the ARA—they preferred to kill communists and Jews instead.

Golder had had a change of heart about the Soviet government since the spring. No longer the "white slaver," as he had written in April, the Bolsheviks now seemed willing to work honestly with the United States for improved relations. From Paris in mid-October, Golder wrote a long letter to Herter, insisting that the best thing for Russia and the world as a whole would be for the United States to establish official relations. He admitted this would strengthen the communists, but only for a time, since by "coming in official contact with the rest of the world, the Bolsheviks will ipso facto become respectable and respectability will kill them." By treating them "as human beings," the Americans stood a good chance of influencing the Bolsheviks and bringing about change to the Soviet state. Regardless what the right might say back in the States, Golder went on, "we have got to do it for the sake of bleeding, suffering Russia. We can bury our pride and eat our words, if necessary, but we must save Russia and she is worth saving." The only other option was to stand by and wait, which would mean the death of millions more Russians.

Herter was unconvinced by Golder's argument. He remained of the opinion that only loans and investment from the West, not diplomatic recognition, might induce the Soviets to change their politics, and these

would not be forthcoming as long as the government there refused to recognize the foreign debts of the previous regime or to guarantee private-
property rights. A copy of Golder's letter was forwarded to both Hoover
and Secretary of State Hughes, and they concurred with Herter.

This volte-face on the part of Golder is surprising. None of the Americans with the ARA knew Russia better than he did, and he, of all people,
must have known that trading ambassadors would not solve the deep di-
visions separating the two countries, nor would it overcome the profound
suspicion toward the United States so prevalent not only within the
Soviet elite, but throughout the entire state machine.

Golder had apparently forgotten the advice of his friend Sergei Oldenbourg. Earlier that summer, he'd asked Oldenbourg, an eminent scholar
of ancient India and minister of education in the Provisional Government,
whether it might not be good for the United States to recognize Soviet
Russia, since this would allow Western capital to flow in and so revive
the economy. Oldenbourg, wiser about the reality in his country than
Golder, told him no, outside help was not the answer to their troubles.
"Our salvation," he said, "can not come from without but must come from
within." Greater American involvement would merely provoke the anger
of the communists and trigger a backlash, igniting a renewed wave of
extremism like the one they had witnessed before NEP. Russians had to
solve their own problems, and he was certain they would. "All the suffering, all the misery we have endured and are enduring is teaching us Russians to think clearly and that is a great step in the line of progress." The
old scholar was correct about the dangers of American involvement, but
tragically mistaken in the notion that the Russians' suffering had taught
them to think clearly, as the bloody horrors of the 1930s would show.

Golder's thinking had been influenced by his now frequent meetings
with Karl Radek—no longer the arch-critic of the Americans—with whom
he had become "quite chummy," as Golder described it, over dinners at
the Pink House. He began supplying Radek with books on American politics and culture and had convinced himself that he had converted the old
communist to more moderate beliefs. His relationship with Radek—and
comments by a few highly placed officials, such as Alexei Rykov, Politburo

member and chairman of the Supreme Soviet of the National Economy, about the benefits of using American capital for the development of key regions of the country—fooled Golder into believing the Soviet government had turned its back on communism for good.

But it wasn't just his reading of the political situation that had changed Golder's thinking. Golder ached over the suffering of his native land. It was hard for him to witness, and he so wanted to see its recovery. On November 5, the day before beginning his journey back to Russia from London, he wrote to a colleague at Stanford that he was as enthusiastic about returning "as I would be going to hell." Russia's problems were so painful it made him weep. "Life here is hard and discouraging and so hopeless," he wrote two weeks later, now back in Moscow. "The nearer we came to Russia the more I felt the gloom settling on me. Misery, depression, oppression, demoralization everywhere." He tried to tamp down the compassionate fellow man in him in favor of the detached intellectual: "But it is all interesting from the point of view of social science. It is a kind of vivisection experiment."

EARLY AUTUMN HAD been a time of good feeling among the ARA bosses in Moscow and their Soviet counterparts. On September 8, *Pravda* published an interview with Haskell in which he praised the Soviet government for its well-intentioned cooperation, singling out "the personal integrity and decency of the Russian citizenry." Four days later, the Soviet government created the Central Commission for the Struggle Against the Consequences of the Famine—known by the acronym *Posledgol*— meant to mark a new, post-famine phase in its efforts to help people suffering the effects of the disaster. On September 16, *Izvestiia* proclaimed, "The backbone of the famine has been broken." Also that month, the decisions made at the July 30 meeting of ARA heads in New York, to end adult feeding and to focus on the neediest children, were also put into effect. The plan for the ARA now envisioned a smaller operation through the winter, with a pull-out before the harvest of 1923.

If the view from Moscow was one of success, things looked different out in the famine zone. From Pugachëv County came reports of crop failure. The local Soviet representative to the ARA told Cyril Quinn that same month that the situation was worse than the previous year, and he pleaded with him not to reduce operations. One relief worker had used the word "holocaust" to describe what he'd seen in Pugachëv. The Soviet leadership, however, didn't care to hear such negative assessments. Moscow wanted the famine to be over, and that was the message it chose to broadcast.

The government held a banquet, complete with performances by dancers from the Bolshoi Theater and a concert by the Stradivarius Quartet, to mark the one-year anniversary of the ARA's efforts in Russia. Lander, Eiduk's successor as Soviet plenipotentiary to the ARA, stood up during the meal to thank the ARA for saving millions of lives and acknowledged the "honest and energetic" work of the Americans—about fifty of whom were there that night—on behalf of the starving masses. At this, Haskell rose to extol the support for their mission by the Soviet authorities, especially two of those seated at the table that night—Lev Kamenev, who had always done everything possible to assist Haskell in his efforts, and "Comrade Dzerzhinsky, to whom millions owed their lives," for his resolute effort in solving the railroad crisis that spring. And then he went a step further, expressing his hope that the experience of the past year would lead to normal relations between the two countries, for the Russians had many friends in America, including Mr. Hoover, and their two peoples had so much in common: "These are the only two nations in the world that ought to be united," *Izvestiia* reported, "and he sees nothing that could keep this from happening." Raising his glass, Haskell stated, to the great delight of his hosts, "No other nation in the world has greater respect and love for the Russians than we Americans." The warm atmosphere lasted until Haskell and the final guests had finished their coffee, around five o'clock in the morning. Everyone, it seems, went home happy.

No sooner had Lander's cordial words left his mouth than the Soviet government sought to tighten the screws on the ARA. On October 1, Lander sent Haskell a letter outlining a new set of rules for the various foreign aid missions. All expenses associated with the rendering of relief would henceforth be shared by the foreign agencies, not just the Soviet government; only in extreme situations would the foreign missions be permitted to open kitchens where Soviet feeding stations were already in operation; the distribution of all clothing and aid to students, teachers, and academics was to be entrusted to the Soviet government, under the guidance of *Posledgol*. Finally, all customs and transportation costs incurred for individual food parcels were to be borne by the recipients themselves, not the Soviet government.

Haskell was furious. He quite rightly saw the new terms as contraventions of the Riga Agreement, and an attempt to hamper the efforts of the ARA to such an extent that their work would become impossible. He fired back a reply, demanding answers to two questions: Did the government want to discontinue the food-remittance program in its current form? Did the government no longer intend to respect the Riga accord as drafted and agreed to? If, Haskell threatened, the ARA was no longer needed, then he would immediately order operations halted, and the Americans would pack up and go home as soon as possible. He gave Lander until noon of October 4 to reply. Haskell informed the London office of Lander's letter, describing the changes as "an effort on the part of the Communist Party to thoroughly Nansenize [i.e., neuter] the A.R.A." He added that any backsliding on the Riga treaty would be "a fatal mistake."

Lander backed down. He showed up at Haskell's office, humble and apologetic, and insisted that this entire business had been nothing but a misunderstanding. The letter had been drafted in haste, "after office hours," and none of the provisions applied to the ARA. The Riga Agreement retained its full authority as before, Lander assured Haskell, and no changes to it would even be considered without mutual agreement between the ARA and the Soviet government.

Haskell naïvely believed the ARA had won and the matter was settled, but the Soviets didn't back down. Before the month was out, the government went back on its promise to Haskell and refused to exempt the ARA from the new restrictions proposed in Lander's letter. On October 31, an order went out imposing new regulations on all foreign kitchens, with the intent of closing as many of them as possible. All foreign relief supplies were ordered to be handed over to Soviet institutions for delivery to the needy. Again, Haskell complained to Lander. This time, he was ignored.

As the Soviet government intensified its campaign against foreign relief, the people suffered. News that the ARA was being pushed out of Russia was met with anguish. That month, a Russian ARA inspector by the name of Chervyakov wrote about a visit to the Bashkir canton of Burzyan-Tangaurovsky: "With the liquidation of the ARA's operations happening at every turn, one can see scenes of the poor peasants' despair in every village upon learning that the kitchens are being closed [. . .] As soon as the news is announced, they begin to weep and pray for more help."

18

ORENBURG

ON THE AFTERNOON OF SEPTEMBER 10, Harold Fleming boarded a train in Moscow for Orenburg. He was carrying with him a large supply of film, reams of crop statistics, and a railway map ten feet long and two feet wide that recorded all the stops along the way, made especially for him by his new draftsman. He was being sent out to review the files of the Orenburg office as it prepared to wind down operations. Fleming was excited to go: this would be his first visit to Asia. His only concern was Paulina, who had been ill with a fever. Her condition had become so severe the previous week that Fleming had had to borrow Haskell's automobile to take her to the hospital. He hoped she'd be all right without him.

One of the
countless orphans
abandoned to fate

Fleming traveled in comfort, in a clean and spacious wagon-lit, while outside, armies of orphans clung to the buffers and perched on the roofs, despite the best efforts of the guards to pull them off.

Unlike the American express trains Fleming was used to, they moved along at a leisurely pace; he felt as if he were part of some "caravan." They passed through Penza Province, where the stations were full of peasants selling milk, apples, and watermelon, and Syzran on the Volga, one of the hardest-hit areas of the famine, its station still overrun with refugees. He changed trains in Samara, where a group of Russians joined him in his compartment. When they learned he was with the ARA, they began rhapsodizing about American condensed milk. He entertained them with stories of the wonders of the New York City subway. The farther east they went, the worse became the evidence of the famine. After three and a half days, Fleming finally reached Orenburg, over nine hundred miles southeast of Moscow, in the shadow of the Ural Mountains, near the border with modern-day Kazakhstan. Crowds of bedraggled refugees filled the station. It was an awful sight. To Fleming, it looked as if he'd ended up in some bleak frontier town out of the Wild West; images from Mark Twain's *Roughing It* came to mind. His heart sank. He couldn't imagine a more depressing place.

Situated on a slight rise over the surrounding steppe on the Ural River, Orenburg was a city of some 150,000. The ARA began feeding fifty thousand children in mid-November 1921, and then soon added more and more to the rolls as the true extent of the need became clear. For the Americans, Orenburg was a hardship post, a fact even the Soviet authorities admitted. Four months after setting up operations, the ARA members were still living in terrible conditions. In February, the local plenipotentiary wrote a letter to Eiduk in support of the Americans' complaints about their arrangements. Thirteen men had been housed in quarters meant to hold no more than three. One of them had been sleeping in a corridor for lack of space; another bunked down on a couch and had to use his coat as a blanket. A couple of the men had to arrange several chairs to create makeshift beds. The office was no better, with three men to a desk. For a long time, there was no typewriter, and just getting paper and pencils proved a challenge. The ARA men, the official wrote, had been put through "a series of the most unimaginable trials."

The first thing every new arrival did was to obtain a gun permit. No one went out at night unarmed. Whatever the temperature, the local ARA man never failed to carry a revolver in his hand as he made his way through the dark streets, frostbite be damned. Twice, burglars robbed the personnel house, and there were many occasions when the men awoke to the sound of intruders and had to chase them off, guns drawn. One American remarked how the sound of gunfire in the streets was never-ending.

The Ural River marked the division between Europe and Asia, and the Americans became acutely aware of just how far they were from head-quarters back in Moscow. Right about the time the ARA showed up, the post-and-telegraph office burned to the ground, further isolating the men. Even after the office had been rebuilt, it took on average two weeks for a telegram from the capital to reach Orenburg. During the winter, snows blocked the rail line for weeks at a time. There was a tale of one train from Moscow that stalled on the line and became stuck in the snow; all the passengers froze to death. During their first winter there, when the line was blocked for six long weeks, the ARA men would scan the horizon with their field glasses, hoping to catch sight of a train carrying one of their couriers with food, supplies, and news of the outside world.

The Russian couriers were the real unsung heroes of the ARA relief mission. No one associated with the operation exposed himself to greater danger. During the winter of 1921–22, for every two couriers shuttling across Russia, one was in the hospital with typhus. The couriers practi-cally lived on the trains, which were home not only to beggars, thieves, and bandits, but also to lice. Rubbing up against the vermin-infested pas-sengers made infection almost a certainty, and avoiding physical contact was impossible. Indeed, so overcrowded were the trains and platforms that the ARA men developed a technique they called the "flying wedge," a sort of blocking formation to create a gap in the human mass so the courier could squeeze through and onto the train. Upon arrival, every cou-rier had to be vigorously brushed with a whisk broom to remove as many of the lice as possible before he was admitted into the ARA office with the mail pouch. And it wasn't just the pouch he was responsible for. The couri-ers brought everything the ARA needed, from commissary supplies, office equipment, and medicine to alcohol, newspapers, and money. At times, couriers handled as many as twenty large crates. They worked in relays, handing their load off to the next courier, who would take it farther down the line. The distances were enormous, and the time spent on the road was long: the four hundred miles between Petrograd and Moscow took four days to travel; the six hundred between Moscow and Tsaritsyn, eight days. Remarkably, none of the ARA money ever went missing, and only one box of personal items was lost. The Russian couriers embodied honesty, commitment, and determination. Some couriers, trapped on snowbound trains for days on end, sold their own underwear for money to buy food instead of laying a finger on their entrusted cargo. Without their efforts, the ARA mission to Russia would have been impossible.

The heavy snow that made contact with Moscow difficult did have its advantages: it covered up the dead animals and human excreta that littered the Orenburg streets. With spring, the snow and ice melted to reveal stomach-turning sights and smells and the threat of disease. More than forty dead bodies were found rotting along the riverbanks in Orenburg. Sanitation was an enormous problem. Only one street was paved; the water supply was susceptible to contamination; garbage cans were not yet invented. Orenburg had just two public bathhouses, and most people couldn't afford to visit them. About 95 percent of the city's residents were infested with lice.

In the summer of 1922, the ARA organized a thousand stranded refugees into a work brigade and sent them out to clean the filth. Once this had been finished, the brigade fortified the banks of the river in advance of the next spring's runoff, repaired several damaged streets, and planted a forty-acre vegetable garden. The ARA installed a permanent filtration system for the city's water supply and convinced the municipal authorities to clean the town's sewage pipes.

Life for the Americans in Orenburg had been particularly difficult. Allen T. Burns, a social worker and reformer, visited on a fact-finding mission in the autumn of 1922 and was shocked by what he saw:

> The boys of the A.R.A. were in a really hyper nervous condition from hard work and memories of the horrors that they worked night and day to alleviate last winter [. . .] It was not in the least necessary for these American boys to tell me what they had been through: I read it in their eyes before they had spoken a word. That same blank, mirthless smile, in which the eyes took no part, that I found among prisoners of war after five years of prison hell, typhus, cholera, smallpox, starvation, and freezing.

He asked one of the men how he and the others could show "such signs of suffering," given that they had plenty of food, clothing, and a warm place to sleep. "How in the hell can a real man eat or sleep in comfort when he knows that in the morning the first thing that will greet his eyes when he looks out the window will be corpses along the street?" the man replied. "Corpses of people that have died during the night from starvation and freezing. And that out in some of the villages people were crazed from hunger until they were eating corpses." The only well-fed creatures in Orenburg, he informed Burns, were the dogs feeding on the unburied dead in the cemetery.

Fleming concurred with the bleak assessment of the place, but it didn't affect his mood. He was working hard at the office, writing a large report on the history of ARA operations in the region, gathering as much statistical information as possible, and going through all the files to determine what should be saved and brought back and what could be destroyed. He wrote his parents on September 21 to say that he'd been "enjoying every moment" since his arrival and had "never felt better in my life." Not only was he too busy to be homesick, he'd yet to visit Asia: "Have looked across the river to Asia but not crossed yet. What's the use?"

On the 23rd, Fleming departed Orenburg for Samara, where he arrived the following day. The drive from the station to the ARA personnel house in one of the mission's Cadillacs proved memorable:

> The driver of this car had a very strange and alarming manner
> of driving us, though our hosts seemed to pay no attention to
> his vagaries. First he drove on one side of the street; then on
> the other; he then concentrated his attention on the telephone
> pole, and running the car full force at it, changed his mind at
> the last moment and dodged it by a quarter of an inch. Then he
> ran up on the sidewalk with two wheels and then off again, just
> flicking a stone post set in the curb with the mudguard, but not
> touching it; he then proceeded to the middle of the street again,
> and decided to stop; changed his mind at the last moment again,

eased the car over a rolling bump, and repeated the reel. Once
or twice he drew up beside a large building and all but stopped;
I thought we had arrived, but we had not and kept going. For
variety and curiosity it certainly was a star performance.

During his brief stay in Samara, Fleming learned that their chauffeur,
like most other experienced drivers, had memorized every last pothole, dip,
crater, and bump and developed this bizarre manner of "zigging and zag-
ging," as Fleming put it, to avoid them all. "It turned out that all the
chauffeurs in all the districts have their little song and dance memorized
for every street in town. It is a remarkable example of adaptation." Aware
of this curious fact, the local governments insisted there was no reason
to waste limited money on fixing the streets, since everyone had learned
what to avoid.

From Samara, Fleming headed to Ufa, stopping the first night at the
station in Buguruslan. He asked a peasant there about conditions and how
the next harvest was looking, to which the man replied that, although he
likely had enough food to last perhaps to February, after that the famine
was certain to hit again and was bound to be worse than the previous year.
When asked what the peasants thought of the ARA, the man had one
word: grateful. He hoped the ARA would not leave and would be around
to help come spring, when the need would again be immense.

Fleming spent just enough time in Ufa to go over the office's files
and then had to get back on the road. By now, he longed to return to
Moscow and Paulina. His father, an agent for the New York Life Insurance
Company in Salem, wrote to Harold at the time that they'd been receiving his letters and had even taken them over to share with their friends
one night at the local grange. He was proud of Harold and his work.
"It should improve the relations between Russia and the United States
and it demonstrates the brotherhood of nations in a magnificent way.
Russia has been the ancient friend of the United States as far back as the
Revolutionary War and it is fitting that our country should be able and
willing to do this large service at this crucial time." He ended by expressing his concerns for Paulina's health and hope that she was feeling better.

Fleming left Ufa and traveled back to Samara, where he embarked on a crowded boat for Simbirsk. Once in Simbirsk he repeated the work he had done in Ufa and also found time to visit the local cinema for a showing of D. W. Griffith's 1916 film *Intolerance*, the copy so old and so often repaired that entire scenes of the movie were missing. After one more stop, in Kazan, Fleming was finally on a train back to Moscow, sharing a compartment with three Communist Party members. They offered him tea and asked him how the working class fared in the United States. Fleming, reciprocating their gift with some evaporated milk, answered that the American worker fared much better than his Russian counterpart. At this, one of them assured him there was going to be a revolution in America in the next few years. Fleming told him that when that happened he'd be sure to ship his money out to Russia. With that, the conversation died and the Russians lit up their *makhorka*.* "Makhorka," Fleming remarked, "is a weed the Russians use for tobacco. While its scent is distinctive, it is not fragrant." To make matters worse, his travel companions refused to crack a window, and so they sat in a choking fug of heavy smoke the entire way. On October 9, their train pulled into Moscow's Kazan Station, a month after Fleming had begun his trip.

He was glad "to get back to blighty." He threw himself into organizing his notes in preparation for writing up a report of his trip, updating all his charts and statistical tables at the office, developing his photographs, and spending time with Paulina, who was now well and out of the hospital.

And then there were the parties. The Pink House, home to the ARA bosses, and the Blue House, where many of the roughly fifty ARA men stationed in Moscow lived, became popular venues for wild revelry fueled by lots of imported alcohol and commissary goods—American cigarettes, candies, and fine delicacies unavailable in Russia—at which the young Americans and their female Russian employees danced the fox-trot until the early hours of the morning. Fleming threw himself headlong into the partying.

---

* *Nicotiana rustica*, as opposed to *Nicotiana tabacum*, the common variety of tobacco plant.

A good number of the Russian women belonged to the old nobility, whose families had been dispossessed after the revolution. Their lives had been especially hard during the civil war, and they were grateful for the opportunity to work for the Americans.

Two sisters, Alexandra and Sofia from the princely Golitsyn clan, whose grandfather had been the popular long-serving mayor of Moscow and a vocal liberal critic of Nicholas II, got jobs with the ARA, as did their cousins, Alexandra and Sofia (Sonya) Bobrinskaya, descendants of Count Alexei Bobrinsky, the illegitimate son of Empress Catherine the Great and Count Grigory Orlov. Alexandra Golitsyna was overjoyed by the "huge wages" the Americans paid, as well as the opportunity to receive food parcels. She and her sister sent one of them home to their family in Bogoroditsk—the estate of the Bobrinskys in Tula Province, to which many in the extended family had fled during the civil war—and it caused a sensation. The entire family gathered around the wooden crate emblazoned with an American flag, opened the lid, and then stood back in wonder at its contents of canned milk, American bacon (something no one had ever seen before), macaroni, rice, and sugar, all of it wrapped up in bright, decorative packaging.

The Russians found working for the Americans exciting. Kirill Golitsyn, another of the young Golitsyn cousins, wrote of the enormous impression the "elegant and independent" Americans made on them, how they behaved so freely and spent their money without the slightest care. They were unlike any people the Russians had ever known. Countess Irina Tatishcheva was hired as a bookkeeper for the ARA and then promoted to secretary. She liked being around the Americans—"They were so merry, not like all those gloomy Soviet officials who were dominated by fear." Sonya Bobrinskaya worked as secretary to the American William Reswick. His interpreter was a "Princess Irina," whom he described as "a girl of rare beauty from one of Russia's great aristocratic clans whose entire family had apparently been murdered by the peasants during the revolution." Reswick was amazed by Irina's energy and boundless compassion for the poor and suffering.

Although they had next to nothing, these "former people" tried to reciprocate their employers' hospitality. They threw parties in the mansion of the Samarin family, at 18 Spiridonovka Street, near the ARA headquarters—a few rooms on the mezzanine had not yet been nationalized, and these became a sort of commune of *jeunesse déclassée* for the Golitsyns, Bobrinskys, Samarins, and other young nobles. The American reporter Edwin Hullinger, who had toured the famine zone with Childs, attended many of these parties at the Samarin home. He was struck by the contrast between his hosts' grim living conditions and their infectious happiness. Everyone was laughing, flirting, and dancing. It made him wonder if the revolution had freed these young people to a lifestyle unknown and impossible to their parents. "Over it all hung an atmosphere of free camaraderie which would not have been possible under the gilded chandeliers and in the stately drawing-rooms of their ancestors. There was an unaffected, frank jolliness that reminded me of our own American Far West." The young women in their "pre-war dress" looked "as charming and pretty as if just home from college." One of these noble daughters told Hullinger: "I am trying to live on the surface of life. I have been in the depths for five years. Now I am going to be superficial. It hurts less."

Sonya Bobrinskaya had an especially sad story. Her father had been arrested more than once and held in a GPU prison in Moscow. She often visited him there, bringing letters and a bit of food. Once, she herself was summoned by the GPU while she was at work. She told Fleming she had to leave immediately, offering that she had no idea when she might be back. It's not hard to imagine the fears that filled her mind as she made her way to the dreaded secret police. Her father didn't make it out alive; he died that year in prison.

The Americans offered an escape from life's depths, and the Russians were grateful. They were fascinated by the Americans and their culture, especially jazz and the fox-trot. They were still young and wanted to enjoy themselves, to be frivolous and silly; they rejected the dour puritanism of official communist culture, which considered fun bourgeois. The Russians and Americans would dance through the night, the latest records from America spinning on their gramophones, and then race through the empty streets in the ARA's automobiles as the sun rose over

Moscow. The American men were besotted with these exotic "Madame Butterflies," as they were known, and their advances were frequently returned. Almost one in ten of the ARA men ended up marrying a Russian woman; Golder dubbed these women "famine brides." In 1923, Alexandra Bobrinskaya married her ARA boss, Philip Baldwin, and not long thereafter left Russia for Italy to live with his mother. Her younger sister Sonya married the Englishman Reginald Witter in 1924, and then they, too, left Russia. Not all of these unions ended happily. There was the story of one Russian woman from the ARA who had departed Russia with an Englishman, only to learn that he had no intention to marry her, but set her up as his mistress. Devastated by his betrayal, she committed suicide.

The Russians who remained behind suffered as well. In 1924, in what became known as "The Fox-Trot Affair," the secret police arrested several of these "former people" who had worked for the ARA and exiled them from the capital as "harmful elements." To the authorities, their past association with the Americans offered undeniable proof of their counter-revolutionary, anti-Soviet attitudes.

"I MUST REPORT again the excellent spirits in which I rejoice all the time," Fleming wrote his parents on October 18. "I almost think it dangerous that I feel so good." He insisted this was the result of neither too much coffee nor too much alcohol, but of the work itself, which he found so fascinating and important. He had a clear sense of the historical significance of the mission he was involved in. Their operation in Russia, he boasted, was "the biggest job of famine fighting ever done in the history of man, not excluding the job Joseph put across, and we do it for free, while Joseph mortgaged the whole nation to the crown in the bargain."* Based on his study of the recent crop yields, he was certain that there would be yet more famine in the coming year and that as many as eight million people would require aid. There was still plenty of work to be done.

---

* A reference to the biblical story of Joseph, who as vizier to Pharaoh devised a plan to store grain in advance of the seven-year famine in Egpyt and so help save the people from catastrophe.

The social opportunities offered by Moscow were no less invigorating than the challenges of work. Paulina ended up back in the hospital and had to have a kidney and her appendix removed, an operation that frightened both of them, but she came through just fine, and Fleming had to admit he loved to visit her: she looked so pretty in her gray uniform bathrobe, her nose pressed against the window as she waited for him to come up the sidewalk, a bouquet of flowers in his hand. By November, he found himself contemplating marriage.

But there were other distractions. With some of his ARA buddies, Fleming frequented the opera and ballet as well as the city's many cafés and clubs. They played chemin de fer and faro and drowned themselves in beer and vodka till the early morning hours, piling drunk into a droshky to take them back home to the Blue House. He started seeing a cabaret singer, and another woman, whom he called his "Sunday night lady." Though he kept both of them secret from Paulina, it seems she had a pretty good idea what he was up to. Hurt, she withdrew from Fleming, and he tried to patch things up between them. They spent Christmas together, but it was a bittersweet holiday: Fleming had just been informed that, after New Year's, he was going to be transferred out of Moscow to the provinces. Paulina was grief-stricken. Fleming wasn't quite certain how he felt, but his concern for her future was genuine. "As for what will become of Paulina," he informed his parents at the end of December, "I do not know."

19

MARXISM PLUS AMERIKANIZM

C HILDS'S RUSSIAN IDYLL came crashing down in the first week of December.

Since arriving in Kazan, Childs had enjoyed frequenting the city's bazaars in search of bargains for antiques, furs, and various tsarist collectibles. He carefully put together a collection of over two thousand rare coins, of which he was most proud. Some of these he had taken with him to Berlin for safekeeping earlier that spring; others he sent out of the country via the ARA mail pouch. All of this was illegal, an unambiguous violation of the Riga Agreement on the export of Russian valuables. He had gotten away with this smuggling until the first day of December, when the Soviet authorities, following up on long-standing rumors of illegal shipments by the ARA, requested that the pouch be opened at the Moscow customs office before the courier departed for Riga. ARA officials were permitted to be present for the inspection. Just as the Soviets had suspected, they discovered a trove of contraband: gold and silver items, diamonds, furs, rugs, paintings, Gobelin tapestries. Included in the haul were dozens of eighteenth-century jewel-encrusted gold snuffboxes belonging to Childs's mother-in-law.

Childs happened to be in Moscow. The next morning, Haskell summoned him to his office to explain himself. Terrified, Childs lied to his boss, insisting that he had had no idea what was in the package Georgina's mother had asked him to send to a certain gentleman in London. Later, in his memoirs, Childs admitted he had known full well what he was doing, although he wished he had heeded a dream he had had just days before, in which Mathilde's collection was discovered and seized by the authorities. Every last piece was confiscated and never seen again. In light of the scandal, Childs knew the only thing to do was resign. He was not the only one. Wahren, Van Arsdale Turner, and Earl J. Dodge, who worked in the Blue House in Moscow, were also implicated and forced to resign.

The incident was a horrible embarrassment for the ARA and offered the Soviets the proof they had been looking for of the Americans' duplicity. *Izvestiia* ran an article under the headline "How They Help Us" excoriating the ARA as little more than a front for the plundering of Soviet Russia of several trillion rubles' worth of cultural patrimony. "This is how the representatives of 'civilized' America behave in 'barbaric' Russia. This is how 'rich' America takes advantage of 'poor' Russia."

Haskell and Quinn leapt into damage-control mode. In total, four men were fired and sent packing, and the ARA worked to convince the Soviet government that the smuggling had been an isolated incident carried out by a few bad actors. Their efforts paid off; days later, Lander published a short notice in *Izvestiia* praising the efforts of Haskell and Quinn in helping to uncover the smuggling activities and declaring that the crimes of these individuals should in no way sully the image of the ARA and its operations in Russia, which remained praiseworthy.

Profoundly embarrassed, Childs returned to Kazan and sought an

Better days. Before his downfall, Childs, center, inspects Student Dining Hall No. 2.

alibi for his departure from Russia. He convinced Dr. John E. Cox, the district physician, to write a letter addressed "To Whom It May Concern" stating that, upon a thorough examination, he found Childs to be suffering from exhaustion and nervous anxiety because of the demands of his job, and recommending he leave Russia for an extended period of rest.

With Cox's letter in hand, Childs informed his co-workers in Kazan on December 11 that he was resigning because of ill health. John H. Boyd would be taking his place. He thanked everyone for their service, praised the work they had accomplished, and told them he'd never forget the heroism of the people of the Tatar Republic.

Childs was swamped with outpourings of gratitude. Letters arrived from all over the republic thanking him for his work. The members of the relief committee in Sarapul sent him "a warm proletarian 'Spassibo' and their heartfelt wishes for your continuing successful work for the welfare of humanity." Some of the local staff acknowledged that many people had viewed the Americans with skepticism when they first arrived, but Childs's energy, humanity, and selflessness had quickly put any doubts to rest. They noted how he had taken "to heart the sorrows of a people entirely strange to you." They would never forget him and were saddened at the loss of "a man whom hundreds of thousands of children, fed by the ARA, will remember forever with gratitude." Childs was treated to a farewell banquet and presented with a traditional Tatar costume—silk robe, embroidered cap studded with pearls, and richly patterned boots—as a parting gift. On the night of the 20th, he and Georgina left for the station amid many teary goodbyes.

They reached Petrograd on Christmas Eve and went straight to Georgina's mother, whom they found in a terrible state. She was barely surviving on a bit of bread and butter and coffee in her small unheated rooms. Her nerves were frayed, and Childs feared she was on the verge of a complete breakdown. He took them out to a Christmas dinner in a deserted restaurant, and they discussed their plans for leaving Russia. On January 3, 1923, Childs and Georgina boarded a train for Helsinki. Since Mathilde had yet to receive permission to leave the country, they decided she would follow as soon as she was allowed. The parting was hard, especially for Georgina, but Childs was relieved once they had crossed the border. "After 16 months in Russia," he wrote his mother, "it is like paradise to be in Finland. My nerves have been shot all to pieces." He didn't breathe a word about the customs scandal in his letters home. He was too ashamed. Instead, he wrote his mother that he had resigned from the ARA so that he could help Georgina and her mother leave Russia. It had been a difficult decision, but he felt it had been the right thing to do, especially since his own health was poor and might well not withstand another winter there. As for what he would do next, he admitted that he had no idea. Everything was up in the air. For Georgina, the separation from her mother was excruciating. She was sick with worry—tinged, no doubt, with guilt at having left her behind—and nothing Childs could do or say helped to calm her. Finally, in late February, Mathilde was able to join them in Berlin. It was an especially gratifying reunion.

They took Mathilde to live with friends in Wiesbaden, and were preparing to travel on to England for the crossing to America when Childs was suddenly stricken with appendicitis and had to undergo emergency surgery. It was not until late March that he was well enough to leave the hospital. Although he was excited about introducing Georgina to his parents, the prospect of returning to Lynchburg left him with a feeling of personal defeat; even before they had begun the long voyage home, he was busy trying to land a job that would take him back to Russia.

A NEW WRINKLE was added to the American mission when Kamenev informed Haskell at a meeting on November 6, 1922, that the Soviet government was planning to export as much as $50 million worth of grain in the coming months. The idea of selling grain abroad in the midst of a famine first arose back in August, in a report by Vasily Mikhailovsky, a noted demographer and the director of the Moscow Soviet's statistical department. He argued that, in light of a likely surplus from the next harvest, it made sense to export this extra grain to earn hard currency that could be used either to buy manufactured goods to sell on the Russian retail market or to invest in plant and equipment vital to modernizing the devastated industrial base. A debate ensued within the Soviet government about the appropriateness of shipping food to foreign countries while millions still faced starvation and the country remained reliant on foreign aid, but the failure to establish trade relations or secure loans from the Western powers at Genoa and The Hague, combined with the now-undeniable fact that world revolution was becoming ever more unlikely, meant that the Soviet state would have to find its own way forward.

At the Fourth World Congress of the Communist International, in November, Lenin told the delegates that heavy industry was vital to Soviet Russia and it could only be developed with state subsidies. "Unless we find them we are lost as a civilized state—let alone as a socialist state." Three days after Kamenev first broke the news to Haskell, he told him that the Soviets would, of course, be willing to forgo the grain exports if the United States would be willing to offer them loans, and even suggested they might consider putting up the Romanov crown jewels as collateral.

Hoover was furious upon hearing the news. He wrote Haskell on November 18: "The A.R.A. [. . .] must protest against the inhumanity of a government policy of exporting food from starving people in order that through such exports it may secure machinery and raw material for the economic improvement of the survivors. Any such action imposes the direct responsibility for the death of millions of people upon the government authorities." If industrialization necessitated so many innocent lives, Hoover was convinced Russia was better off remaining a traditional agricultural society.

This did not mean, however, that Hoover was against exploring economic activities with the Russians. In early August of that year, Chicherin and Leonid Krasin had informed Stalin, who had become general secretary of the Communist Party's central committee in April 1922, that, on Hoover's initiative, a commission of about thirty leaders from the American industrial, financial, and trade sectors were preparing to visit to explore the possibility of establishing trade relations with Soviet Russia. Stalin's response is not known, and in the end no American delegation ever visited. In what Chicherin referred to as a defense of Russia's "national honor," the Soviets insisted no American commission would be permitted to investigate the Soviet market unless the United States permitted a reciprocal delegation to do the same in America. The principle of reciprocity was more than the Americans, especially Secretary of State Hughes, were willing to accept, which left the Soviets little choice but to refuse the American economic mission.

Matters did not end there, however. Sometime later in November, Lenin and Haskell met to discuss the possibility of enlisting Hoover's help in the economic reconstruction of Russia. According to Haskell, the idea had come from Lenin, who had requested that Haskell deliver a letter from him to Hoover back in Washington. According to Lenin, in a note addressed to the Politburo, the idea had been Haskell's, first brought up in conversation with Kamenev and then repeated at this November meeting with Lenin. In his note, Lenin remarked that he had told Haskell he fully endorsed his plan and then began showering the American with compliments, an admission that suggests the idea had been Lenin's all along, and that heaping flattery on Haskell was a conscious move in the Soviet leader's plan to win over the Americans and gain their help.

Haskell had met Lenin on several occasions before and had developed a great appreciation for the man he called "the bearded little chief." He was taken by Lenin's remarkable political and personal gifts and found him to be among the most magnetic and convincing speakers he'd ever met. In their meetings, Lenin was not above admitting the mistakes of his government and its lack of expertise in business and economic matters. Haskell later wrote that he was stunned by Lenin's desire to write directly to Hoover and to request his services as, in Haskell's words, "Economic Dictator of Russia." Lenin's admiration for American efficiency, technological know-how, and relentless dynamism was both well known and shared by other Soviet leaders. At a speech in February 1923, Nikolai Bukharin stated that what Russia needed to move the economy forward was "Marxism plus Amerikanizm." This did not mean, however, that the Soviets had any intention of turning their backs on communism. Rather, they intended to use America's strengths against it. "Amerikanized Bolshevism," Trotsky proclaimed in 1924, "will triumph and smash imperialist Amerikanizm."

The Politburo approved Lenin's plan; shortly before Haskell left for the United States, he received a letter from Lenin, dated November 22, expressing his strong desire for The Chief's help.

Dear Mister Hoover!

Mister Colonel Haskell has told Comrade Kamenev, with whom he meets regularly in regard to matters of the ARA, and then conveyed to me in a special meeting that under certain conditions you are prepared to come to Russia and devote yourself to her economic reconstruction. I welcome this offer with extraordinary interest and thank you in advance for it. Allow me to repeat what I told Mister Haskell, namely that assistance from an outstanding expert of organization and "captain of industry" in a country whose economic foundations are so contrary to ours would be of singular importance and we would find this both a great benefit and a pleasure.

In accordance with Mister Haskell's wishes, this entire matter will remain strictly confidential until you have made your decision.*

It is a stunning and in many ways humiliating letter: the great leader of world proletarian revolution supplicating before a titan of American capitalism. After Haskell departed Russia for Washington with the letter, Lenin began to have second thoughts and feared he had made a mistake. He even instructed Litvinov to rush a cable to Haskell in London telling him not to deliver the letter to Hoover if he thought it might be "awkward or inopportune." Haskell did, however, present it to Hoover, but Lenin's overture went nowhere. Hoover never replied, and didn't even share his thoughts on the matter with Haskell.

None of this should have been a surprise. From the start, the mission of the ARA had been to feed a starving nation, not to rebuild its economy, especially since Soviet Russia was a country that not only had no diplomatic relations with the United States but had been founded on an ideology of world revolution and the overthrow of the capitalist West. Haskell, like Childs and many other ARA men, believed that Russia was changing, that it had abandoned its radical roots and could be brought back into the fold of the Western countries through political recognition, financial assistance, and economic cooperation. Earlier, Hoover had been open to the possibility of such cooperation, but he came to see matters differently. He disgreed with Haskell and the others who thought that the actions of the Western governments could change Soviet Russia. Hoover, it must be said, was correct. Exchanging ambassadors would do nothing to revive the Russian economy. If the Soviets were serious about attracting large capital investment, private property had to be guaranteed full legal protection, for without it the risk to investors would outweigh any potential reward,

---

* The letter was written by Lenin on the 22nd, but the final version, presented to Haskell, bore the date of November 28 and Chicherin's signature.

a fact that was lost on the Soviet leadership. Moreover, it wasn't clear just what Russia had to offer prospective trade partners. Lenin may have been a brilliant theoretician of capitalism, but he was startlingly ignorant of its practical realities. When Parley P. Christensen, the presidential candidate for the Farmer-Labor Party in 1920, asked Lenin on a visit to Russia the following year what exactly his country could offer America's farmers in return for grain, he replied, "We can put furs on your wives." The fact was, Russia produced almost nothing of value to the American market, something that hasn't changed in a hundred years.

On top of all this, the Soviets had taken a series of actions that autumn to make the ARA's already difficult work that much harder. In contravention of the Riga Agreement, they insisted that the ARA now pay for its Moscow offices and housing as well as the salaries of all the Russian personnel. They reduced the number of railcars at the disposal of ARA staff from thirteen to five. Despite the continued need, the government forced the Americans to close their feeding operations in four Ukrainian territories, a move that was so outrageous it elicited an angry article in the pages of *Izvestiia*, no less. New restrictions were imposed on the food-remittance program as well. More and more Soviet citizens were stricken from the rolls, and those who did continue to receive parcels found themselves the victims of harassment or, in some cases, even arrest. Deliveries coming in from abroad were suddenly subjected to long customs delays, and various bureaucratic hurdles were thrown up to slow down the courier runs. A ban was placed on the import of all alcohol unless it was under the control of the Commissariat for Public Health.

All of this, combined with the decision to export grain, convinced Hoover that the Soviets had not changed in any fundamental way. Back in December 1921, Hoover had been optimistic about the chances for U.S.-Soviet cooperation, writing to Secretary of State Hughes that "the relief measures already initiated are greatly increasing the status and kindliness of relations and their continuation will build a situation which, combined with other factors, will enable the Americans to undertake the leadership in the reconstruction of Russia when the proper moment arrives." Now it was obvious this was never going to happen. Even Haskell, a true friend and supporter of the Soviets, had to shake his head in disbelief. In early 1923, he wrote to Quinn: "In regard to the Lenin matter, nothing tangible has developed except that I carry verbal messages to him. I think that they can thank their own stupidity and their failure to cooperate with the A.R.A. for a lack of results in that direction."

By January 1923, Hoover had decided it was time to prepare for the end of the mission and an orderly exit from Russia. Upon his instructions, Quinn put together a detailed plan for liquidating the operation, which he sent to the ARA office in New York on the 11th, proposing that they would pull out of the country by early June. Hoover approved Quinn's plan; after further discussions back in New York, they decided to keep the plan a secret from the Soviets in order to limit the likelihood of having more roadblocks thrown up in the final months. They also agreed that it would be best to drop any objections to the recent backsliding by the Soviets on the provisions of the Riga Agreement. The New York office wired Moscow on the 23rd: "The Chief feels that the Soviet authorities are trying to crowd us out of Russia and will endeavor to put us in the wrong; so we need to keep peace temporarily and make arrangements for our final exit." Quinn dubbed this "samovar diplomacy," and he instructed all the district supervisors to make sure everyone was on his best behavior when interacting with local officials.

News of the end of the mission did not go over well with many of the ARA men, because there were still so many hungry people in need of their help. Although the numbers being fed had fallen drastically by November— when just over eight hundred thousand children and adults were receiving food—these shot back up again in the following months, soon reaching about three million. *Izvestiia* reported, on the last day of January, that the harvest in Samara Province would be only 30 percent of normal. The local ARA district supervisor was equally pessimistic, noting in a report: "As to be expected the second part of the winter is sharpening the famine. Stores of grain are running out." Nevertheless, Lander wanted the ARA to close down in that province's Syzran district, citing favorable harvest statistics supplied by the local *Posledgol* representative, statistics that the ARA as well as Soviet district officials knew to be overly optimistic.

The extent of the famine remained a hotly debated matter back in the States. In November, Paxton Hibben, a former diplomat now in charge of the American Committee for Relief of Russian Children, attacked the ARA in *The Nation* for underestimating the number of starving people in Russia and not doing enough to help. He cited a figure of over seven million facing starvation, put the blame for this on the failures of the ARA, and even defended the Soviet government against responsibility for the famine. On January 7, at a large rally in New York City in favor of recognizing Soviet Russia, Hibben joined the speakers denouncing Hoover as a man who opposed relations simply because he saw no way to make a personal profit out of it. Russia, Hibben went on, was both morally and politically superior to the United States, with its "race wars" and "murderers." There "people may criticize the government to their heart's contents [. . .] and still view the world with no [prison] bars to intervene." Hoover typically ignored these critics, dismissing them in private as irresponsible "pinks and reds." Even the ARA men who wanted good relations with the Soviets would have no truck with left-wing critics like Hibben. "I feel that we are so near a successful conclusion of our work," Haskell wrote to an ARA colleague in late February, "that we can stand almost anything for the few remaining months, rather than have a break with these people and give the radicals in America the opportunity to attack us for deserting these people and forcing a fight with them."

Part of the problem lay with the simple fact that only people who had actually gone to Russia to work the famine had any idea of just what an enormous job it was. To those who had, there was a natural and not unwarranted bewilderment at just what they had managed to accomplish. "When one stops to think it over, the work of the ARA in Russia has certainly been a most remarkable undertaking and probably in many ways one of the greatest operations in history," Walter Bell wrote from Ufa to a colleague back in New York in late December. "After a year's close contact with all the usual and <u>unusual</u> difficulties that those in all other districts have had to contend with, I do not think that any of us Americans can really tell how we managed to put the job over."

1923

20

MORE HUNGRY
SOULS TO FEED

O N JANUARY 8, 1923, Frank Golder wrote to his friends Tom and Sigrid Eliot back on the Oregon coast to thank them for their Christmas letter, which had warmed him with memories of pleasant times spent together. The Eliots shared Golder's desire for better relations with Russia, although they saw the reasons for the tensions between the two countries very differently. They suggested in their letter to Golder that Hoover and Hughes were the problem, which he disagreed with. He told them that the U.S. government had been doing everything possible in the past year to improve relations, but its efforts had failed because of the pettiness of the Soviet leadership. "The Reds," he noted, "are eager to get our goodwill and more eager still to get our bourgeois capital," but were constantly throwing up roadblocks and doing things that impeded their own interests. Golder admitted there were some "noble men" among the leaders, "but large numbers of them are rascals who are crushing the spirit of the movement." It grieved him to read the attacks on the ARA in publications like *The Nation*, or to hear of the words of men like Paxton Hibben about how the Soviet government was the only honest one in the world. He'd never understand how good people back home could run down Hoover and the ARA and praise the Soviets.

Discouraged though he was, Golder remained an advocate for recognition. He laid out his thinking on U.S.-Soviet relations that month in a long confidential letter to Hoover's assistant Christian Herter, which he asked him not to share with the State Department. Bad though the tensions were at the moment, he was still convinced that, by establishing political relations, the United States might exercise a moderating influence on Russian domestic life, helping to further its move away from the radicalism of the early years following the revolution. The process would be gradual, however, and there could be no hope of any "immediate material profit." In Soviet Russia "there are no fundamental laws, no basic principles of justice as in England, no constitutional guarantees as in the United States for the individual or his property." Life here was characterized by the arbitrary use of power. People could be arrested at any moment, for any reason, with no warrant, and their property taken without explanation. In such a chaotic and uncertain environment, there could be no foreign investment in the economy. "The financial conditions are so disturbed," he concluded, "that it is impossible to do big business." No one in Russia could make any plans for tomorrow, and so they all lived only for today.

If America had little to gain materially from Russia, Golder believed she had much to gain spiritually. He had spent a recent weekend in Petrograd, taking in some ballet and opera, and came away deeply moved by the artistry and beauty of the productions. It pained him to see the terrible conditions in which Russia's artistic community was forced to live and try to carry on its proud tradition. Nonetheless, Golder took comfort in the fact that many of the young American men attached to the ARA had been attending the theater, and its influence was clear to him.

"We are giving Russia bread, but it is giving us something more precious in turn." He was convinced that their encounter with Russian culture had changed these young and, in his opinion, unrefined Americans, and they would take this enlightened sensibility back home and release it into American life.

IN MID-JANUARY, the vice-president of the Dagestan Republic arrived at the Moscow offices of the ARA to ask for help in feeding the starving people of his mountainous region. Dagestan, a beautiful land of dizzyingly diverse ethnicities and languages located on the western shore of the Caspian Sea north of Azerbaijan, had declared independence in 1917 as the Mountainous Republic of the Northern Caucasus before becoming engulfed in the bloody violence of the civil war. Initially welcoming the Red Army as their liberators from the Whites, the Mountaineers, as they were known, soon found themselves robbed of their independence and forcibly incorporated into Soviet Russia in early 1921.

On the evening of February 12, Golder left Moscow on the Tiflis Express to investigate the situation in the Caucasus. Along the way, he noticed that there now appeared to be plenty of food available in the stations they passed. Once they had traveled beyond Rostov-on-Don, conditions improved considerably; food here in the south was both cheap and abundant. The train pulled into Petrovsk, the capital of Dagestan, on the morning of the 16th. It was cold and dark outside, and Golder found the town dirty and smelly. He spent two days surveying Petrovsk and gathering information on the needs of the local people before setting out for the rugged mountains of Dagestan. Traveling with him were five local men: Abdulah, his liaison officer, an intelligent, well-informed, and physically imposing young man who'd fought in the civil war, with whom Golder quickly formed a good bond; Abdulrachman, from the republic's Department of Education, a cynical, pessimistic, and prematurely old middle-aged man who seemed to carry the weight of the world on his shoulders; Mohammed, their driver; and two bodyguards, Ali Khan and Haji, a peasant from the Dagestani lowlands, decorated Red Army soldier, and wonderful young man with whom Golder established an immediate rapport. Each one of them was armed with a rifle, a revolver, and a dagger.

Golder was struck by the beauty of the mountains, whose peaks rise over fourteen thousand feet, and the auls, or villages, constructed of stone, clinging to the steep ridges as a defense against attack. Much of the time, they had to travel on sturdy ponies along treacherous narrow paths through sheer river gorges, with the ground falling away thousands of feet off to their sides. The children's homes here were in terrible shape—the children dirty and half starved, living on nothing more than a bit of watery cornmeal soup. The higher up into the mountains the men traveled, the worse the conditions became. In some villages, the children were practically left on their own, because there weren't enough adults to care for them. Amazingly, some of the American corn had managed to find its way to these remote mountain villages, but it wasn't much, and the people, Golder found, were barely surviving. Many people told him they had nothing left to do but pray for the mercy of Allah. By the 24th, he

A couple dancing the lezginka for Golder and his traveling companions

had seen enough to know help was desperately needed, and he sent a telegram back to Moscow to ship food and medicine as soon as possible.

Despite the gnawing scarcity, the legendary hospitality of the Caucasus greeted Golder everywhere he went—tables heavy with food and wine, attractive pairs of young men and women dancing the lezginka to the accompaniment of the choghur and tambourine.

The feasts could be so large, and long, as to be almost intimidating; polite refusals to the host's entreaties to more food or drink were futile. Frequently, Golder was taken for an important communist official from Moscow, since most of the villagers had never heard of America. His attempts to explain proved fruitless. In Khunzakh, the old village sage told Golder, "America is the lower world," a place "so far that no man can go there." Golder insisted that the man was mistaken, that he in fact lived there. The villager paused and then admitted it might well be possible and offered the theory of a hole in the earth that linked America, the lower world, with Dagestan, the upper world. (Dagestan literally means "land of mountains," and its inhabitants quite naturally considered themselves to live on top of everyone else.) This idea posed a problem, however: if, some of the villagers asked, America was beneath Dagestan, then how could the people walk there? Wouldn't they be upside down? This seemed to stump them all until the wise man solved the conundrum by asking them to consider the fly. Did it not walk on the top and bottom of things without falling? The men nodded in agreement.

Word of the exotic American spread. Upon arriving in one aul, Golder and his party found the road lined with the local men as a sign of respect. They'd heard that the American visitor was carrying a large bag of gold with him to buy Dagestan from the Soviets. When Golder told them of their mistake, they asked that he simply buy them instead and take them with him. He apologized and said he'd have to decline their offer; with that, the travelers rode on to the next aul past a line of crestfallen faces.

They returned to Petrovsk on March 6. Golder was delighted to see that an ARA representative had already arrived in response to his telegram and was busy making preparations to receive a large shipment of food and medical supplies. The people of the town, amazed by the speed with which the ARA worked, told Golder that Americans were a very clever people who "can do anything." By the middle of the month, he was back in Moscow. He wrote Herter of his trip and the "most interesting experience among those wild mountaineers and bandits."

He also wrote of a conversation he had had the previous day with Radek, who told him what he knew about Lenin's devastating stroke just days earlier, which had left him unable to speak and partially paralyzed. Lenin had already suffered two serious strokes, in May and then December 1922. After this latest stroke, there appeared little hope of recovery. Golder and Radek wondered aloud what might happen if he died. Radek was certain Stalin would become the leader of the party, which he thought would be a good thing. "He has a very high opinion of the Georgian," Golder informed Herter. Lenin's health improved that autumn, but he was just an empty shell of his former self. The country was now in the hands of his old Bolshevik comrades. Lenin died on January 21, 1924, most likely from cerebral arteriosclerosis, although rumors persist to this day that the cause of death was syphilis.

IN EARLY JANUARY 1923, Fleming was sent to Samara. He wrote his parents from there on the 15th to tell them he'd been busy setting up his room with a desk, typewriter, reading lamp, row of books, icon, and two photographs of his dear "Politchka," whom he had left back in Moscow. He included Paulina's photograph in his letter, adding with feigned drama that should it get lost, he would quit the ARA and drown himself in the Irish Channel. His letter completed and his bags packed, he set off on a two-week inspection tour later that day.

Fleming, like many other of the young Americans, reveled in the authority entrusted in him as a representative of the ARA. He recalled of this trip:

> My travel orders and official duties, I was informed, were a carte
> blanche to every part of provincial life in Russia, without fear

of the government nor favor of the old bourgeoisie. I had an open sesame to all doors and all classes. In the same day I might threaten the chairman of a county ispolkom,* the biggest man in the county, with closing all the kitchens in his county if he did not come to order; I could then talk with a former well-to-do merchant now proscribed and ostracized by the government, and finish the day by attending a peasant wedding where the most violent liquor ever concocted was poured out for the guests.

The richest man in two counties, I was also the only man in two counties who could afford to laugh at the name of the Government Political Department.† I was privileged to talk on equal terms with heads of provincial departments, to open or close kitchens feeding thousands of children, and to give carpet talks to small-town officials for negligence in the discharge of their duties.

Traveling with Fleming was his Russian interpreter, George. A Jewish anarchist in his late twenties, George had been exiled from tsarist Russia and eventually wound up in the United States. With the fall of the Romanov dynasty, he joined a group of fellow political exiles intent on returning home and devoting themselves to the revolution. They left the East Coast by train for Vancouver, where they embarked on a ship to take them to Vladivostok and from there to Moscow by way of the Trans-Siberian Railway. Short, chatty, and something of a ladies' man, George endeared himself to Fleming, and the two men got along splendidly during their travels throughout the province.

Their first stop was the town of Syzran, where they met with the local chairman of the executive committee, a Comrade Ageev, and an ARA-employed subinspector named Almazov, whom Fleming called an expert in uncovering embezzled American sugar and village committees not carrying out their duties. After a thorough examination of the books

---

* Executive Committee.
† The GPU.

and some tea, Fleming was satisfied that everything was shipshape, and
then he and George, accompanied by Almazov, left for the station and
an overnight train to Gorodishche, the next stop on the tour. Given the
many tales of railway bandits, the men slept with their shoes on. Fleming
kept his Mauser pocket pistol at the ready.

The men got off the train at the village of Chadaevka in the early
morning and climbed into a sleigh for the ride to Gorodishche, some dozen
miles away. They raced across the heavily packed snow, exposed to an icy
wind that froze their faces and cut through their clothing, and had to stop
along the way at a peasant hut to warm up; three hours later they reached
Gorodishche. The district of Gorodishche, roughly 210,000 people, had
suffered terribly in the famine. Dr. Mark D. Godfrey of the ARA had visited in the summer of 1922 and found the conditions in the children's
homes to be especially deplorable. A free ARA medical dispensary was set
up to help address the more than twenty thousand cases of trachoma in
the area, as well as a plague of syphilis that afflicted 60 percent of the
population.

The next morning, the men set off in two sleighs to inspect the surrounding countryside. Not taking any more chances with the cold, Fleming donned a twenty-pound sheepskin *tooloop* over his fur coat. The
cloak's collar extended several inches over his head, and the skirt reached
to the ground; it was so thick and heavy that he required help to put it
on and climb into the sleigh. Walking more than a few steps was out of
the question.

They made slow progress, and soon it grew dark. The area was full
of wolves, hungry for the taste of horsemeat, and so they kept on, in the
hope of finding a place to put in for the night. Eventually, the lights of
the village came into view. They made their way to the home of the village head, stabled their exhausted horses, and went in to warm up and get
some much-needed food and rest.

Just then, a boy arrived to invite them to a wedding. Fleming wanted
to beg off, but George insisted they go. The party was in full swing when
they arrived. The room, filled with peasant girls and young men singing
traditional folk tunes in high-pitched voices, fell silent as soon as the

strangers entered, and every eye followed as they were shown to a large table covered with an assortment of salted fish, sausages, cabbage, fried meats, and a large tank. The head of the village held a dipper in his hand and began filling small tin cups that Fleming immediately recognized as retooled cans of ARA condensed milk.

It looked like water, but smelled like a mix of gin, three-in-one oil, and kerosene. George refused the cup offered to him, but Fleming graciously accepted. "My stomach did not object, but my tongue did," he recalled. He didn't dare light his pipe for fear his breath might ignite. When he had drained the cup, he returned it to his host with a large smile. "Tell them I could make a hundred miles to the gallon on that," he said to George. Fleming began to fear the drink was affecting his eyes after he began to see black spots scurrying up and down the walls. But then he felt something move on his neck and looked down to see insects crawling all over his coat. The room was infested with vermin. Having seen enough, the two men got up, excused themselves, and left.

After inspecting the ARA kitchen the next morning, they set out with fresh horses for the Tatar village of Vyselki, where they arrived at twilight. It was a neat, peaceful-looking village—"the dream of a New England town," Fleming thought. They rode up to the finest house, knocked, and were shown in by the owner, who proceeded to seat them before a steaming samovar. Their host then went to fetch the village head, the Orthodox priest, the Tatar mullah, and the members of the ARA committee. The mayor informed them that nearly all of the village's five hundred inhabitants were relying on food substitutes to get by—millet husks, ground bark and bone, and *lebeda*. Although no one had starved to death that year, quite a few had perished the previous year. "Only the ARA rations saved the whole village from starvation," he told them. As they went through the records of the ARA kitchen, Fleming treated the men to several cups of warm cocoa, which they drank with evident relish. Before the meeting broke up and the exhausted travelers prepared for bed, the mullah asked Fleming to do him the honor of visiting his mosque the next day.

A light snow was falling when Fleming and George were awoken in the morning and told the mullah had sent a sleigh to collect them.

Melting the ice on the windows with their breath, they looked out to see a horse covered in frost. Icicles hung from its nostrils, and Fleming noticed how its frozen breath gave the poor beast the appearance of a skeleton. They stepped out into the cold. Columns of smoke drifted lazily from the village's white chimneys. "For a second I did not feel it," Fleming recalled. "Then a painful sensation developed around my forehead, eyes and nose, the only parts of my body exposed to the air. They seemed to be gripped by pincers." The driver's face was white with snow to match his steed. They set off at a gallop, the horse's hooves shooting clumps of hard-packed snow at the men as they hurried to the mosque.

It was a large, barnlike building with a high roof and a spire finished with a crescent. The mullah met them at the door, explaining that he had postponed the service to await their guests. He led them upstairs into an expansive hall where about fifty men in Tatar robes stood, and then showed them to seats at the back of the congregation. With a sign from the mullah, the men dropped to their knees and prostrated themselves in the direction of the morning sun. The service lasted some twenty minutes, while Fleming and George watched with curious eyes.

Afterward, the mullah led one of the congregants up to Fleming. This man told him that during their ceremony they "had invoked the mercy and blessing of Allah upon the soul of the American Relief Administration and upon the American people for the good which they had done to this little town of Vyselki," something they had been doing in their services for the past year and would continue to do as long as at least one of them was alive. He said to Fleming:

> Without the American corn which we received last spring almost no one in this village would now be alive and standing here. It seems wonderful that the great American people, so distant from us, should have heard of the little town of Vyselki and sent corn so many thousands of miles to us during the months of the famine. The authorities no further away than Gorodishche send us nothing, and did not even answer our entreaties for assistance.

Then he told Fleming that if they did not receive help again this year from the Americans, many more would die. "Can you help us?" he asked. Fleming assured him that he would speak to his superiors, but he could not promise that there would be any more food. Still, he wanted to do whatever he could for these people. "I like the Tartars [*sic*]," he remarked. "They seem like an intelligent lot."

Fleming and George next traveled to the city of Penza, where they checked in to the shabby and run-down Grand Hotel. Since their room was too cold to stay in, they went off to the theater. The production was excellent, and George knew one of the actresses, so they invited her out for a drink after the play. Over a bottle of wine and cigarettes, Nadezhda Galchenko told them her tragic story.

Before the Great War, she had lived well in Kazan with her husband and children. They'd had a fine apartment, servants, and large landholdings in Ukraine, but lost everything in the revolution, and her husband was arrested by the Cheka as a counterrevolutionary. He was soon freed, and they fled to their former lands in Ukraine, where the peasants welcomed them back and gave them food. But the area became another battleground in the civil war, and again her husband was arrested. He was taken to Ufa and forced to join the Red Army. Nadezhda managed to meet up with him there.

"Ufa was a charnel house," she told them. "The dead from starvation were more than the living could bury. Refugees from the villages wandered about the streets in desperation, searching for food, committing horrible deeds of violence at night—killing and stripping late pedestrians and selling their clothes in the marketplace for food." To help feed her family, Nadezhda began acting in the theater. She won the favor of some Red officials, who gave her gifts of bread, meat, and cabbage. Then the Americans came, and they, too, helped the family with food. Eventually, they were permitted to move to Penza. Her husband had family here, and she managed to find work at the theater. And then, one day, her husband vanished. Though she wasn't sure why he'd left them, she was not sorry to see him go. Sometime later, she married another man, who now worked as an inspector for the ARA. When she had finished her story, they sat in silence, smoking and eating chocolate. Then George escorted Nadezhda home.

Fleming found her beautiful and intriguing. He saw Nadezhda again, and soon thought he might be falling in love. He convinced her to leave her husband; sometime during that winter, she moved to Samara with her children to be near him. He would have her over to his room for dinner and then put a record on the phonograph and take her to his bed. In the early-morning hours, they'd dress, and Fleming would walk Nadezhda back home, while her children were still asleep. Young and naïve, he had no notion of what he'd done and how he was ruining Nadezhda's life.

For the next three months, Fleming made a series of tours—back to Syzran and Gorodishche and Penza, as well as to Stavropol, Buguruslan, and Sorochinsk. The travel conditions remained brutal, with temperatures reaching minus thirty degrees Fahrenheit. Still, he loved it. One trip had him traveling for two whole days along the Volga, "a beautiful ride in sun and snow," he wrote in a letter to his parents. He was taken with the vast treeless steppes that resembled the ocean. "The wind blows the snow into the form of waves, and for miles one sees about him only this restless rough expanse of snow like the surface of a bay under a small breeze—in one place a village stood out like an island, and the two domes of the church rose among the village huts on the horizon exactly like the twin lighthouses on Baker's Island in Salem Harbor."

Fleming encountered hunger and want nearly everywhere he went, but by April he had become convinced that conditions had improved markedly and the Russians should be able to pull through until the next harvest. Their work, as far as he could tell, was over.

21

FINISHING THE JOB

PLEADING FOR FOOD, RUSSIA SELLS GRAIN
Petrograd Has 35,000 Tons Ready to Ship, Says American Relief Worker
FAMINE MENACES 8,000,000

THIS WAS THE HEADLINE for *The New York Times* on February 21, 1923. The story was based largely on an interview with James B. Walsh, who had just returned home after serving with the ARA in the city of Rybinsk. He told the newspaper that he had learned about the grain while traveling through Finland on his way out of Russia. Over three thousands tons of grain had already arrived in Finland by rail from Russia, and he'd been told that Petrograd was making plans to ship thirty-five thousand tons in the coming months. The article went on to state that Mr. Walsh's figures were likely too conservative, and that nearly one hundred thousand tons of rye, barley, and wheat from the Volga region had already left for Europe on ships from Odessa and Novorossiisk, on the Black Sea. According to official Soviet sources, there were plans in place to export as much as seven million bushels of grain that year.

The tone of the article left little doubt that the newspaper found this news incomprehensible, especially given that the ARA was still feeding one and a half million children a day and, according to at least one recent report, as many as eight million Russians would need to be fed before the end of the year. As justification, Kamenev was quoted as saying that the amount of grain being exported was small and only involved cereals that for a variety of reasons could not be used in the famine districts. *Izvestiia* later confirmed that roughly four hundred thousand tons of grain had been exported around this time.

The New York Times followed up on March 4, blasting what it described as "this preposterous movement of grain out of a country that has been facing famine and depending on foreign charity." As to the reason for this action, the *Times* surmised that it may well have been an act of desperation, what it characterized as "the last card played by a government vainly trying to obtain resources to enable it to continue its exercise of power in the expectation that a world revolution may solve the deadlock between the Communist and the anti-Soviet governments of the world."

In February, the Moscow correspondent for the *Times*, Walter Duranty, asked the questions on many Americans' minds: "What is the real truth about the famine situation in Russia today? Has Russia a surplus of grain available for export? Is foreign relief needed to save millions from starving?"

Haskell was among those who both understood and endorsed the Soviets' decision to export grain. The Associated Press reported on March 7 that Haskell had informed Hoover that what Russia needed now was not more famine aid, but credit or loans to rehabilitate its transportation and agricultural sectors. This article noted that Haskell had discussed the matter thoroughly with Kamenev, and both were in agreement that the country now had enough grain on hand to address the lingering famine, but Russia could not make a real step forward unless it received money from the West. Haskell had conveyed his thoughts to Hoover in a cable on the 6th, noting that, without greater economic assistance to the Soviet government, "misery and suffering by millions over a long period of years" would be a certainty. Hoover released to the press Haskell's cable justifying the ARA's decision to end Russian famine relief, but only after he had quietly excised Haskell's comments endorsing Soviet grain exports and arguing for more general economic aid and cooperation.

Hoover's underhanded attempt to control the story blew up in his face when one of the ARA employees in New York accidentally gave out the full text of Haskell's cable to a reporter and it made its way to *The Nation*. "Mr. Hoover Stabs Russia," the magazine accused on March 21, insisting that Hoover was grossly underestimating the need for further famine aid and trying to sabotage Soviet-American economic cooperation. Hoover's anti-Bolshevism blinded him to the realities of Russian suffering and the basic needs of her people, the article stated.

Hoover stuck to his guns, however, and refused to back down on his decision either to end the mission or to recognize the Soviet government officially. Top ARA officials had held different opinions on these matters for some time, but up until then they had been kept private. Now the disagreements exploded into the open. Fisher and Herter sided with Hoover; Haskell and John R. Ellingston, director of the historical division in Moscow, opposed him. "Complete condemnation of [the Bolsheviks] and the spirit behind the revolution is, it seems to me," Ellingston wrote to Fisher, "no more just, though just as natural, as British condemnation of the French revolution, and I suspect that no one in America in 50 years from now will regret the Russian revolution or feel that its big results were other than good." Hoover and the ARA, in his estimation, suffered from "a lack of vision."

The Soviet government handed Hoover and his supporters a gift later in March, when it put more than a dozen clergymen on trial for anti-Soviet agitation. The trial was a sham, and their guilt a foregone conclusion. All of the accused were sentenced to long terms in prison except Monsignor Konstantin Budkevich, a Catholic priest and an organizer of

peaceful resistance to the seizure of church property, who was sentenced
to death. The verdict unleashed an international outcry. Appeals for leni-
ency poured in from political and religious leaders across Europe and the
United States, including Pope Pius XI. All of these were brushed aside,
and the Soviet prosecutor insisted that Budkevich had to pay for the
clergy's role in centuries of oppression of the working class. He was executed on Easter weekend, and his body disposed of in a mass grave. For
Hoover, no greater proof of the Bolsheviks' fundamental iniquity was
necessary.

Confused about the conflicting reports coming out of Russia on the
extent of the need for continued aid, Hoover had written in late January to
Lincoln Hutchinson—one of his special investigators, then in Italy recovering from pleurisy—to ask him to go back to Russia and see what he could
find out. Hutchinson, who had made a similar tour of the Caucasus with
Frank Golder the previous year, replied that he was happy to do what he
could, but that any information he might gather would amount to little
more than "a new set of guesses." He had noticed the past spring and summer how the Soviet authorities had cracked down on all efforts to conduct
independent investigations into the food situation. Officials throughout
the country had been given special orders not to hand out to foreign relief
operations any statistics that had not first been sent back to Eiduk in Moscow for approval, and these orders had been followed with ever greater efficiency as the year progressed. Nonetheless, he promised to try his best, even
though he held out little hope of coming back with any definitive answers.

In the meantime, the ARA moved forward with its plan to liquidate
the operation. On March 1, Haskell wrote New York for authorization
to begin the process, which he likened to a military mobilization that,
once begun, would be difficult to undo or change in direction. The idea
was first to stop all medical supplies, then the food-remittance program,
next to close the remaining kitchens, and finally to shut down headquarters in Moscow and pull everything out of Russia. Their intention was not
to inform the Soviets of this plan, in the hope of preventing them from
causing trouble. Samovar diplomacy—the policy of appeasing Soviet demands wherever possible—would remain in force throughout the process.

The goal was to avoid as many quarrels as they could and make the pull-out smooth and uneventful. On the 13th, Haskell got the go-ahead from New York, aiming to get the ARA out of Russia by June 1.

On April 3, Hutchinson issued a report supporting the Soviet government's officially stated view that the country now had enough grain, and corroborating its estimates for a large harvest. If hunger was to be a problem, he commented, then this would be due only to poor distribution, not to a serious shortage of food. The famine, he affirmed, was over. Two weeks later, the ARA released to the Associated Press an interview with Ronald Allen, district supervisor of Samara Province. He concurred with this growing consensus: "Samara, the blackest spot of last year's Volga famine, is emerging from the catastrophe with an excellent chance of having a surplus of grain when the summer crop is harvested." Allen said Russia would have no more need of the ARA after the first week of June, a view that was shared by the other district heads across Russia.

Hoover was delighted with the news. A State Department officer wrote to Secretary of State Hughes on May 4 of their recent conversation: "Mr. Hoover said that he had never been so glad to finish a job as this Russian job; that he was completely disgusted with the Bolsheviks and did not believe that a practical government could ever be worked out under their leadership."

Haskell notified Kamenev of their intention to complete the liquidation in the first week of June. This didn't come as a surprise: the Soviets had been aware of the general plan since late April. Once they knew, the Russians had started making things difficult for the Americans, just as Haskell had feared. They slowed down deliveries of food and supplies, and began stalling and dragging their feet. The less food the ARA dispensed to the hungry, the more that would be left for the government to confiscate.

On May 18, Lander sent a top-secret directive to all officials working with the ARA not to permit the Americans to take any photographs, films, or negatives with them out of the country unless these had first been inspected and approved by the GPU at the Moscow headquarters. A nervous inspector from Syzran came to speak in private with Ronald Allen in Samara and told him that orders were being sent out to the Russian personnel from Comrade Karklin to inspect the Americans' bags, and to confiscate all cameras, binoculars, and firearms unless the Americans had special permission to leave the country with them. Every effort was to be made so that the ARA automobiles and trucks ended up in the possession of *Posledgol*, and every piece of "valuable literature"—regardless of the language it was written in—was to be seized. And, most important, they had been ordered to stop feeding operations and begin stockpiling as much American food as possible. When the inspector ignored this directive and continued to give out food, he was threatened with arrest. He managed to get away, and ran straight to Allen in Samara.

On June 3, the plenipotentiary attached to the ARA in Yekaterinburg Province, a certain Comrade Vilenkina, sent a secret letter to the regional representative chairman of the RSFSR* for the Bashkir Republic and Urals that showed just how poisonous relations had become. "The presence of the ARA in our Workers' region is no longer desired," she wrote. "I have secretly given out the order to confiscate all the Americans' property immediately upon their departure." According to the letter, the ARA had been giving out food parcels "left and right to prostitutes and suspicious persons." Among the persons she singled out for special attack were Boris Elperine ("a provocateur [. . .] We must discredit him in the eyes of Bell") and his boss, the Ufa district supervisor Bell ("an old geezer [. . .] a degenerate and a drunk"). In another letter, Vilenkina characterized the Americans as a bunch of unemployed war veterans who had come to Russia to make a profit off the Russian people; there wasn't a humanitarian among them. They were to a man a drunk, unruly, debauched, and dishonest group. A few of them, she claimed, had raped women in Ufa and had to be spirited out of the country to avoid a scandal.

Lander sent a coded cable to Ufa as the ARA was preparing to leave, instructing officials there that any expressions of thanks must be of "an absolutely official nature." He went on: "Under no circumstances are there to be any large displays or expressions of gratitude made in the name of the

---

* With the establishment of the Soviet Union in late 1922, the RSFSR—its name now slightly changed to the Russian Soviet Federative Socialist Republic—became the largest of the republics that made up the USSR.

Two happy
Russian children
eating their ARA
rations in Ufa

people themselves." In the case of Bell, however, this proved impossible. Everyone who knew Bell loved him. Elperine considered him "a master handler of men," and Harold Fisher called him "a genius" who overcame more obstacles than anyone else in the organization. Olga Kameneva, the wife of Lev Kamenev and sister of Trotsky, who had also been involved in famine relief, agreed, saying he had done the best job of all the district supervisors.

Up until the last moment, Bell was working like mad to improve life in Ufa: organizing labor brigades to erect bridges, repair roads, and refurbish schools, and overseeing the reconstruction of the city's glass factory, which, after he got it up and running, would employ five hundred workers. His efforts even won the praise of *Pravda*.

The people of the Bashkir Republic showered Bell with honors and gifts. He was made an honorary mayor of Ufa, honorary chairman of the Ufa City Council, and an honorary life member of the fire department of the town of Miass. People flocked to his office to present tokens of their gratitude, including six wolf cubs (which he had to politely decline) and a richly embroidered Bashkir costume presented by one of the Bashkir leaders. Bell was moved by this gesture. "I have lived with them through the worst period of suffering and hardship they have ever endured [. . .] They nursed me through typhus. I feel as though I am part of their new existence, and as they want me to come back and help them, I am determined to do so."

Before catching the train back to Moscow for the last time, Bell called his young assistant, Aleksei Laptev, into his office and thanked him for all the wonderful work he had done for the ARA. He gave him a letter conveying the gratitude of the ARA and expressing his own personal desire to hear from him sometime in the future. Finally, Bell presented Aleksei with a gift: a brand-new American Underwood typewriter. It was a generous act, one that neither man knew at the time would change Laptev's life.

In early May, Golder departed Moscow by train for Odessa, where he embarked on a U.S. naval vessel for Constantinople. About forty years earlier, Golder had made the same trip across the Black Sea, then as a boy fleeing the anti-Jewish violence of tsarist Russia with his family for a better life in America. His heart was breaking, and he was overcome with conflicting emotions as he sailed away from what he called "that sick country."

> As I stood on the destroyer looking over Odessa, tears almost came into my eyes at the thought of the misery and suffering endured by those big hearted and fine people and I felt so sorry for them. That, no doubt, is the feeling of every ARA man when he leaves Russia. Yet there is nothing more that we can do. We are leaving and that is right. We have done a monumental piece of work, for in addition to feeding the hungry we have started forces at work that are bound to have results. I do not feel like a deserter, but more like one who fights and runs away and will live to fight another day.

On June 13, the last ship carrying food from America arrived in Riga. On the 15th, a final liquidation agreement was signed by Haskell and Kamenev, stating that both countries were satisfied with the fulfillment of all promises and commitments by the two sides, including the payment of all moneys due the ARA by the Soviet government. The next evening, the ARA hosted a farewell banquet in Moscow, whose guests included Kamenev, Dzerzhinsky, Litvinov, Radek, and Lander. Haskell greeted everyone with a few brief remarks, thanking all of them, and especially Comrade Dzerzhinsky, for their energy and help over the past two years, and stating that the representatives of the ARA were now convinced that the Soviet government was working for the well-being of the Russian people and that no barriers remained to prevent America's recognition of the USSR, something he hoped to see very soon.

Then came warm, grateful speeches by Kamenev and Radek in praise of America's selflessness, altruism, and idealism. Chicherin captured the spirit of the evening when he said:

> The work of the ARA is in fact the work of the entire American people, who came to the aid of the Russian people during hard times and in so doing set down a solid foundation for a future of unshakeable friendship and mutual understanding between us [. . .] In the name of future relations between the American and Russian people, which are sure to be both fruitful and rich, we honor today the mighty work of the ARA and, surveying the enormous scope, and future results, of its operations, we proclaim with all our hearts: Long Live the ARA!

The Council of People's Commissars reciprocated with a banquet for the ARA on July 18. It was a sumptuous affair for about fifty persons, the top ARA representatives and Soviet officials, plus members of the international press corps and foreign dignitaries. As the men feasted, an orchestra played behind a bank of potted palms. Coffee, liqueur, and cigars were served in the garden after dinner, and then the guests returned to the great state dining room for a round of speeches and toasts in recognition of the ARA's monumental efforts, and expressing the firm belief of better relations to come between the two countries.

Kamenev presented Haskell with a commemorative enamel plaque and then read aloud the official proclamation of gratitude from the Council of People's Commissars:

In the garden at the banquet on the evening of July 18. From left to right:
Maxim Litvinov (largely obscured), Lev Kamenev, Cyril Quinn, Mr. Volodin
(Lander's secretary), Karl Radek, Nikolai Semashko, William Haskell,
Georgy Chicherin, Karl Lander, and Leonid Krasin

During difficult times of enormous natural calamity, the
American people, represented by the A.R.A., responded to
the needs of a population, already exhausted by intervention
and blockade, suffering from famine in Russia and the Union
Republics, and unselfishly came to its assistance by organizing on
the broadest scale the supply and distribution of food and other
goods of primary necessity. Thanks to the enormous and entirely
disinterested efforts of the A.R.A., millions of people of all ages
were rescued from death, and whole towns and cities were saved
from the horrible catastrophe that threatened them. Now, with the
enormous work of the A.R.A. coming to an end, the Council of
People's Commissars, in the name of the millions who have been
saved as well as the working masses of Soviet Russia and the Union

Republics, is honor bound before the entire world to express its most profound gratitude to this organization, to its leader Herbert Hoover, to its representative in Russia Colonel Haskell, and to all its employees and to declare that the peoples of the Union of Soviet Socialist Republics will never forget the help the American people showed them by way of the A.R.A. and recognizes in this help the pledge of future friendship between both peoples.

An emotional Haskell accepted the gift. "I am proud to say that I consider all of you my personal friends," he told his hosts, "and part from you now not by saying 'Farewell,' but 'Do svidaniya,' until we meet again."

The ARA had saved millions of lives. According to the Soviet press, it had fed eleven million people—almost a tenth of the population—in twenty-eight thousand towns and villages and distributed over 1.25 million food parcels. It had restored fifteen thousand hospitals serving eighty million patients and inoculated ten million people against a variety of epidemic diseases. No reliable records were kept on the number of famine victims; the estimates range from as many as ten million to as few as one and a half million. A reasonable figure would be over six million excess deaths from starvation and disease, making this one of the worst famines in world history, behind the Chinese famines of 1877–79 (over nine and a half million dead) and 1959–61 (over fifteen million) and the Indian famine of 1876–79 (roughly seven million excess deaths).* And how many lives did the ARA save in the end? This is even more difficult to answer, although, when one considers both food relief and medical intervention, an estimate of more than ten million does not seem exaggerated.

But it was more than just saving lives. The ARA had given the people hope. A thank-you note from one village in Samara Province expressed a sentiment shared by millions of other Russians, Ukrainians, Jews, Tatars,

---

* The figures come from the distinguished Irish historian Cormac Ó Gráda's *Famine: A Short History.* The excess death rate, or excess mortality, refers to the death toll above a noncrisis norm and is the most widely used standard for judging the severity of famines. Ó Gráda notes that, in the typical absence of reliable census figures and civil registers, the mortality figures for practically all of history's famines remain largely guesses.

Bashkirs, Avars, Mordvins, and Udmurts: "Saving our children from death by starvation, you saved the future of our country. We may perish for our sins, but thanks to you, our children will grow up and make for themselves promising futures, not repeating our mistakes."

In the spring of 1921, the Soviet government had faced daunting threats to its existence on a number of fronts. When famine erupted, and Soviet officials began to realize the horrifying dimensions of this fast-moving catastrophe, Lenin knew he had to turn to the capitalist West to save his communist regime. Several countries heeded the call, and every contribution was important, but America provided the lion's share, some 90 percent of all relief. The ARA had helped to stabilize a country teetering on the edge of a precipice, and in so doing allowed the Soviet regime to consolidate its power.

On July 20, Haskell and the few remaining Americans in Moscow closed down the ARA headquarters and departed for home. They left not only with a deep sense of satisfaction at what they had accomplished, but also with a conviction that a new chapter in Russian-American relations had begun, one of friendship, trade, and cooperation, for which they could rightly claim no small role.

22

CHARITY AND
COMPASSION

F LEMING LEFT SAMARA for Moscow on May 14. Three days later
he boarded the Moscow-Vladivostok Express with plans to sail
home across the Pacific from the Russian Far East. As his train
pulled out of Moscow, he was overcome with emotion. Nadezhda had rid-
den the train with him part of the way from Samara to the capital, and
it was only then that he realized the depth of her feelings for him. He
had taken her talk of love as mere words, a sort of game they were playing
with each other, and had given no thought to their future. At Syzran she
left him, devastated at how she had misread his feelings for her. Fleming
was a confused mess of emotions. On the 18th, an anguished cable arrived
at the ARA office in Moscow from Nadezhda, addressed to Fleming: "Life

intolerable. Death preferable. Telegraph." Headquarters took the matter seriously. They sent a cable to Ronald Allen, still in Samara, and instructed him to find Nadezhda and see about the situation. It wasn't that anyone at headquarters was especially concerned for her welfare; rather, the ARA felt that everything possible had to be done to avoid a scandal.

Fleming changed his plans while crossing Siberia, and at Chita, on the far side of Lake Baikal, he boarded a train for Peking. He found that he was not ready to return home, and wanted to see if there wasn't some chance of getting back to Russia. "I was never so homesick in all my life as I was for Russia when I left it," he wrote a friend back in the States in mid-August. Just writing the date of his departure from Moscow he found painful. Their train had passed by the monastery at Sergiev Posad, north of the capital, and seeing its towers and domes brought back memories of a visit there one moonlit night the previous summer with Paulina. He couldn't stop thinking about her, and was awash in regret for not having asked her to marry him. He managed to get by as a freelance reporter in China, but all the while his thoughts were directed toward Russia. Throughout the rest of the summer and on into the autumn, he sent out application after application for any sort of job in Russia, but nothing came through. He tried to get a position at the U.S. Embassy in Tokyo, in the hope this might offer some opportunity to go back, but the job never panned out. The end of December found him in Shanghai, writing for a local newspaper and waiting for a Soviet visa that had been held up for a month. "I dreamed the other night that I was in battered old Samara," he wrote his parents, "looking for Nadezhda Mikhailovna but in vain." He received a handful of letters from Paulina and Nadezhda, but then these, too, stopped coming.

Fleming never did get a Soviet visa. By March 1924, he had run out of money and hope. Nothing was going his way. The articles on his experiences in Russia that he'd been submitting to newspapers and magazines in the States kept coming back in the mail with rejection letters. His writing, one editor commented, "lacked exactness." He left Shanghai that month on the *Empress of Asia*, sailing for Vancouver, and from there went south by train to Seattle. When he checked in to the Sigma Chi fraternity at the University of Washington, he found a letter waiting for him from Arthur T. Dailey of the ARA. Dailey had written to inform him that his query about being hired back on had been received, but, unfortunately, at this time the ARA no longer needed his services.

Fleming moved to New York City, found work as a financial journalist, and later married. A decade later, he was still struggling to get over Russia. He tried to fill this hole in his life through his work as editor for the quarterly *A.R.A. Association Review*, a position he held for thirty years. He contributed this notice in 1932: "Wanted: By a number of former ARA relief workers. A famine, earthquake or pestilence. In going condition. Guaranteed to run indefinitely, or until Prosperity gets around the corner." Twelve years later, he wrote in the review that he was still living on Washington Square with the "same wife, same cat, same typewriter, same pictures on the wall." Nothing could take the place of his Russian adventure.

Fleming always looked forward to the annual ARA reunions held in New York at the Harvard Club or Waldorf Astoria Hotel. He was there for the last one, on April 24, 1965. Times had been hard for Fleming of late. His wife had died a slow, painful death that had almost destroyed him. For nearly a year, he'd lived on little more than whiskey. He would have gone on drinking, but his liver finally gave out, and he had to get off the bottle. Seated next to him at that last reunion was Aleksei Laptev. A few years after the ARA left Ufa, Laptev traveled to Moscow, bringing with him the expensive American Underwood typewriter that Bell had given him before departing. He found a hard-currency store willing to buy it from him for a good price, and with his newfound wealth he bought himself a one-way ticket on an ocean liner to America.

That night was Holy Saturday, the day before Easter, the most sacred time of the year in the Russian Orthodox calendar. When Laptev mentioned this to Fleming, he saw his face light up at the memory of the holiday in Russia some forty years before. He invited Fleming to be his guest at the midnight service, and the two men walked out of the Waldorf together. They joined the clergy and congregation as they made their procession around the church, candles in their hands. Afterward, Laptev brought Fleming back for the Easter meal with his small circle of family and friends. It was the last time they ever saw each other. Fleming died in 1971.

RUSSIA HAUNTED MANY of the ARA men, not just Fleming. The experience had been difficult, frustrating, at times even dangerous, but it had also been profoundly rewarding, intense, and meaningful, and it had made them feel important. In Russia, they were big men, rich and powerful, exotic and alluring. Back in the States, they were just regular Joes again— no big deal, nothing out of the ordinary. The transition wasn't always easy.

In September 1923, while vacationing in Savoy, Bell wrote to a fellow ARA veteran, R. H. Sawtelle: "I found that the Russian experience had pretty well knocked me about physically, which was not strange when one considers what Ufa did to me in the way of typhus, rheumatism and malaria." Regardless, it remained the best thing he'd done in his life: "My association with the ARA has always been the greatest pleasure and satisfaction of anything I have ever been connected with and the spirit of loyalty shown throughout the entire organization, as exhibited by the difficult and dangerous work in Russia, where the only motto seemed 'Carry on' made it a greater honor to have been part of the organization." A month later, Bell was busy trying to find a way to go back to Russia as soon as possible and get involved in some sort of business venture. He was excited by what he'd been hearing about the changes there. It seemed that a new "light," as he called it, was emanating from Moscow.

Bell never made it back. He settled in Danbury, Connecticut, and got a job with the American Hotel Corporation. Ufa never left his thoughts, however. Later, he helped raise a fund among his ARA colleagues to help bring their dear old comrade Boris Elperine to New York City. Bell died, aged seventy-two, in 1946.

In the summer of 1922, William Kelly took a room at the Harvard Club on New York's West Forty-fourth Street and began looking for work. Unlike his old boss, Kelly hadn't the least desire to return to Russia. His job inquiries at Doubleday, Page & Co. Publishers, Funk & Wagnalls, and the U.S. Department of Commerce went nowhere. Even though money was tight and his prospects were not looking bright, he and Jane decided to go ahead and get married, and eventually Kelly found a position with an advertising agency on Madison Avenue. He remained in advertising for the rest of his life, and died in 1977 at the age of eighty-one.

Childs returned to Lynchburg with Georgina in the spring of 1923. He sat for the Foreign Service examination, and then received word he'd been hired by *The Christian Science Monitor* as their Moscow correspondent. The couple's Soviet visas were issued, and they were all set to leave when Georgina had a change of heart. There was simply no way she could go back. Given what she'd been through, and what awaited them, Childs understood, and he informed the newspaper he'd not be taking the job after all. That autumn, Childs joined the State Department and began what would become a thirty-year career, with postings across the Middle East and Africa, including ambassadorships to Saudi Arabia and Ethiopia. Upon his retirement, he and Georgina settled near her mother in Nice, France, in an apartment with a view of the sea. Childs never gave up on his dream of a literary career; he penned a couple of adventure novels and established a reputation as one of the world's leading authorities on Casanova. Georgina died in 1964, and eleven years later Childs took her ashes home with him to Lynchburg so they could be buried together. In 1975, he made one last trip to the Soviet Union. Upon his arrival, Childs mentioned to an airport official that he had been in Russia fifty years earlier with the ARA. The man's face lit up. "Ah-RA," he whispered with reverence. That one moment made the entire trip worthwhile. Twelve years later, Childs died of heart failure in Richmond, Virginia. He was ninety-four.

Frank Golder arrived back at Stanford in the autumn of 1923 in time to begin teaching his classes on Russian history and to start the arduous task of sorting and compiling the vast collection of books, periodicals, and ephemera that he had acquired in Russia for the Hoover War Library. Immersed in Russia's recent past, he soon struck upon the idea of creating an institute for the study of the revolution that would bring together American and Soviet scholars in joint research projects.

Together with Lincoln Hutchinson, Golder traveled to the USSR in late 1927 to try to interest the Russians in his plan for a research institute, and to witness the celebration of the ten-year anniversary of the Bolshevik Revolution. Life, he observed, was still a struggle, and ragged orphans still filled the streets, but food was plentiful, and a sense of normality had returned. The big cities showed undeniable evidence of a material prosperity that had been lacking when he'd left four years earlier. He witnessed the military review and listened to the speeches on Red Square on November 7. The scene called to mind moments of his past: 1914, when he'd seen Tsar Nicholas II bless the army on the eve of World War I; 1917, when he'd listened to Alexander Kerensky, head of the Provisional Government, exhort the troops to keep up the fight against the Germans; and 1923, when he'd watched Trotsky review the victorious Red Army. Today's celebration seemed monotonous and uninspired, as if everyone was simply going through the motions. "How the mighty have fallen and how much blood has been wasted in those thirteen years!" he wrote. "How little there is to show for it!"

The visit convinced Golder that the Soviet Union was moving ever further away from communism. "The Stalin progressives," he told a gathering of ARA alumni in New York City upon his return, were defeating the party of Trotsky, which would mean the abandonment of "the sacred tenets of the revolution." Soviet Russia now realized its fate lay with the West and the investment and credit it alone could provide, he assured his former colleagues.

As for his institute, matters hadn't gone as Golder had hoped. After reviewing one of the initial manuscripts, Soviet officials took umbrage at how the authors had depicted the Bolsheviks' treatment of the peasants, and expressed serious doubts about the advisability of a scholarly body that tried to combine what they believed to be outdated Western bourgeois history with their more advanced scientific school of Marxism-Leninism. Such theoretical concerns became moot a few years later, when most of the scholars Golder had wanted to work with were imprisoned under Stalin. Golder himself died in January 1929 after a brief illness. It was perhaps something of a blessing that he did not live to see his beloved Russia descend into the dark madness of Stalin's terror.

GOLDER WAS NOT the only American convinced of Russia's bright future. "Communism is dead, and Russia is on the road to recovery," Haskell wrote to Hoover in late August 1923, after returning to the United States. "The realization by the Russian people that the strong American system was able and contained the spirit to save these millions of strangers from death that had engulfed them must have furnished food for thought [. . .] To America, this is a passing incident of national duty, undertaken, finished, and to be quickly forgotten. The story will be lovingly told in Russian households for generations."

Haskell, of course, was wrong. Communism was not dead, and Russia, or at least official Russia, was soon looking upon this experience with the ARA in less-than-loving terms.

The first arrests appear to have begun not long after the Americans' departure in July 1923. The GPU arrested a former nobleman by the name of Palchich who had worked for the ARA and accused him of being a spy and having provided the Americans with secret maps of the Baku oil fields for use in a planned American invasion. A certain N. Belousov, the son of a tsarist officer and an inspector for the ARA in Simbirsk, was arrested; he purportedly admitted under questioning that his anti-Soviet views had led him to cooperate with American agents embedded in the ARA. Among his supposed crimes was gathering information for the ARA on the economic conditions and food supply in one remote district. One of Childs's assistants, a woman named Molostova, was also imprisoned as an agent of the United States. Proof of her treachery was that, upon Childs's request, she had translated Russian books about the Soviet economy and agriculture.

In May 1924, under the headline "ARA Spies in Role of Philanthropists," *Izvestiia* reported the arrest of two Soviet citizens on charges of economic espionage. One of them was sentenced to ten years in prison; the other, five. Hoover was outraged. "While the imprisonment of those assistants continues," he told the press, "it will form an impassable barrier against any discussion of the renewal of official relations." Secretary of State Hughes agreed with Hoover, as did first President Harding and then his successor, Calvin Coolidge. Official recognition of the Soviet Union would have to wait another decade, until November 1933, when President Franklin D. Roosevelt established normal diplomatic relations between the two countries.

Although this recognition did not come until a full decade after the end of the ARA mission, relations between the Soviet Union and the United States had not stagnated during the 1920s. Just the opposite. Harding and Coolidge, with the support of Hoover as secretary of commerce, may have opposed official relations, but they did nothing to prevent American firms from doing business in Russia, and even began to encourage them. Between 1923 and 1930, the sale of American goods to the USSR grew more than *twentyfold*, from $6 million to $140 million per year, and overall trade between the countries during that period surpassed $500 million, most of which consisted of American exports to Russia. A quarter of all Soviet imports came from the United States, representing a range of products but especially heavy equipment for use in mining, agriculture, construction, metalworking, and the oil-and-gas industry. Large credits flowed into the Soviet economy from banks such as Chase National, Guaranty Trust, and Equitable Trust and firms such as General Electric and the American Locomotive Sales Corporation, especially after Hoover lobbied the administration to loosen restrictions on private loans. By 1928, American companies were offering Moscow large, long-term financing deals, as much as $25 million over five years. Trade with the United States surpassed that with countries such as Britain, which had signed a trade pact with the Soviets in 1921 and established diplomatic relations three years later.

Trade and loans, however, had not convinced the Soviets to embrace capitalism or to forsake communism, as many Americans had believed they would. The logic of the Soviet Union's internal development proved resistant to external influence. Haskell visited the Soviet Union in 1931, during the first Five-Year Plan. The country was in the midst of Stalin's "revolution from above," intending to erase all traces of capitalism and build the world's first fully socialist state. Stalin had launched the USSR on a gargantuan program of crash industrialization. Bewildered at what he saw, Haskell only now began to entertain doubts about Russia's future. "The people are allowed what the government prescribes—and nothing more—whether it be shelter, food, or clothing," he noted. "Russia is at war; she is fighting a five-year battle against her own backwardness [. . .] The sacrifices that the people are making stagger the imagination."

Forced collectivization of agriculture was the second pillar of Stalin's revolution. Haskell toured the Russian heartland and spoke with the peasants. They admitted to being confused about what was happening and what the future held for them and their traditional way of life. They were worried, and suspicious of the government. Haskell shared their fears. "The kulak still remains earmarked for elimination 'as a class.' His 'crime' was that he got along fairly well." By American standards, he'd be considered "a poor wretch," but since he'd managed to raise his head just above the masses, it was to be "cut off." Haskell asked the Russians he met what they remembered of the ARA. Most had never heard of it, and those who had wanted to know if it was true that the Soviet government, not the Americans, had paid for all the food.

Collectivization amounted to a new war against the peasants, eerily reminiscent of the bloody violence of a decade earlier. The state planned to ensure a surplus of grain, both to pay for industrialization and to feed the growing number of workers in the cities, by forcing the peasants off their individual plots and into large state-controlled collective farms. This second serfdom was met with fierce resistance in the countryside, and millions of people were deported to Siberia and other lands far to the east. The chaos resulted in another epic famine, in which at least five million perished between 1931 and 1934. Once more, the starving, driven mad by hunger, resorted to eating human flesh. But this time there would be no appeal for relief from the outside world.

By the early 1930s, Hoover was in no position to come to Russia's aid even if he'd been asked. America's great humanitarian had become a national hero after his exploits in Belgium and then Russia, and so, when, in the spring of 1927, heavy rains caused the Mississippi River to burst its levees and unleash a flood that destroyed one hundred thousand homes and displaced over six hundred thousand people in several southern states, it was only natural that President Coolidge looked to Hoover to head the relief effort. Working with the American Red Cross, Hoover directed one of the largest fund-raising efforts in U.S. history to bring food and supplies to the area. Although the operation was in large part successful, horrible atrocities were inflicted on African Americans. Denied the decent food and shelter provided to white American refugees, blacks were forced to live outdoors, amid miserable conditions. They did most of the difficult work in the immediate aftermath of the flood, under the watch of armed National Guard troops. Men who tried to rest were beaten. White planters feared African Americans would leave the area for the North, thus depriving them of cheap labor, so the white troops, and local law enforcement, placed many of them into what Hoover himself called "concentration camps" and forced them, at gunpoint, to remain. The exact number of African Americans murdered is still unknown.

Hoover enlisted the press to cover up the scandal and present a false picture of the relief operation as one of racial harmony and cooperation. He wished to avoid a scandal during his run for the presidency, and wanted to squeeze as much positive publicity out of the disaster as possible, even going so far as to commission the first-ever presidential campaign film—*Master of Emergencies*. Riding the wave of a booming economy, Hoover won the 1928 election in a landslide.

The stock-market crash of 1929 and ensuing Great Depression proved Hoover's undoing. The "Master of Emergencies" now became the face of poverty and ineptitude. The shantytowns that sprang up in cities across America were dubbed "Hoovervilles"; the homeless tried to keep warm under "Hoover blankets," old newspapers; cardboard inserted into worn-out shoes was "Hoover leather." Hoover had not caused the economic calamity, but he'd also not been able to end it. To most Americans, Hoover seemed distant, aloof, untouched by the suffering of his fellow citizens. To others, he was downright cruel. Promising to defend American jobs for so-called real Americans and to remove the burden on relief agencies of what many considered the undeserving poor, Hoover and his administration organized the forced deportation from the United States of persons of Mexican descent. The Mexican repatriation—a form of ethnic cleansing—resulted in the expulsion of perhaps a million people, over half of them legal American citizens. Needless to say, the policy did nothing to end the Depression. Hoover lost the 1932 election to Roosevelt in a bigger landslide than his victory four years earlier. Even his home state of Iowa and adopted home of California went for Roosevelt. Hoover's failure as a president erased all of his earlier successes.

Back in the USSR, the history of the ARA was being expunged or distorted beyond recognition. Workers took down the signs outside the Blandy Memorial Hospital and the Blandy Children's Home soon after the ARA pulled out of Ufa. If the proposed monument to Blandy was ever built, it's no longer there now. In Odessa, the Haskell Highway and Hoover Hospital were quietly renamed. Several of the officials with whom the Americans had worked and who knew the truth about the ARA's mission fell victim to Stalin's terror in the late 1930s. Kamenev, Radek, Eiduk, Lander, Kashaf Mukhtarov, Rauf Sabirov—all were executed as enemies of the people. Trotsky was butchered on Stalin's orders in Mexico City in 1940. Olga Kameneva was shot in a grove outside Orël in 1941. A few managed to escape a violent end. Dzerzhinsky dropped dead of a heart attack in the Kremlin in July 1926 after delivering a fiery speech denouncing his old comrades Trotsky, Kamenev, and Zinoviev. Georgy Chicherin died a decade later of diabetes. Gorky died a month before, in June 1936. Rumors have long persisted that he had been killed on Stalin's orders. Doctors removed Gorky's brain and deposited it in Moscow's Brain Institute alongside Lenin's and those of other exceptional figures, so that researchers could dissect it in their search to uncover the material basis of genius.

There was no statute of limitations for the crime of having worked for the Americans. In 1948, a full quarter-century after the ARA left Russia, a man by the name of Gorin was arrested as an American spy. During his interrogation, he confessed that he had first been recruited by Blandy in August 1921 as part of a plot to overthrow the government. He had gathered sensitive information for the Americans and divulged the identities of the Russian staff working for the GPU. He also told them that the Americans had not given up their nefarious plans. Just last year, he said, Colonel Haskell's son had visited Moscow and had tried to get in contact with former Russian personnel of the ARA. It required no further comment that the purpose of his visit had been to reinvigorate the anti-Soviet operations begun by his father.

The rhetoric against the ARA heated up during the Cold War. According to the 1950 edition of the *Great Soviet Encyclopedia*, the ARA had been established solely "to create an apparatus in Soviet Russia for spying and wrecking activities and for supporting counterrevolutionary elements." Not a single reference was made to the Americans' relief operations. A standard history textbook from 1962 explained to schoolchildren that Hoover had sent the ARA to Soviet Russia "to secretly organize an insurrectionary force," but thanks to the vigilance of the Cheka and GPU, his plot was uncovered, the ARA's Russian counterrevolutionary agents were arrested, and America's plans to overthrow the first communist government were thwarted.

In 1958, *Izvestiia* attacked Hoover after he spoke at the Brussels World's Fair: "It was he who headed the notorious American Relief Administration, which so shamelessly covered its relief to all and sundry enemies of Soviet rule with its alleged concern for the hungry." The following year, on a visit to the United States, Nikita Khrushchev was willing to admit that, even if, thanks to the ARA, "thousands of people were rescued from famine on the Volga," the world should remember that it was American intervention that had brought about the Russian civil war and thus the famine. "American aid?" he sneered. "You have to sell your soul to get it." Hoover found the vilification hurtful. "My reward was that for years the Communists employed their press and paid speakers to travel over the United States for the special purpose of defaming me," he wrote in his memoirs.

Although Russia had turned her back on Hoover, one place where he could always count on getting a warm reception was the annual reunion

Moscow, March 14, 1922, noon. Four girls enjoying their meal of bread, rice, beans, and cocoa outside the ARA kitchen in the old Hermitage Restaurant. The ARA provided lunch for four thousand children at this one location every day.

of ARA employees in New York. He was a regular speaker at these events, and the men, now old and gray, loved nothing more than to listen to The Chief recount the tale of their glorious mission to Russia. Hoover continued to attend the reunions for decades, until his death in 1964.

The mission of the American Relief Administration was not the last chapter in the history of American aid to Russia. Under the Lend-Lease program, signed into law by President Roosevelt in March 1941, the United States delivered $12 billion in supplies to the Soviet Union between 1941 and 1945 to support the war against Nazi Germany. Along with matériel, which included 15,000 airplanes, 9,000 tanks, 362,000 trucks, and 15.4 million pairs of army boots, America shipped millions of tons of food (powdered eggs, grits, dried peas and beans, coffee, sugar, flour, and Spam), which by 1945 amounted to 10 percent of the entire agricultural output of the Soviet Union.

During a ballet performance at Leningrad's Mariinsky Theater in October 1954, the *New York Times* reporter Harrison Salisbury met a middle-aged survivor of the nine-hundred-day siege of the city. Salisbury asked the man what Russians thought of Americans and whether they recalled their help during the war. "Of course we remember," he said. "American Spam . . . we still make jokes about it but we were glad to eat it at the time. American butter . . . American sugar . . . We haven't forgotten that America helped us. We Leningraders never forget a friend."

The official government attitude, however, was to play down American help. Not everyone went along. Marshal Georgy Zhukov, the brilliant Soviet military commander, insisted on acknowledging the significance of Lend-Lease: "Now they say that the Allies never helped us, but it can't be denied that the Americans gave us so many goods without which we wouldn't have been able to form our reserves and continue the war." American support had been crucial in sustaining the Soviet struggle against the Nazis.

The United States came to Russia's aid once more in the 1990s, when the collapse of the Soviet Union led to severe economic hardship. Millions lost their jobs or went without pay; basic necessities were in short supply; the stores were empty of food. In 1993, 70 percent of Russian households were experiencing hunger. By the end of the decade, almost half of the population was living below the poverty line. The United States, together with Western Europe, stepped in to help. Between 1992 and 2007, the U.S. government provided $28 billion in assistance to the countries of the former Soviet Union. In 1999 alone, Russia requested five million tons of food aid from the United States, worth nearly $2 billion. The European Union added several hundred million dollars' worth of food assistance as well. For 1999–2000, U.S. and European food aid to Russia surpassed that given to the entire continent of Africa.

IN "THE AMERICAN CENTURY," published in *Life* magazine in February 1941, Henry Luce wrote that Americans had "to accept wholeheartedly our duty and our opportunity as the most powerful and vital nation in the world and in consequence to exert upon the world the full impact of our influence." With the world at war, it was no time for Americans to be gloomy or apathetic. He urged the United States to take up its role as "the

Good Samaritan of the entire world" in words that echoed the spirit of Woodrow Wilson two decades earlier.

According to Luce, it was not just power that made America exceptional, it was her values as well. "We are the inheritors of all the great principles of Western civilization—above all Justice, the love of Truth, the ideal of Charity." Americans, he argued, had a sacred duty to use the nation's great might to lift "the life of mankind from the level of the beasts to what the Psalmist called a little lower than the angels."

Luce's idea of the American Century was always more aspirational than real, and it is a mistake to think that America still exerts the kind of global power it did in the second half of the last century. Just as America's power has waned, so, too, has Americans' belief in the fairy tale of their ability to redeem the world, which can only be seen as a change for the better. Nonetheless, even if the United States can't be the world's Good Samaritan, Americans should never forget that their country possesses enormous wealth that can do much to relieve suffering throughout the world. A century ago, Maxim Gorky praised the generosity of the American people "at a time when humanity greatly needs charity and compassion." May the story of the ARA inspire that same spirit of generosity today toward all humanity, abroad and at home.

A NOTE ON SOURCES

The story of the ARA's mission to Russia has been told before, most recently by Bertrand M. Patenaude in *The Big Show in Bololand* (2002). Mr. Patenaude's magisterial study, based on exhaustive archival research, is the definitive book on the subject, and anyone seeking to learn more should begin there. *The Big Show* proved invaluable in my research and in helping me formulate my own thinking about the subject. Also of note are H. H. Fisher's *The Famine in Soviet Russia, 1919–1923* (1927) and Benjamin M. Weissman's *Herbert Hoover and Famine Relief to Soviet Russia: 1921–1923* (1974).

Along with printed sources, this book draws on a wealth of unpublished archival materials, especially for reconstructing the lives of the main characters. The University of Virginia Library houses the J. Rives Childs collection, whose letters and other writings I made extensive use of. The New York Public Library contains important materials on Harold Fleming, and Columbia University's Rare Book and Manuscript Library has a large collection of ARA photographs, in addition to other documents on the work of the ARA (such as the personal papers of Aleksei Laptev) and on the famine more generally. I received a good deal of biographical information on the employees of the ARA from the Herbert Hoover Presidential Library and Museum in West Branch, Iowa. The State Archive of the Russian Federation in Moscow revealed a number of interesting finds—especially official Soviet documents pertaining to the famine and the work of the ARA—that for the most part have not been consulted by Western historians. Important and still little-known Soviet documents on the famine from the Samara Region State Archive of Social and Political History are available online on the "Istoricheskaia Samara" (Historical Samara) Web site at: историческая-самара.рф/каталог/самарские-тайны-хх-века/1921-год.html.

The vast archives of the ARA are kept at the Hoover Institution at Stanford University. These materials are of supreme importance, not only in reconstructing the official organizational history of the ARA, but also because they include many of the personal papers of men associated with it, including William Kelly, Colonel William Haskell, and Frank Golder. In addition to manuscripts, printed materials, and ephemera, the Hoover Institution has the largest collection of photographs on the Russian mission, some of which are reproduced in this book.

Since *The Russian Job* is aimed at a general audience, I have chosen not to include notes to sources for quotes and specific facts. All statements concerning dates, statistics, events, and biographical details have been carefully sourced from reliable publications or archival documents listed in the bibliography. All quotations have been reproduced verbatim. Editorial omissions are marked by an ellipsis placed inside brackets: [. . .]; ellipses in the original sources are left as is, without brackets.

SELECT BIBLIOGRAPHY

ARCHIVAL SOURCES

Albert and Shirley Small Special Collections Library, University of Virginia
Bakhmeteff Archive of Russian and East European Culture, Columbia University
Herbert Hoover Presidential Library and Museum
Hoover Institution Library and Archive, Stanford University
New York Public Library, Division of Manuscripts and Archives
Samara Region State Archive of Social and Political History, Samara, Russia
State Archive of the Russian Federation, Moscow, Russia

PUBLISHED SOURCES

NEWSPAPERS AND JOURNALS

Izvestiia
The Nation
The New York Times

Pravda
Soviet Russia
The World's Work

BOOKS AND ARTICLES

Adamets, Serguei. "Famine in Nineteenth- and Twentieth-Century Russia: Mortality by Age, Cause, and Gender." In *Famine Demography: Perspectives from the Past and the Present*, ed. Tim Dyson and Cormac Ó Gráda. Oxford, 2002.

———. *Guerre civile et famine en Russie: Le pouvoir bolchevique et la population face à la catastrophe démographique, 1917–1923*. Paris, 2003.

Alekseev, V. V., and Z. S. Boncharov. "Deiatel'nost' ARA v Rossii v osveshchenii russkoi emigrantskoi pechati." In *Sotrudnichestvo i sviazi Rossii i SSSR s narodami zarubezhnykh stran XX vv.*, eds. V. M. Koz'menko and V. V. Kerov. Moscow, 2010.

"The Amazing Dr. Edward Ryan and the Work of the American Red Cross in Estonia." No author. Accessed at: https://photos.state.gov/libraries/estonia/99874/History%20stories/The-Amazing-Dr_-Edward-Ryan.pdf on 1 June 2017.

Anshakova, Iu. Iu. "Gumanitarnaia missiia ARA v Kazani vo vremia goloda 1921–1922 gg." *Izvestiia Samarskogo nauchnogo tsentra RAN*, vol. 9, no. 2 (2007).

———. "Nachal'nyi etap raboty Amerikanskoi administratsii pomoshchi v Samarskom okruge vo vremia goloda 1921–1922 gg. (Po materialam missii)." *Izvestiia Samarskogo nauchnogo tsentra RAN*, vol. 7, no. 2 (2005).

———. "Sovetskaia Rossiia nachala 1920-kh godov glazami amerikanskogo ochevidtsa." *Izvestiia Samarskogo nauchnogo tsentra RAN*, vol. 10, no. 4 (2008).

Applebaum, Anne. *Red Famine: Stalin's War on Ukraine*. New York, 2017.

"'ARA k nam idet bez zadnikh myslei, no vozni s nei budet mnogo': Deiatel'nost' Amerikanskoi administratsii pomoshchi v Rossii. 1921–1923 gg." *Istoricheskii arkhiv*, no. 6 (1993).

Arkhiv VChK: Sbornik dokumentov. Moscow, 2007.

Arnold, David. *Famine: Social Crisis and Historical Change*. Oxford, 1988.

Asquith, Michael. *Famine: Quaker Work in Russia, 1921–1923*. London, 1943.

Bacevich, Andrew J., ed. *The Short American Century: A Postmortem*. Cambridge, Mass., 2012.

Badmaeva, E. N. *Kalmykiia v nachale 1920–kh godov: Golod i preodolenie ego posledstvii*. Elista, 2006.

Baer, Brian James, and Susanna Witt. *Translation in Russian Contexts: Culture, Politics, Identity*. New York, 2017.

Balderrama, Francisco E., and Raymond Rodríguez. *Decade of Betrayal: Mexican Repatriation in the 1930s*. Albuquerque, 2006.

Baranov, Sergey. "Lend-Lease: How American Supplies Aided the U.S.S.R. in Its Darkest Hour." *Russia Behind the Headlines*, March 14, 2016.

Bechhofer, C. E. *Through Starving Russia*. London, 1921.

Beeuwkes, Henry, M.D. *American Medical and Sanitary Relief in the Russian Famine, 1921–1923*. American Relief Administration Bulletin. Series 2, no. 45. April 1926.

Belokopytov, V. I. *Likholet'e. (Iz istorii bor'by s golodom v Povolzh'e 1921–1922 gg.)*. Kazan', 1976.

Blackburn, Marc K. *The United States Army and the Motor Truck*. Westport, Conn., 1996.

Brovkin, Vladimir. *Russia After Lenin: Politics, Culture and Society, 1921–1929*. London, 1998.

Bukhman, K. "Golod 1921 goda i deiatel'nost' inostrannykh organizatsii." *Vestnik statistiki*, bk. 14, no. 4/6 (1923).

Bulletin of the American Relief Administration, ser. 2, nos. 25–35 (June 1922–April 1923).

Cabanes, Bruno. *The Great War and the Origins of Humanitarianism, 1918–1924*. Cambridge, U.K., 2014.

Chamberlain, Lesley. *Lenin's Private War: The Voyage of the Philosophy Steamer and the Exile of the Intelligentsia*. New York, 2007.

Childs, J. Rives. *Black Lebeda: The Russian Famine Diary of ARA Kazan District Supervisor J. Rives Childs, 1921–1923*. Edited by Jamie H. Cockfield. Macon, Ga., 2006.

———. *Let the Credit Go: The Autobiography of J. Rives Childs*. New York, 1983.

———. *Vignettes, or Autobiographical Fragments*. New York, 1977.

Courtois, Stéphane, Nicolas Werth, Jean-Louis Panné, et. al. *The Black Book of Communism: Crimes, Terror, Repression*. Translated by Jonathan Murphy and Mark Kramer. Cambridge, Mass., 1999.

Dokumenty vneshnei politiki SSSR, vol. 4 (March 19–Dec. 31, 1921).

Dubie, Alain. *Frank A. Golder: An Adventure of a Historian in Quest of Russian History*. Boulder, Colo., 1989.

Dubrovina, E. N., compiler. *Golod v Srednevolzhskom krae v 20—30–e gody XX veka: Sbornik dokumentov*. Vol. 1. Samara, 2014.

Edgar, W. C. *The Russian Famine of 1891 and 1892: Some Particulars of the Relief Sent to the Destitute Peasants by the Millers of America in the Steamship* Missouri—*A Brief History of the Movement, a Description of the Relief Commissioners' Visit to Russia, and a List of Subscribers to the Fund*. Minneapolis, 1893.

Engelstein, Laura. *Russia in Flames: War, Revolution, Civil War, 1914–1921*. New York, 2017.

Fen, Elisaveta. *Remember Russia*. London, 1973.

Fisher, H. H. *The Famine in Soviet Russia, 1919–1923*. New York, 1927.

Fitzpatrick, Sheila, ed. *Russia in the Era of NEP: Explorations in Soviet Society and Culture*. Bloomington, Ind., 1991.

Foglesong, David S. *The American Mission and the "Evil Empire."* Cambridge, U.K., 2007.

Fry, A. Ruth. *A Quaker Adventure: The Story of Nine Years' Relief and Reconstruction*. New York, 1926.

Galitzine, Alexandre, ed. *The Princes Galitzine: Before 1917—and Afterwards*. Washington, D.C., 2002.

Genkina, E. B. *Gosudarstvennaia deiatel'nost' V. I. Lenina, 1921–1923*. Moscow, 1969.

German, A. A. "Gumanitarnaia pomoshch' Zapada nemtsam Povolzh'ia v bor'be s golodom 1921–1923 gg." In *Blagotvoritel'nost' i miloserdie: Sbornik nauchnykh trudov*, ed. V. N. Iarskaia. Saratov, 1997.

Glenny, M. V. "The Anglo-Soviet Trade Agreement, March 1921." *Journal of Contemporary History*, vol. 5, no. 2 (1970).

Goldberg, Harold J., ed. *Documents of Soviet-American Relations*. Vol. 1, *Intervention, Famine Relief, International Affairs, 1917–1993*. Gulf Breeze, Fla., 1993.

Golder, Frank. *War, Revolution, and Peace in Russia: The Passages of Frank Golder, 1914–1927*. Compiled, edited, and introduced by Terence Emmons and Bertrand M. Patenaude. Stanford, 1992.

Golitsyn, K. N. *Zapski*. Moscow, 1997.

Golitsyn, Sergei. *Zapiski utselevshego*. Moscow, 2006.

Golitsyna, I. D. *Vospominaniia o Rossii: 1900–1932*. Moscow, 2005.

Gorev, M. *Golod.* Moscow, 1922.

Gor'kii, Maksim. *O russkom krest'ianstve.* Berlin, 1922.

Gorodnichii, N. F. "Maloizvestnye stranitsy deiatel'nosti ARA v Sovetskoi Rossii." *Voprosy istorii,* vol. 12 (1968).

Gorsuch, Anne. *Youth in Revolutionary Russia: Enthusiasts, Bohemians, Delinquents.* Bloomington, Ind., 2000.

Gregory, T.T.C. "Stemming the Red Tide." *The World's Work,* vol. 41 (April 1921) and vol. 42 (May and June 1921).

Gribble, Richard. "Cooperation and Conflict Between Church and State: The Russian Famine of 1921–1923." *Journal of Church and State,* vol. 51, no. 4 (Autumn 2009).

Gul', Roman. *Dzerzhinskii: nachalo terrora.* 2nd ed. New York, 1974.

Hammond, Frederic G. "Patriarch Tikhon and the Controversy over the Treasure of the Russian Orthodox Church, 1921–1922." Yale College, 1981. Unpublished paper.

Herbigny, Michel d'. *L'Aide pontificale aux enfants affamés de Russie.* Rome, 1925.

Hiebert, P. C. *Feeding the Hungry: Russia Famine, 1919–1925.* Scottdale, Pa., 1929.

Hohenberg, John. *Foreign Correspondence: The Great Reporters and Their Times.* New York, 1964.

Hoover, Herbert. *Memoirs.* Vol. 2, *The Cabinet and the Presidency, 1920–1933.* New York, 1952.

Hudson, Hugh D., Jr. *Peasants, Political Police, and the Early Soviet State: Surveillance and Accommodation Under the New Economic Policy.* New York, 2012.

Hullinger, E. W. *The Reforging of Russia.* London, 1925.

Ingulov, S. *Golod v tsifrakh.* Moscow, 1922.

———. "Zametki o golode." *Krasnaia nov',* no. 2 (1922).

Itogi bor'by s golodom v 1921–1922 gg.: Sbornik statei i otchetov. Moscow, 1922.

Karpinskii, K. "Rol' Amerikanskoi administratsii pomoshchi (ARA) v dele spaseniia golodaiushchikh v 1921–1923 gg." *Osinskii ezhegodnik,* no. 6. (1998).

Kas'ianenko, V. I. *Strana Sovetov i SShA: Opyty i uroki sotrudnichestva v 20–kh—nachale 30—kh godov.* Moscow, 1989.

Kennan, George F. "Our Aid to Russia: A Forgotten Chapter." *The New York Times,* July 19, 1959.

Khmelevskaia, Iuliia. "Desiat' millionov rtov." *Vokrug sveta,* Nov. 2011.

———. "Missiia vypolnima? Amerikanskaia filantropiia protiv pervogo Sovetskogo goloda." *Vestnik Permskogo universiteta,* vol. 3, no. 17 (2011).

Kniga o golode: Ekonomicheskii, bytovoi, Literaturno-Khudozhestvennyi sbornik. Samara, 1922.

Kogan, A. N. "Antisovetskie deistviia Amerikanskoi administratsii pomoshchi (ARA) v Sovetskoi Rossii v 1921–1922 gg." *Istoricheskie zapiski,* vol. 29 (1949).

———. "Sistema meropriatii partii i Sovetskogo pravitel'stva po bor'be s golodom v Povolzh'e." *Istoricheskie zapiski,* vol. 48 (1954).

Kramer, Mark. "Food Aid to Russia: The Fallacies of US Policy." Harvard University PONARS Policy Memo 86, Oct. 1999.

Latypov, R. A. "Amerikanskaia pomoshch' Sovetskoi Rossii v period 'velikogo goloda' 1921–1923 godov." In *Nuzhda i poriadok. Istoriia sotsial'noi raboty v Rossii, XX v. Sbornik,* eds. E. Iarskaia and P. V. Romanov. Saratov, 2005.

———. "'Kul'turnyi shok' v mezhdunarodnykh otnosheniiakh: opyt raboty ARA v Rossii v 1921–1923 gg." *Novyi istoricheskii vestnik,* no. 1 (2005).

Leggett, George. The *Cheka: Lenin's Political Police*. New York, 1987.

Lenin, V. I. *Collected Works*. 4th ed. Vol. 45. Moscow, 1970.

———. *Neizvestnye dokumenty. 1891–1922 gg.* Moscow, 2000.

———. *On the Foreign Policy of the Soviet State*. Moscow, 1964.

———. *Polnoe sobranie sochinenii*. 5th ed. Vols. 44, 53–55. Moscow, 1970, 1975.

Leyda, Jay. *Kino: A History of the Russian and Soviet Film*. Princeton, 1983.

Lin'kova, A. P. "Dokumenty Syzranskogo filiala TsGA Samarskoi oblasti o deiatel'nosti ARA v Povolzh'e v 1921–1923 gg." *Otechestvennye arkhivy*, no. 1. (2009).

Long, D. *Istoriia Rossii: Dialog rossiiskikh i amerikanskikh istorikov*. Saratov, 1994.

Lunze, Karsten, Elena Yurasova, Bulat Idrisov, et al. "Food Security and Nutrition in the Russian Federation: A Health Policy Analysis." *Global Health Action*, vol. 8 (2015).

Machiavelli, Niccolò. *The Quotable Machiavelli*. Edited by Maurizio Veroli. Princeton, 2016.

Makarov, V. G., and V. S. Khristoforov. "Gangstery i filantropy: ARA pod zorkim nabliudeniem chekistov." *Rodina*, vol. 8 (2006).

———. "K istorii Vserossiiskogo komiteta pomoshchi golodaiushchim." *Novaia i noveishaia istoriia*, no. 3 (2006).

McMeekin, Sean. *The Russian Revolution: A New History*. London, 2017.

McMurchy, Myles. "'The Red Cross Is Not All Right!' Herbert Hoover's Concentration Camp Cover-Up in the 1927 Mississippi Flood." *Yale Historical Review*, Fall 2015.

Mizelle, Peter Christopher. "'Battle with Famine': Soviet Relief and the Tatar Republic, 1921–1922." University of Virginia, 2002. Ph.D. dissertation.

Narskii, I. V. *Zhizn' v katastrofe. Budni naseleniia Urala, 1917–1922*. Moscow, 2001.

Nash, George H. *The Life of Herbert Hoover: The Engineer, 1874–1914*. New York, 1983.

———. *The Life of Herbert Hoover: The Humanitarian, 1914–1917*. New York, 1988.

———. *The Life of Herbert Hoover: Master of Emergencies, 1917–1918*. New York, 1996.

Neverov (Skobelev), Aleksandr. *Ia khochu zhit'*. Moscow, 1984.

———. *Polnoe sobranie sochinenii*. Vol. 4, *Golod*. 2nd ed. Moscow-Leningrad, 1927.

Neverovu. No author. Moscow, 1924.

Ó Gráda, Cormac. *Eating People Is Wrong, and Other Essays on Famine, Its Past, and Its Future*. Princeton, 2015.

———. *Famine: A Short History*. Princeton, 2009.

Patenaude, Bertrand M. *The Big Show in Bololand: The American Relief Expedition to Soviet Russia in the Famine of 1921*. Stanford, 2002.

Payne, Muriel. *Plague, Pestilence and Famine*. London, 1923.

Pipes, Richard, *Russia Under the Bolshevik Regime*. New York, 1994.

———, ed., with the assistance of David Brandenberger. *The Unknown Lenin: From the Secret Archive*. New Haven, 1996.

Poliakov, V. A. "Golod v povol'zhe, 1919–1925 gg.: proiskhozhdenie, osobennosti, posledstvie." Volgagrad State University, 2009. Ph.D. dissertation.

———. "K voprosu o prodolzhitel'nosti pervogo sovetskogo goloda v 1920–e gody: Na materialakh Povolzh'ia." In *Problemy agrarnoi istorii i krest'ianstva srednego Povolzh'ia*, ed. N. V. Zavariukhin. Yoshkar-Ola, 2002.

———. "Komissiia M. I. Kalinina: Iz istorii gosudarstvennoi pomoshchi golodaiushchim (1921)." *Novyi istoricheskii vestnik*, no. 2 (2007).

———. "Povolzhskii golod nachala 1920–kh gg.: K istoriografii problemy." *Novyi istoricheskii vestnik*, no. 1 (2005).

Pomoshch': Biulleten' Vserossiiskogo komiteta pomoshchi golodaiushchim, no. 1 (Aug. 16, 1921) and no. 2 (Aug. 22, 1921).

Reswick, William. *I Dreamt Revolution*. Chicago, 1952.

Rhodes, Benjamin D. "American Relief Operations at Nikolaiev, USSR, 1922–1923." *The Historian*, vol. 51, no. 4 (Aug. 1989).

Robbins, Richard G., Jr. *Famine in Russia, 1891–92: The Imperial Government Responds to a Crisis*. New York, 1975.

Robinson, Geroid Tanquary. *Rural Russia Under the Old Regime*. Berkeley and Los Angeles, 1932.

Rogger, Hans. "Amerikanizm and the Economic Development of Russia." *Comparative Studies in Society and History*, vol. 23, no. 3 (July 1981).

Salisbury, Harrison E. *American in Russia*. New York, 1955.

Schmemann, Serge. *Echoes of a Native Land*. New York, 1997.

Sebestyen, Victor. *Lenin: The Man, the Dictator, and the Master of Terror*. New York, 2017.

Service, Robert. *Lenin: A Biography*. Cambridge, Mass., 2000.

———. *Spies and Commissars: Bolshevik Russia and the West*. London, 2011.

Shapovalov, Veronica. *Remembering the Darkness: Women in Soviet Prisons*. Lanham, Md., 2001.

Shenk, Robert. *America's Black Sea Fleet. The U.S. Navy Amidst War and Revolution, 1919–1923*. Annapolis, Md., 2012.

Shubin, Daniel H. *A History of Russian Christianity*. Vol. 4. New York, 2006.

Siegel, Katherine A. S. *Loans and Legitimacy: The Evolution of Soviet-American Relations, 1919–1933*. Lexington, Ky., 1996.

Skariatina, Irina. *A World Can End*. New York, 1931.

Slezkine, Yuri. *The House of Government: A Saga of the Russian Revolution*. Princeton, 2017.

Smele, Jonathan D. *The "Russian" Civil Wars, 1916–1926: Ten Years That Shook the World*. New York, 2015.

Smirnova, T. V. "*. . . Pod pokrov Prepodobnogo*": Ocherki o nekotorykh izvestnykh sem'iakh, zhivshikh v Sergievom Posade v 1920–e gody. Sergiev Posad, 2007.

Smith, Douglas. *Former People: The Final Days of the Russian Aristocracy*. New York, 2012.

Smith, Harold F. "Bread for the Russians: William C. Edgar and the Relief Campaign of 1892." *Minnesota History*, Summer 1970.

Sorokin, Pitirim. *Leaves from a Russian Diary*. New York, 1924.

Starr, S. Frederick. *Red and Hot: The Fate of Jazz in the Soviet Union*. New York, 1983.

Stout, Mark. "World War I and the Birth of American Intelligence Culture." *Intelligence and National Security*, vol. 23, no. 3 (2017).

Tarnoff, Curt. "U.S. Assistance to the Former Soviet Union." CRS Report for Congress, March 1, 2007. Order Code RL32866.

Trotsky, Leon. *How the Revolution Armed: The Military Writings and Speeches of Leon Trotsky*. Vol. 4, *1921–1923*. London, 1981.

Trubetskoi, A. V. *Puti neispovedimy (Vospominaniia, 1939–1955 gg.)*. Moscow, 1997.

Usmanov, N. V. "Amerikanskaia pomoshch' golodaiushchim na Iuzhnom Urale v 1921–1923 gg.: Dokumenty gosarkhivov Respubliki Bashkortostan." *Otechestvennye arkhivy*, no. 1 (2009).

———. *Deiatel'nost' Amerikanskoi administratsii pomoshchi v Bashkirii vo vremia goloda 1921–1923 gg*. Birsk, 2004.

———. "Pomoshch' amerikantsev golodaiushchim v sovetskoi Rossii v 1921–1923 gg. (po materialam Urala)." *Istoricheskii vestnik*, vol. 4, no. 151 (2013).

Vasil'evskii, L. M. *Zhutkaia letopis' goloda (Samoubiistva i antropofagiia)*. Ufa, 1922.

Veil, Charles. *Adventure's a Wench: The Autobiography of Charles Veil As Told to Howard Marsh*. New York, 1934.

Vins, O. V. "Pomoshch' inostrannykh organizatsii golodaiushchim Avtonomnoi oblasti nemtsev Povolzh'ia v 1921–1922 gg." *Kul'tura russkikh i nemtsev v Povolzhskom regione*. no. 1 (1993).

Völgyes, Iván, ed. *Hungary in Revolution, 1918–19: Nine Essays*. Lincoln, Neb., 1971.

Volkogonov, Dmitri. *Lenin: A New Biography*. New York, 1994.

Volkov, Oleg. *Gorodu i miru: Povest', pis'ma*. Moscow, 2001.

Weeks, Albert L. *Russia's Life-Saver: Lend-Lease Aid to the U.S.S.R. in World War II*. New York, 2004.

Wehner, Markus, and J. A. Petrova. "Golod 1921–1922 gg. v Samarskoi gubernii i reaktsiia sovetskogo pravil'stva." *Cahiers du monde russe: Russie, Empire russe, Union soviétique, États indépendants*, vol. 38, nos. 1–2 (January–June 1997).

Weissman, Benjamin M. *Herbert Hoover and Famine Relief to Soviet Russia: 1921–1923*. Stanford, 1974.

Whyte, Kenneth. *Hoover: An Extraordinary Life in Extraordinary Times*. New York, 2017.

Williams, William Appleman, ed. *The Shaping of American Diplomacy*. Vol. 1. New York, 1956.

Zhurkin, A. "Deiatel'nost' Amerikanskoi Administratsii pomoshchi v Rossii: K istorii sovetsko-amerikanskikh kontaktov." In *Istoriia mirovoi kul'tury, traditsii, inovatsii, kontakty*. Moscow, 1990.

ACKNOWLEDGMENTS

For their help in the research and writing of this book, I wish to thank Natalya Bolotina, Yelena Mikhailova, Yelena Matveeva, Craig Wright, Tanya Chebotarev, Meredith A. Self, Anatol Shmelev, Sarah Patton, David H. Sun, Nigel Raab, Willard Sunderland, Yuri Slezkine, Daniel Beer, Rachel Polonsky, Rebecca Manley, Robert Service, Andrew Kahn, Fritz Hammond, Cormac Ó Gráda, Stephen Wheatcroft, Neal Bascomb, Jeffrey L. Ward, Shaun Walker, Derek Butler, and the staffs of the Columbia University and University of Virginia libraries, the New York Public Library, the Herbert Hoover Presidential Library and Museum, the State Archive of the Russian Federation, and the Hoover Institution Library and Archives.

I would also like to acknowledge Bertrand M. Patenaude of the Hoover Institution, author of *The Big Show in Bololand*, the definitive study of the ARA's mission to Soviet Russia. His book served as both an inspiration and an irreplaceable resource.

I am grateful to my agent, Melissa Chinchillo, and everyone at Fletcher & Company, for their hard work and support, as well as to my editors, Eric Chinski and Georgina Morley. As always, it's been a pleasure to work with the excellent team at Farrar, Straus and Giroux, including Julia Ringo, Jeff Seroy, Devon Mazzone, Flora Esterly, Nancy Elgin, and Terry Zaroff-Evans.

Thank you to my family, especially Emma, Andrew, and Stephanie, to whom this book is dedicated, for all things big and small.

INDEX

Page numbers in *italics* refer to illustrations.

Eiduk, Alexander, *60*; ARA and,
60–61, 75–76, 78, 91–92; Haskell
and, 158–59; in *Izvestiia*, 91
Elabuga, 69
Eliot, Sigrid, 235–36
Eliot, Tom, 235–36
Elperine, Boris: Bell and, 101–102,
135, 253, 262; Kelly and, 101–102,
109, 170, 172, 179
Emma (ARA laundress), *62*, 62–63
exiles, 114
exports, of Russian grain, 226–27, 230,
248–49

famine: ACRFR, 122; Bolsheviks
and, 16; brides, 220; cannibalism
and, 92–93, 113–14, 146–51, *147*;
children dying of, *66*, *117*; children's
home in, 52, *52*, 84, 117; Childs on,
65–67, 73, 81–82, 84, 166; corn
in, 160–64; drought and, 10–11; of
1891, 10–11; Fleming on, 212, 220;
food in, 66–67, 133–34; Golder on,
50–51; Haskell on, 178; Hibben on,
232; Kelly on, 116–18; Lenin on,
11; morgue, *65*; of 1921, 11, 16–17;
number of deaths in, 257; orphan
of, *211*; refugees of, 16–17, *17*, *51*,
53, *55*, 66, 132; relief, 23, 93, 126;
in Samara Province, 28, 51–52,
231; shock, 64; Sorokin on, 111–14;
Soviet government on, 16, 143–44,
192, 258; starvation and, 112;
thatched roofs and, 167; on Volga
River, 48
Famine: A Short History (Gráda), 257*n*
Famine Museum in Samara, 146–47,
147, 147*n*
farewell banquet for ARA, 254–57, *256*
February Revolution, 44
Fechin, Nikolai, 74, *75*, 119, 200–202,
202
First World War, 11, 21–22
Fisher, Harold, 203, 253
Five-Year Plan, 266–67

Fleming, Harold, *194*; in ARA,
192–93, 211–12, 221, 240–45;
Bobrinskaya, S., and, 219; Brown
and, 193; in China, 260; Dailey
and, 260–61; on famine, 212; on
famine fighting, 220; Galchenko
and, 245–46, 259–60; George and,
242–45; Haskell and, 210; kitchen
inspections by, 243; Laptev and,
261–62; in Moscow, 194–95, 217,
221, 259–60; in New York City,
261; in Orenburg, 210, 212, 215;
on Russia, 260–61; Russia tour,
240–46; in Samara, 215–16, 240; in
Ufa, 216–17; Zhirnova and, 194–95,
216–17, 221
Floete, Carl, 100
floods of 1927, U.S., 267–68
food: bread, 10–12, 15, 34, 118; corn,
127–29, 140–41, 156–57, 160–64,
162, 244; in famine, 66–67,
133–34; shipping, 48; transport
trains, 129–30, 132, *133*; United
States Food Administration, 23–24,
87; as weapon, 25, 36
Ford, Henry, 35
foreign aid, appropriations bill, 88–90,
93, 127
Fourth World Congress of the
Communist International, 226–27
Fox-Trot Affair, the, 220

Galchenko, Nadezhda, 245–46,
259–60
Garner, William, 137, 143
Genoa Conference, 157–58, 176–77
George (Russian interpreter), 242–45
Germany, 22, 25, 157–58
Gest, Morris, 188–89
Gibbs, Philip, 64–65
God, 112–13
Godfrey, Mark D., 185–86, 242
gold, 93
Golder, Frank, *45*, 46, 53, 67;
in ARA, 45, 48, 76–78, 130, 177;

PAGE 4: Henry Wolfe with evidence of cannibalism: Courtesy of Albert and Shirley Small Special Collections Library, University of Virginia, J. Rives Childs Papers

PAGE 11: Vladimir Lenin: Heritage Image Partnership Ltd / Alamy

PAGE 17: Refugees in search of food: Courtesy of the Herbert Hoover Presidential Library and Museum

PAGE 23: Herbert Hoover: Glasshouse Images / Alamy

PAGE 43: J. Rives Childs: Courtesy of Albert and Shirley Small Special Collections Library, University of Virginia, J. Rives Childs Papers

PAGE 45: Frank Golder: Courtesy of the Hoover Institution Library and Archive, Stanford University

PAGE 47: ARA Moscow headquarters: Courtesy of the Hoover Institution Library and Archive, Stanford University

PAGE 49: Children at the Alexander Palace ARA kitchen: Courtesy of the Hoover Institution Library and Archive, Stanford University

PAGE 51: Refugees on a train: Courtesy of the Herbert Hoover Presidential Library and Museum

PAGE 52: Inside a children's home: Courtesy of the Hoover Institution Library and Archive, Stanford University

PAGE 55: Young famine victims: Courtesy of the Hoover Institution Library and Archive, Stanford University

PAGE 56: Muddy street in Kazan: Courtesy of the Bakhmeteff Archive of Russian and East European Culture, Columbia University

PAGE 60: Alexander Eiduk: Courtesy of the Hoover Institution Library and Archive, Stanford University

PAGE 61: Haskell and Quinn: Courtesy of the Hoover Institution Library and Archive, Stanford University

PAGE 62: Emma: Courtesy of the Hoover Institution Library and Archive, Stanford University

PAGE 65: Bodies piled in a morgue: Courtesy of the Herbert Hoover Presidential Library and Museum

PAGE 66: Child dying of hunger: Courtesy of the Herbert Hoover Presidential Library and Museum

PAGE 68: Childs and Simson at an ARA kitchen: Courtesy of Albert and Shirley Small Special Collections Library, University of Virginia, J. Rives Childs Papers

PAGE 70: Loading supplies: Courtesy of Albert and Shirley Small Special Collections Library, University of Virginia, J. Rives Childs Papers

PAGE 75: Fechin's portrait of Childs: Courtesy of Albert and Shirley Small Special Collections Library, University of Virginia, J. Rives Childs Papers

PAGE 82: Dining Hall No. 1: Courtesy of Albert and Shirley Small Special Collections Library, University of Virginia, J. Rives Childs Papers

PAGE 83: Childs and Skvortsov: Courtesy of Albert and Shirley Small Special Collections Library, University of Virginia, J. Rives Childs Papers

PAGE 91: ARA warehouse in New York City: Courtesy of the Hoover Institution Library and Archive, Stanford University

PAGE 100: William Kelly: Courtesy of the Herbert Hoover Presidential Library and Museum

PAGE 103: ARA mascot Mischka: Courtesy of the Hoover Institution Library and Archive, Stanford University

PAGE 105: Colonel Bell: Courtesy of the Hoover Institution Library and Archive, Stanford University

PAGE 117: "Harvest of Hunger": Courtesy of the Hoover Institution Library and Archive, Stanford University

PAGE 125: ARA transport column: Courtesy of the Hoover Institution Library and Archive, Stanford University

PAGE 128: SS *Winneconne*: Courtesy of the Bakhmeteff Archive of Russian and East European Culture, Columbia University

PAGE: 129: Simbirsk by the Volga: Courtesy of the Hoover Institution Library and Archive, Stanford University

PAGE 133: Russian soldiers guarding food: Courtesy of the Herbert Hoover Presidential Library and Museum

PAGE 137: William Kelly and Harold Blandy: Courtesy of the Hoover Institution Library and Archive, Stanford University

PAGE 138: Piet Hofstra and William Kelly: Courtesy of the Hoover Institution Library and Archive, Stanford University

PAGE 147: Three arrested women: Courtesy of the Hoover Institution Library and Archive, Stanford University

PAGE 149: Mukhin Pyotr Kapitonovich: Courtesy of the Hoover Institution Library and Archive, Stanford University

PAGE 159: Felix Dzerzhinsky: Pictorial Press Ltd / Alamy

PAGE 160: Karl Lander: Courtesy of the Hoover Institution Library and Archive, Stanford University

PAGE 162: Children waiting for corn: Courtesy of the Hoover Institution Library and Archive, Stanford University

PAGE 165: Tetiushi ARA office: Courtesy of Albert and Shirley Small Special Collections Library, University of Virginia, J. Rives Childs Papers

PAGE 171: Corpse in snow: Courtesy of the Hoover Institution Library and Archive, Stanford University

PAGE 174: Harold Blandy's funeral: Courtesy of the Hoover Institution Library and Archive, Stanford University

PAGE 180: Aboard the *Pecherets*: Courtesy of the Bakhmeteff Archive of Russian and East European Culture, Columbia University

PAGE 181: Baseball in Simbirsk: Courtesy of the Bakhmeteff Archive of Russian and East European Culture, Columbia University

PAGE 185: ARA inoculating children: Courtesy of the Herbert Hoover Presidential Library and Museum

PAGE 187: Children in Odessa: Courtesy of the Hoover Institution Library and Archive, Stanford University

PAGE 188: Pavlov with his dog: Courtesy of the Hoover Institution Library and Archive, Stanford University

PAGE 194: Harold Fleming: Courtesy of the Herbert Hoover Presidential Library and Museum

PAGE 202: Fechin's portrait of Georgina: Courtesy of Albert and Shirley Small Special Collections Library, University of Virginia, J. Rives Childs Papers

PAGE 211: Abandoned orphan: Courtesy of the Hoover Institution Library and Archive, Stanford University

PAGE 224: Student Dining Hall No. 2: Courtesy of Albert and Shirley Small Special Collections Library, University of Virginia, J. Rives Childs Papers

PAGE 238: Dancing the lezginka: Courtesy of the Hoover Institution Library and Archive, Stanford University

PAGE 253: Children eating ARA rations: Courtesy of the Hoover Institution Library and Archive, Stanford University

PAGE 256: In the garden at the banquet: Courtesy of the Hoover Institution Library and Archive, Stanford University

PAGE 271: Children at an ARA kitchen in Moscow: Courtesy of the Herbert Hoover Presidential Library and Museum

A NOTE ABOUT THE AUTHOR

Douglas Smith is an award-winning historian and translator and the author of *Rasputin* and *Former People*, which was a bestseller in the United Kingdom. His books have been translated into a dozen languages. The recipient of a Guggenheim Fellowship, he has written for *The New York Times* and *The Wall Street Journal* and has appeared in documentaries on the BBC, National Geographic, and Netflix. Before becoming a historian, he worked for the U.S. State Department in the Soviet Union and as a Russian affairs analyst for Radio Free Europe/Radio Liberty. He lives with his family in Seattle, Washington.